KT-232-308

VOCATIONAL EDUCATION
AND TRAINING INSTITUTIONS
A management handbook and CD-ROM

Vocational education and training institutions

A management handbook and CD-ROM

Designed and edited by
Vladimir Gasskov

International Labour Office   Geneva

Copyright © International Labour Organization 2006

First published 2006

Publications of the International Labour Office enjoy copyright under Protocol 2 of the Universal Copyright Convention. Nevertheless, short excerpts from them may be reproduced without authorization, on condition that the source is indicated. For rights of reproduction or translation, application should be made to the Publications Bureau (Rights and Permissions), International Labour Office, CH-1211 Geneva 22, Switzerland, or by email:pubdroit@ilo.org. The International Labour Office welcomes such applications.

Libraries, institutions and other users registered in the United Kingdom with the Copyright Licensing Agency, 90 Tottenham Court Road, London W1T 4LP [Fax: (+44) (0)207 631 5500; email: cla@cla.co.uk], in the United States with the Copyright Clearance Center, 222 Rosewood Drive, Danvers, MA 01923 [Fax: (+1) (978) 750 4470; email: info@copyright.com], or in other countries with associated Reproduction Rights Organizations, may make photocopies in accordance with the licences issued to them for this purpose.

V. Gasskov (designer and editor)

Vocational education and training institutions: A management handbook and CD-ROM

Geneva, International Labour Office, 2006

Guide; training management; vocational training; vocational education; training institution.

ISBN 92-2-117104-3 (book + CD-ROM)

The designations employed in ILO publications, which are in conformity with United Nations practice, and the presentation of material therein do not imply the expression of any opinion whatsoever on the part of the International Labour Office concerning the legal status of any country, area or territory or of its authorities, or concerning the delimitation of its frontiers.

The responsibility for opinions expressed in signed articles, studies and other contributions rests solely with their authors, and publication does not constitute an endorsement by the International Labour Office of the opinions expressed in them.

Reference to names of firms and commercial products and processes does not imply their endorsement by the International Labour Office, and any failure to mention a particular firm, commercial product or process is not a sign of disapproval.

ILO publications can be obtained through major booksellers or ILO local offices in many countries, or direct from ILO Publications, International Labour Office, CH-1211 Geneva 22, Switzerland. Catalogues or lists of new publications are available free of charge from the above address, or by email: pubvente@ilo.org

Visit our web site: www.ilo.org/publns

Photocomposed and printed in Switzerland   WEI/SRO

PRINCIPAL CONTRIBUTORS

Peter Noonan, Australia
Anne Deschepper, Australia
George Preddey, New Zealand
Beryl Pratley, United Kingdom

The ILO wishes to acknowledge the generous assistance provided by the Government of Japan in the preparation of this publication.

ABOUT THE AUTHORS

Vladimir Gasskov has a diploma in engineering, an advanced degree in industrial sociology and a Ph.D. in management sociology. He worked in an electronics assembly company as a technologist and then for ten years at the International Institute for Management Studies in Moscow. He has been involved in various management consulting and technology transfer projects. Since 1989, Dr. Gasskov has been employed by the International Labour Office (ILO) as a vocational training specialist. His research and advisory activities focus on management, financing and the evaluation of vocational education and training (VET) systems and institutions. His main publications include: *Managing vocational training systems: A handbook for senior administrators*; *Alternative schemes of financing training*; and *Skills promotion funds*.

Peter Noonan, who trained as a teacher, is an independent consultant and researcher in education and training and an associate of the Faculty of Education at Monash University, State of Victoria, Australia. He was a senior public servant at state and national levels in VET and post-compulsory education for over 20 years and played a key role in the development of Australia's national training system. He was awarded a Fulbright scholarship in 1993. He works with state and national training agencies, education and training providers and enterprises and also undertakes research projects. He is currently the principal adviser for an occupational skills standards project in Papua New Guinea.

Anne Deschepper has worked in the VET sector in Australia as a teacher and administrator for more than 25 years. Her experience as a teacher of basic education, language and communication skills underpins an interest in the ways in which educational organizations focus their attention on the needs of their learners. This has led her to become involved in and lead teacher development programmes, curriculum and learning resource development, the design of training delivery and of assessment protocols and tools, and the implementation of new learning technologies in the classroom. She is the manager of

Educational Development Services at Chisholm Institute of Technical and Further Education (TAFE) in the State of Victoria.

George Preddey worked for seven years as an ionospheric physicist, for 13 years teaching at two New Zealand polytechnics and a university, for three years as a futurist, and for three years as a civil defence manager. He was then employed by New Zealand's Ministry of Education for a ten-year period which covered the country's major reforms in tertiary education. He was chief adviser tertiary when he left the Ministry in 1997. Since then he has worked under contract as a tertiary education consultant to various international agencies in Chile, Ghana, Hungary, Malaysia, Nepal, Oman and the Philippines. He has also worked under contract to the Tertiary Education Advisory Commission, a precursor of New Zealand's Tertiary Education Commission.

Beryl Pratley has spent most of her career as a teacher, teacher trainer and manager in the English tertiary education sector. After six years as a college principal, she worked with government agencies responsible for curriculum development and assessment, before joining Her Majesty's Inspectorate (HMI) of schools and colleges. In 1993, when HMI for the tertiary sector was disbanded, she became head of the School of Education at Kingston University, Surrey. From 1997, she was the senior inspector for the south-east region of England at the Further Education Funding Council. Since retiring, she has worked as an independent consultant (mainly concerned with strategic planning and quality improvement in tertiary education) for a number of British and international bodies, including the British Council.

ABBREVIATIONS

APSDEP	Asia and Pacific Skill Development Programme
CAD/CAM	Computer-aided design/computer-aided manufacture
EFTS	Equivalent full-time student
EU	European Union
FTE	Full-time equivalent
GAAP	Generally accepted accounting practice
GST	Goods and services tax
HMI	Her Majesty's Inspectorate
HRD	Human resource development
ICT	Information and communication technology
ILO	International Labour Office/Organization
ILT	Information and learning technology
ISO	International Organization for Standardization
IT	Information technology
ITO	Industry training organization
KPI	Key performance indicator
MIS	Management information system
PC	Personal computer
QMS	Quality management system
SCH	Student contact hour
SSP	Statement of service performance
SWOT	Strengths, weaknesses, opportunities and threats (analysis)
TAFE	Technical and further education
TEFMA	Tertiary Education Facilities Management Association
VAT	Value-added tax
VET	Vocational education and training
VLE	Virtual learning environment

INTRODUCTION

Vocational education and training institutions: A management handbook and CD-ROM has been produced under the aegis of the International Labour Organization (ILO) and the Asia and Pacific Skill Development Programme (APSDEP) with the aim of increasing the professionalism of managers and administrators in the vocational education and training (VET) sector. For this purpose, the handbook provides general benchmarks for the management practices of responsive, flexible and efficient VET institutions. The countries and institutions willing to bring about management reform in their VET sectors will find in this instructional material a considerable knowledge base.

Effective public governance and management continue to be the key issues in the VET sector. Most countries operate large numbers of VET institutions, which absorb a large share of their government budgets. More and more of these public service systems are facing growing demand for skills development and, at the same time, zero growth or a drop in funding.

National VET systems and institutions vary from country to country and their management practices reflect the conditions in which they operate. However, no matter the national conditions, all governments wish their VET institutions to operate flexibly and cost-efficiently and to respond quickly to changes in the labour markets.

In many countries, publicly funded VET institutions are part of governments, with their budgets part of government budgets and their staff civil servants. Evidence, however, suggests that responsive, operationally flexible and cost-efficient VET institutions can best be achieved by delegating to them sufficient management, financial and academic autonomy, and, correspondingly, by strengthened professional and management competence of their staff. Lack of autonomy often translates into fewer incentives for staff initiative and improvement of performance.

A very different set-up has been introduced through the public-sector reforms in some countries where governments, instead of being direct operators of public VET institutions, have limited their role to that of founders, regulators, major financiers and performance assessors. In these cases, public VET institutions are administered by their governing councils, whose members are appointed by governments and include major stakeholders. The governing councils, therefore, become the employers of their staff and assume important strategic management responsibilities. Institutional autonomy is strengthened further through the appointment of the chief executive/chief executive officer (director/principal) who manages day-to-day operations.

Although the ownership of VET institutions' assets may be transferred to their governing councils, governments usually retain considerable ownership interests. VET institutions are given all the means and freedom to achieve the agreed outputs and benefit from improved efficiency. Operational autonomy for VET institutions implies that their managers know what they have to do and how to do it if they are to achieve their objectives and maintain long-term institutional viability. In autonomous public VET institutions, a new sense of institutional ownership develops, which differs from traditional government ownership. Greater institutional autonomy helps inspire motivation and encourages VET managers and staff to improve their capabilities in order to achieve better results.

The modern concept of administration distinguishes between governance and management, and is comprised of three levels: the government, the institution's governing council and the chief executive of the institution. In practising this concept, the principal issue is how to establish and exercise optimum freedom and authority at all these levels. This handbook describes the experiences of governance and management structures and procedures established in autonomous public VET institutions.

Vocational education and training institutions: A management handbook and CD-ROM is based on the view that the VET institutions' responsiveness to market demand and their ability to operate flexibly and efficiently are strongly determined by the degree of their management, financial and academic autonomy, as well as by the competence of their managerial, teaching and non-teaching staff, to utilize this autonomy for the benefit of their stakeholders. However, this autonomy, while opening up new opportunities for efficiency and service productivity, may also lead to greater operational and financial risks. These risks need to be managed through new accountability arrangements introduced by governments for VET institutions.

This instructional material is based on systematically documented experiences from Australia, New Zealand and the United Kingdom, countries that have successfully pioneered the governance and management reform of public VET institutions. The VET institutions' management structures and operational practices as well as the legal, policy and organizational environments that have been created in these countries may be viewed as a benchmark against which other training systems may wish to measure themselves. This handbook was developed by reputable professionals who participated in these reforms and so have first-hand knowledge of existing practices.

In these countries, VET institutions have developed as large-scale market operators in the national education and training industry. They cater to thousands of full-time and part-time students of all ages and employ large numbers of staff. Their financial turnover is significant and they generate large amounts in revenue. They operate as public companies and serve the interests of their governments, students, industry and the community.

The documented experiences of autonomous public VET institutions in Australia, New Zealand and the United Kingdom suggest that their administrators direct their attention to managing their institutional balance sheets and operational efficiency, assuring the quality of education and training, and maintaining transparent accountability to their stakeholders. These major strategic concerns are monitored by continuously focusing on learner interests through the development and delivery of innovative VET programmes that companies and individual students want. These are the principal areas of management practice that are described in detail in this handbook.

This handbook is accompanied by a CD-ROM that is not an exact replica of the text of the book but rather has been designed along the same lines. The CD-ROM provides summaries of national management practices ("National Practices") in the VET sector and contains copies or summaries of national training policies, reports and legal documents, as well as real-life management instruments applied by VET institutions in the aforementioned countries. These documents comprising institutional charters, agreements, questionnaires, guidelines, and so forth, can be easily downloaded, enabling users to check their day-to-day management practices against them and improve them if need be. These documents are published on the CD-ROM, courtesy of the government VET agencies, private organizations, and individual public VET providers in Australia, New Zealand and the United Kingdom, whose important contributions are gratefully acknowledged by the writers.

This handbook is intended both as a self-learning tool as well as a means to upgrade the skills of national VET administrators, chief executives and managers of VET institutions, and members of their governing councils.

The handbook and CD-ROM consist of three components:

1. The text of the handbook
The text is not country-specific and provides general approaches to the management of autonomous VET institutions. It is also available on the CD-ROM and its units are hyperlinked to other parts of the instructional material.

2. "National Practices"
The "National Practices" of managing VET institutions are country-specific and refer to colleges in Australia and the United Kingdom, and to polytechnics in New Zealand. They are only available on the CD-ROM. The aim of these

"National Practices" is to illustrate the concepts outlined in the handbook. The titles of corresponding modules and units of the handbook and of "National Practices" are the same.

3. "Resource Documents"

A large number of "Resource Documents" originated from the aforementioned countries which are available only on the CD-ROM. They are arranged alphabetically and structured by subject and country. The "Resource Documents" are also directly accessible through clicking on their titles in the text of "National Practices".

The handbook and "National Practices" consist of 11 modules with 43 learning units, while "Resource Documents" provide access to more than 400 titles recorded on the CD-ROM.

The "Resource Documents" on the CD-ROM were collected and recommended to the ILO by the authors of this handbook. The copyright arrangements and acknowledgments regarding these documents can be found on the CD-ROM.

It is hoped that *Vocational education and training institutions: A management handbook and CD-ROM* will contribute to the implementation of the ILO Human Resources Development Recommendation, 2004 (No. 195), concerning education, training and lifelong learning, the text of which is also available on the CD-ROM.

Reference to the names of individual VET institutions, companies and commercial management products mentioned in this handbook does not mean that the ILO approves or recommends them to users.

This handbook and CD-ROM were approved by the ILO/APSDEP meeting of experts, which took place in February 2005 in Chiba, Japan. The meeting was attended by 16 VET management experts from nine of Asia's most advanced countries.

We hope that this instructional manual will make a significant contribution to the management reforms taking place in the VET sector, and that the individual user will find the handbook and CD-ROM interesting and useful. Our team believes that this learning product will eventually become a foundation for accredited national qualifications in vocational education and training management.

The designer and editor of this volume would like to thank the team of writers for their dedication and passionate commitment to this handbook and CD-ROM that has taken over two years of intensive writing and editing to produce.

CONTENTS

Module 6   Student management

Module 7   Staff management

Module 8   Course development and evaluation

Module 9   The management of training delivery

Module 10   Quality assurance in education and training

Module 11   Performance monitoring and reporting

MODULE 1

Enabling policies and the legal environment

THE LEGAL ENVIRONMENT FOR AUTONOMOUS PUBLIC VET INSTITUTIONS

1.1.1 THE SCOPE AND SET OF LEGAL PROVISIONS APPLIED TO PUBLIC VET INSTITUTIONS

The demand for operational efficiency, flexibility and responsiveness was a major argument behind the reforms of the early 1990s that gave VET institutions in some countries considerable freedom. However, given the large amount of public funding invested in VET institutions and the need to assure balanced and equitable national training provision, the process towards further autonomy has become constrained in recent years.

Autonomous public VET institutions are sometimes called "quasi-autonomous organizations". Managers of these institutions need to have a clear understanding of what their quasi-autonomy ("almost but not quite" is how "quasi" is defined in most dictionaries) means, namely that these institutions still mostly use public money for which they are accountable. Therefore, VET institutions are guided by national policy statements as well as by certain regulations of the agencies and other institutions that finance them. The form of quasi-autonomous organization has also been applied to other non-VET organizations.

The chief executives (directors/principals) of public VET institutions need to immerse themselves in the network of legislation, national policies and regulations in order to comprehend when, where and by what degree they are expected to be autonomous. They also need to learn as much as possible about the network of other quasi-autonomous organizations that surround them and set limits on their autonomy.

Each VET institution's governing council and chief executive need to identify the *degree* of autonomy assigned to their institution. The major questions that need to be asked are:

☐ Is the VET institution controlled by specific clauses in legislation or statutory regulations issued by a government minister or other authority?

☐ Is the VET institution strictly directed by financial regulations and codes or forms of inspection and monitoring by the ministry or other authority?

☐ Is the VET institution generally advised and directed by policy statements and advice, and from which sources?

☐ Is the VET institution's network silent on the matter, giving the institution full autonomy but nevertheless expecting it to work to other general principles required in the public sector?

The answers to these questions may not lie in a single source but in the interaction between sources. Each chief executive needs to understand this network and have some points of influence on it/be able to influence it.

Public VET institutions are likely to be consulted when new legislation and regulations are being drafted. Furthermore, they are likely to lobby government agencies and legislators in order to facilitate desirable reform. Therefore, it would be helpful for the chief executives of these institutions to be aware of examples of good practice in other legislatures to assist them in their lobbying. This unit focuses on what needs to be legislated and regulated, and how, to enable public VET institutions to achieve appropriate operational freedom.

Several pieces of legislation may be required to introduce the proper legal environment for autonomous public VET institutions. Such legislation may cover:

☐ their status and autonomy;

☐ the employment of staff;

☐ performance and accountability frameworks;

☐ assets and financial operations, and so forth.

In countries with federal government structures, autonomous training institutions operate under legislation enacted by the level of government that has constitutional responsibility for education. Legal provisions encompass the purpose of the institutions, governance arrangements and accountability requirements. There may be a need for complementary VET legislation involving formal agreements between national and state (or provincial) governments.

For more details on the sets of legal provisions applied in different countries, consult **Unit 1.1: The legal environment for autonomous public VET institutions** on your CD-ROM.

1.1.2 THE DEFINITION AND LEGAL STATUS OF PUBLIC VET INSTITUTIONS

Public VET institutions may be generally defined and given legal status in legislation. A definition of public VET institutions in legislation may deal mostly with their ability to deliver a diversity of pre-employment VET programmes and adult continuing education and training courses, to promote community learning and undertake applied research, and so on. The legislation may recognize different types of public VET institutions, such as, for instance, general education schools, colleges, vocational training centres, polytechnics, and so forth, and may provide for their establishment and disestablishment.

Organizational forms available for autonomous public VET institutions commonly include state companies, statutory corporations and trusts. *State companies* are those firms that operate under conditions of competitive neutrality with private-sector companies but are owned by and accountable to the government as shareholder. The public institutions registered as *statutory corporations* are more centrally controlled by government but they have some of the freedoms of a state company, including the right to own property. Public institutions registered as *trusts* are controlled by a trust board acting in place of the government as owner.

Each of these organizational forms represents an entity that is legally separated from and able to operate at a distance from the government. All have inherent advantages and disadvantages, determined to an extent by the legislative and regulatory environment within which the public VET institution is required to operate.

The VET institution as state company

Constituting a public institution as a state company clearly establishes the State as the legal owner of the institution. This organizational form may support consistent government ownership policies, including the appointment of governing bodies, authority over the use of assets and the use of incentives/sanctions regarding the VET institution's performance.

Both the state company and statutory corporation organizational forms allow for considerable variations in design to reflect a public institution's characteristics, but neither form focuses on commercial (as distinct from efficiency or financial viability) as opposed to educational objectives. The company form includes the implicit expectation that public VET institutions operate in a business-like manner.

As a state company, a public VET institution may have full powers to borrow and invest in its own name. In exercising these powers, the institution is not able to rely on a government guarantee to underwrite its liabilities. The success of each public VET provider is in the hands of each governing body.

The state company offers legally tested and proven governance and account-ability arrangements in the education and training sector.

The umbrella enabling legislation for public VET institutions should contain provisions reflecting the character and needs of tertiary education, along with the aims and operating principles unique to the VET sector. The powers of the State, as the owner, to direct the governing body is greater than those of ordinary shareholders in a private company, but should still be limited.

Generally, the state company form may be most appropriate in cases where:

□ the education and training services are to be provided in a competitive market;

□ the State is happy to see entities diversify (consistent with policy objectives and financial performance targets, particularly relating to efficiency);

□ the environment is constantly changing, particularly in terms of consumer expectations;

□ the State has residual liability.

The VET institution as statutory corporation

The statutory corporation form is typically less flexible than the state company, as any significant changes in objectives, organizational arrangements and other details are likely to require legislative change. The State is expected to assume residual liability for the debts of public institutions and so requires a strong set of ownership levers to manage the financial risks.

Generally, the statutory corporation form may be most appropriate in cases where:

□ the government's or the public VET institutions' educational objectives are more likely to conflict with their ownership objectives;

□ diversification from the State as the predominant source of revenue is not desirable;

□ contracting is relatively straightforward, with readily specified and meas-ured services, and would stimulate public institutions to operate more effi-ciently.

The VET institution as trust

The trust form may not provide the government with sufficient ownership powers to manage the financial risk it would face if a public institution suffered financial failure. However, in the long term the trust type of structure may also prove to be effective for highly flexible institutions capable of responding quickly to local needs.

For more details on the comparisons of these organizational forms applied in different countries, consult **Unit 1.1: The legal environment for autonomous public VET institutions** on your CD-ROM.

1.1.3 OWNERSHIP OF PUBLIC VET INSTITUTIONS

The issue of ownership is an important component of governance and is central to asset management. Autonomy presumes an ability to acquire or dispose of assets, predetermined by who owns them. Public ownership of VET institutions is commonly held to be necessary to safeguard the State's objectives as well as its resourcing (funding) interest in VET. If the government does not own the public VET institutions, it might prove difficult to ensure that the institution's training delivery is meeting the government's overall training strategy and goals.

Clearly, the State does have (unspecified) ownership responsibilities in the case of autonomous public VET institutions. A clear test is whether the State carries the ultimate risks of ownership, including residual liability, of VET institutions. As an illustration, the net equity of public tertiary education and training institutions may be included in a government's statement of financial position, recorded in an annual budget. This inclusion is not academic, since governments may, on occasion, have met the contingent residual liabilities of failed public VET institutions.

The ownership of public VET institutions is a complex issue that raises the question of whether an institution is more than the sum of its buildings, lands, equipment, curricula, intellectual property, and so forth. Ownership may extend beyond physical and financial assets to include intangibles such as reputation and traditions.

Current practice is that most assets of autonomous VET institutions are owned by the institutions themselves. The government may, from time to time, transfer a land title and other assets from the State to the VET institution (institution's governing council) as a corporation.

For more details on the ownership of public VET institutions in different countries, consult **Unit 1.1: The legal environment for autonomous public VET institutions** on your CD-ROM.

1.1.4 THE ESTABLISHMENT, DISESTABLISHMENT
AND MERGER OF PUBLIC VET INSTITUTIONS

There should be provisions in legislation for the establishment, disestablishment and merger of public VET institutions. Such provisions may be necessary because the establishment, disestablishment or merger of public VET institutions may have implications for the operation, viability and reputation of other public and private institutions as well as for the allocation of public resources.

An important education and training policy issue is whether the numbers and types of public providers should be regulated. There are various ways in which a VET sector can be structured. These range from the government centrally regulating, protecting and determining the numbers and types of providers, to the government allowing the providers to decide for themselves the type of education and training they wish to offer, the names under which they operate and the quality characteristics they seek to establish.

Regulating public provider numbers and types in this manner ensures that a wide range of VET services continues to be available. For example, confusion might arise if any training provider was entitled to call itself a "polytechnic". Regulation could oblige providers to meet minimum standards before being allowed to appropriate titles consistent with the public's common understanding of a polytechnic.

However, regulating types and numbers of providers could also constrain others from entering the market or from shifting from one class to another, perhaps resulting in a shortfall in training in areas of economic growth or increased student demand. More specialized training should also be allowed to develop.

For more details on the legal arrangements for the establishment and disestablishment of public VET institutions, consult **Unit 1.1: The legal environment for autonomous public VET institutions** on your CD-ROM.

1.1.5 MANAGERIAL AND ACADEMIC AUTONOMY

Governing and management autonomy

The autonomy of a public VET institution is determined by the activities that its governing council and management are able to undertake without a government agency intervening. The four concepts of a fully controlled, directed, advised and fully independent institution may be more about nuance and represent a continuum of degrees of autonomy. Legislation may specify that VET institutions are given the autonomy to make their own academic, operational and management decisions, in accordance with the services they provide and the demands of accountability.

Even where institutions have a substantial degree of formal legislative independence, governments may influence their operations through their role as a shareholder in appointing and dismissing governing councils, through specific powers to issue directions to institutions as well as through determining structures of financial incentives and accountability frameworks.

Governments may also influence the nature of VET programme provision and require adherence to policies and guidelines through contracts or performance and funding agreements with the public institutions.

The management activities by which a public VET institution's level of autonomy may be assessed include its ability to:

☐ determine the numbers and types of staff employed, and appoint and dismiss staff;

☐ introduce organizational and management structures;

☐ determine staff conditions of service (remuneration, superannuation, and so forth);

☐ develop courses and curricula and issue awards;

☐ enrol students, set entry standards, assess student progress;

☐ operate bank accounts;

☐ generate, retain and manage revenue and surpluses;

☐ borrow, rent or lease;

☐ purchase and dispose of assets;

☐ maintain and expand buildings and other assets.

Legislating governing councils

In its *Principles of corporate governance* (1999), the Organisation for Economic Co-operation and Development (OECD) describes corporate governance in terms of the structures and processes for making decisions. Corporate governance specifies the distribution of rights and responsibilities among many different participants in the corporation, such as the board, managers, shareholders and other stakeholders, and spells out the rules and procedures for decision-making.

The roles, responsibilities and accountabilities of the governing council, its chairperson, council members, the chief executive and the academic board of the autonomous VET institution should all be clearly defined in order to differentiate between governance and management. For instance, it is commonly believed that the functions of chairperson and chief executive in corporations need to be separated so as to maximize openness about strategy, mission, and accountability. Mature governance and management in the public VET sector should be ensured by legislative measures placing more reliance on the capabilities of the institutions themselves.

Legislation may prescribe the numbers and composition of governing councils of public VET institutions, including staff, student, industry, profession and community representation, as well as persons appointed by the relevant minister. Legislation may also determine the rules and procedures for appointing the chairperson of the governing council and the chairperson's functional relations with the chief executive.

Some of the general elements of good governance in autonomous VET institutions are:

☐ transparency (the free flow of information, which is accessible to all interested parties);

☐ accountability to stakeholders (the institution's council and managers are accountable to the government, general public, customers and communities);

☐ equity (all men and women should be able to benefit equally from education, training and employment);

☐ responsiveness (the institution's flexibility and commitment to identify and meet demand for services);

☐ participation (all stakeholders have a voice in decision-making); and

☐ efficiency (while producing results that meet needs, institutions should protect public assets and make the best use of their resources).

Legislation may prescribe in detail the functions of the VET institution's governing council and its powers, which include the power to:

☐ appoint its chief executive;

☐ determine the institution's general mission, perhaps specified by its charter, which has been approved by the relevant minister;

☐ approve the institution's objectives, perhaps specified in its annual statement of objectives;

☐ ensure that the institution is managed properly, for example, in accordance with its charter and its statement of objectives.

Academic autonomy

Legislation may also contain provisions determining the academic freedom that allows:

☐ the academic staff and students to question and test received wisdom and to state controversial or unpopular opinions;

☐ the academic staff and students to engage in applied research;

☐ the institution and its staff to regulate the content and duration of taught courses;

☐ the institution and its staff to teach and assess students as they consider best.

Although delegating powers to public VET institutions may enable greater institutional flexibility, improve responsiveness to demand, enable full command of resources, cost-efficiency and accountability and increase incentives for better staff performance, it can also place institutions' financial stability and utilization of funding and assets at greater risk. To address the possible rise in risk, there may be a need to improve governance and management as well as to enhance monitoring and accountability.

For more details on the managerial and academic autonomy of public VET institutions, consult **Unit 1.1: The legal environment for autonomous public VET institutions** on your CD-ROM.

1.1.6 LEGISLATIVE PROVISIONS REGARDING THE EMPLOYMENT OF STAFF

The employment conditions for the staff of autonomous public VET institutions can also be dealt with by legislation. This legislation should ensure that every employer in the state services is a good employer.

VET institutions basically fall into two broad categories: those which directly employ their staff and those where the staff are in law employed by central or local government and are only seconded to a VET provider. In the latter case, only procedures concerning discipline, staff competence, and transfer in and out of the institution can be dealt with by the VET institution's management in any detail.

Where VET institutions employ their own staff, the individual council or board of governors must determine the whole range of procedures which will make the organization function successfully and properly within a broad framework of what the national government regards as good practice.

Legislation may preclude the negotiation of employment contracts by public VET institutions at a national level or, alternatively, may allow individual employees to negotiate collective employment contracts for their particular institution. A recent trend has been towards negotiating individual employment contracts at senior managerial level.

Legislation may also determine provisions for pensions, health insurance and other social security matters applicable to the staff of public agencies. The sources of funding and contribution levels by the employers (VET institutions) and employees to the pension and social security funds are normally regulated by individual funds. The government, as the VET institution owner, may wish to accept liability for financial contributions that are normally funded by employers. The government may need to make provisions for the staff of public autonomous institutions to remain eligible to join the national pension and other social security schemes and for the institutions to contribute to these funds. These social security funds commonly provide services to various government institutions.

There are two ways of making such provisions. One option would be that the VET institution's owner (the government) agrees to contribute to the social security funds; this would need to be reflected in the institutional charter and/or service agreements. Another option would be to provide such contributions to the social security funds by making it part of the institution's total salary budget. In this case, the cost should be reflected in the overall unit delivery cost.

In some countries, however, governments have been decreasing their coverage of social security contributions for the staff of autonomous VET institutions, with the consequence that these institutions feel they are increasingly required to meet these and other increased salary costs from other revenue. Education and training sector employees could set up a collective voluntary superannuation fund for their members, funded by members' contributions. Such funds would be private, and VET institutions as corporations may or may not have an obligation to contribute to them.

For more details on the legislative provisions regarding the employment of staff in public VET institutions in different countries, consult **Unit 1.1: The legal environment for autonomous public VET institutions** on your CD-ROM.

1.1.7 LEGISLATIVE PROVISIONS REGARDING THE FINANCING OF VET INSTITUTIONS

The financial framework within which public VET institutions operate may be specified in generic legislation that applies to the whole public sector. Such legislation could, for example:

☐ determine the limits of the training institution's financial autonomy;

☐ provide a framework for scrutinizing the management of the State's assets and liabilities, including the assets and liabilities of public institutions and, most importantly, their control over the disposal of major assets such as land and buildings;

☐ establish lines of responsibility for the use of financial resources provided to public institutions;

☐ establish financial incentives to encourage the effective and efficient use of financial resources in departments of state and state agencies, including public VET institutions;

☐ specify the minimum financial reporting obligations;

☐ safeguard public assets by providing statutory authority and controls for the raising of loans, the issuing of securities and guarantees, the operation of bank accounts and the investment of funds.

Legislation may also establish constraints on the financial powers of the VET institution's governing council through the imposition of restrictions on the amount it may borrow or on the value of the institutional assets of which it wishes to dispose.

For more details on the legislative provisions regarding the financing of VET institutions in different countries, consult **Unit 1.1: The legal environment for autonomous public VET institutions** on your CD-ROM.

1.1.8 LEGISLATIVE PROVISIONS REGARDING ACCOUNTABILITY

Performance-related accountability

Generic legislation pertaining to the public sector should ensure efficiency and the responsible management of state services, including public VET institutions. This objective can be achieved by, for example, legislation which requires that all state agencies, including public VET institutions, provide their responsible minister with a document (in effect a business plan) that sets out the:

☐ objectives of the institution;

☐ nature and scope of activities proposed to be undertaken;

☐ performance targets and other measures by which the performance of the institution may be judged in relation to its objectives;

☐ institution's accounting policies.

Public institutions may be legally required to report to the responsible minister on achieved outputs and outcomes. The format and timing for such reporting may also be determined.

Financial accountability

Generic legislation could also require public institutions to prepare financial statements in accordance with generally accepted accounting practice (GAAP), including financial statements that display the financial position of the institution and a balance sheet that accounts for all the assets under its control. Such an accounting regime would require measurable outputs that could serve as a basis for public funding.

For more details on the legislative provisions regarding the accountability of public VET institutions, consult **Unit 1.1: The legal environment for autonomous public VET institutions** on your CD-ROM.

THE REGULATORY ROLE
OF NATIONAL EDUCATION
AND TRAINING POLICIES

1.2.1 THE CONTENT OF NATIONAL VET POLICIES

National training policies are rarely set out in a single policy document. Different government agencies operating in the fields of employment, education and training may be assigned responsibilities for the development and implementation of VET policies in their respective areas. For instance, one agency might be responsible for policies in qualifications development, skills assessment and certification, while another agency might be in charge of policies for lifelong learning, and so forth. Furthermore, training and other labour market-related policies may change with the election of a new government. However, despite this pluralism, the national training policy development process is becoming increasingly multipartite, involving a broad representation of the stakeholders and agencies concerned.

Managers of VET institutions have to be aware of the consequences of changes in education and training policies, since it is their responsibility to translate these changes into their day-to-day operations. New regulations and even legislative amendments are likely to follow significant policy changes, as are new public funding priorities. National VET policies should be underpinned by high-quality research and evaluation, following consultation with all the relevant parties. Some training policy issues may be particularly sensitive, for example, those that determine principles of access to publicly subsidized education and training services.

National training policies should, at a minimum, include:

(a) Assumptions about the role of education and training

A national VET policy will make certain assumptions about the role of education and training in the economic and social development of a country. It is usually held that a minimum level of education is necessary for an individual to function properly in society and to ensure a degree of social cohesion by individuals participating in democratic processes, and that it helps maintain law and order as well as public health. Training policies also commonly assume that equal access to education and skills will promote equal employment and income opportunities.

Some of the frequently quoted assumptions regarding education and training are that:

☐ education and training can generate private and social benefits;

☐ improved vocational skills is a principal factor in improving productivity; therefore, vocational participation should be encouraged;

☐ educated and trained workers produce and earn more than the less educated and trained;

☐ education and training improves a person's employability and labour mobility, and also increases their ability to adapt to changing technologies;

☐ abundant skills can influence the path of economic development, attract foreign investment and promote growth;

☐ a degree of foundation skills and some job-specific skills are necessary for an individual to become vocationally oriented and be capable of participating fully in lifelong learning;

☐ education and training can reduce the incidence of crime and improve lawful behaviour and general health awareness;

☐ although VET alone cannot create jobs, skills development programmes can contribute to the promotion of employment, and so forth.

(b) The VET system's mission statement (major policy objectives)

The VET system's mission statement sets out its major policy objectives. Depending on national circumstances, these objectives may include:

☐ providing job-related knowledge and skills in order to help people find employment or self-employment (skills for employment promotion);

☐ providing vocational knowledge and skills to any citizen who desires them and to increase the proportion of people with formal vocational qualifications (skills training for the social development of citizens);

☐ ensuring a more equitable access to skills, employment and income (skills training for equitable access to employment and income opportunities);

☐ meeting the training needs of industry, and addressing the national skills shortages, and so on.

16

(c) National training goals, priorities and benchmarks

Broad national goals, priorities and benchmarks may be introduced to guide the overall training provision. These targets or benchmarks can be defined in terms of:

☐ the percentage of young people within certain age limits participating in VET programmes (vocational participation);

☐ the percentage of the population that has achieved a vocational qualification at a stated level;

☐ the percentage of people of working age participating in lifelong-learning programmes;

☐ the agreed groups of the population that will have received priority assistance in education and training (priority target groups that are often defined in terms of a desired equality of access);

☐ the agreed priority areas of economic and social development (such as territories and industrial sectors) requiring priority skills development.

(d) The configuration of a national training system

A national training policy commonly involves the configuration of the training system. It may specify the types of public and private agencies involved and their most important functions, such as, for instance, the government ministry, the national training authority, the vocational qualifications authority, industry training bodies, and so forth. A national training policy determines the organizations that have the right to accredit VET providers, develop the national qualifications framework, assess knowledge and skills, issue awards, and recognize prior learning, and, above all, it outlines the structure of relationships between the organizations that make up the VET system.

(e) Training providers

A training policy should also determine the types of institutions that are authorized to deliver programmes leading to national VET qualifications. As far as the training providers are concerned, the policy determines whether:

☐ their numbers are regulated and, if so, by which authority;

☐ the names of providers, such as "college" or "polytechnic", and so on, are regulated and protected;

☐ public providers are supposed to compete or coordinate VET programmes with each other and with private institutions.

A VET policy may establish or eliminate boundaries in the training markets between different types of training providers. For instance, any VET institution may be authorized to deliver any type of programme for which they are accredited.

A training policy may acknowledge the complementary roles of public and private training providers, and the circumstances under which, if any, private training institutions may be able to access public resources. Another related issue is whether public and private providers are encouraged to compete for public funding and for customers on a "level playing field".

(f) Major learning avenues

The policy should specify the VET programmes that are national in nature as well as the agencies and institutions responsible for delivering them, such as:

- ☐ school-based pre-employment training (conducted in a college or training centre);
- ☐ formal apprenticeship (involving combinations of school-based and workplace experience);
- ☐ adult learning (initiated by the learner for personal career development needs);
- ☐ employer training (initiated by the employer for the employees);
- ☐ training of the unemployed (initiated by the State to reduce dependence and raise inclusiveness).

Policies may also introduce levels of educational and occupational attainment and specify the learning avenues leading to them. The levels of attainment may involve:

(1) semi-skilled, basic training;

(2) skilled workers, clerical workers;

(3) highly skilled, supervisory, junior technicians, senior clerical;

(4) senior technicians, managerial, semi-professional workers;

(5) university graduates, professional workers.

(g) Lifelong learning

Lifelong learning has increasingly become an important part of national training policy. This concept views learning as a process that allows the user to move freely between different stages of learning. One of the practical applications of this concept is that VET avenues should not be a dead end but should provide access to higher education and continuing education and training.

There is also a need for policies at the level of basic education. All modern workplaces require their workers to have basic competency in numeracy, reading and writing in the language of the workplace (which may not be the same as the mother tongue of the worker). Most modern workplaces also require that their workers have basic information technology (IT) skills. An educational system that does not provide these basic skills is failing the future workforce. At the same time, a modern adult and community educational system must address the fact that many adult workers (who left school many years ago) may lack these basic skills, and correspondingly need to deal with this issue.

(h) National priorities for VET system development

A national training policy may establish directions for a reform of the VET system, aiming at improving vocational participation, obtaining greater equity in access to training and cost-efficiency in training provision, and so forth. The most popular current reforms are those that seek to decentralize training systems, introduce competence-based vocational qualifications, apply the international quality management standards of the International Organization for Standardization (ISO) – the ISO 9000 family – in VET institutions, introduce the modular-based learning and distance learning, and so forth.

(i) The division of responsibilities for providing and financing VET

A training policy should provide a clear picture of who is responsible for the provision and financing of VET institutions, particularly where that responsibility is shared between national and state governments, and between governments and the social partners.

Governments frequently are responsible for: ensuring that an appropriate legislative and regulatory environment is in place; governing the national skills development process; maintaining public and private investment in education and training at socially desirable levels; ensuring equitable access to education and training opportunities; assuring quality of the education and training provision. Where national, state or local governments are involved in VET regulations and funding, their roles and responsibilities should be described in ongoing agreements in order to avoid duplication and cost shifting.

Employers may also accept responsibility for the provision and funding of vocational training, and may be charged with identifying sectoral skills development needs. In some countries, labour laws determine that employers must train their employees. Trade unions have a responsibility to ensure that their members have access to education and training that is relevant to their needs.

Employers and trade unions as well as other important stakeholders should be involved in developing national VET policies as well as in assessing training shortages. Their support in promoting learning and defining the training targets and content of VET programmes is crucial to success.

Training policies tend to indicate that private individuals have a responsibility to take advantage of existing opportunities by participating in education and training to develop their own skills and potential, and to share the costs of training delivery, since they are the beneficiaries. The principles of co-funding VET by respective levels of government as well as by industry and private individuals may also be specified in the training policy.

The national policies will influence operations of VET institutions through government directives. VET managers need to handle various policy dimensions sensitively as national priority target groups may change as well as public funding priorities, and the government resources may be allocated to different types of VET programmes.

For more details on the content of national training policies applied in different countries, consult **Unit 1.2: The regulatory role of national education and training policies** on your CD-ROM.

1.2.2 POLICY REQUIREMENTS REGARDING EQUITY, EFFICIENCY, RESPONSIVENESS AND ACCOUNTABILITY

(a) Equitable access to education and training

Although the importance of equality of access to skills training and employment opportunities is generally recognized, the government will need to require VET institutions to develop internal policies and procedures. Equal access is an issue that arises frequently and from a number of dimensions.

Each VET provider needs to examine its own communication, enrolment, training funding and delivery practices in detail in order to see what it can do to improve equality of access. Even the most simple decisions may need to be reviewed. When and how often does the VET institution offer open days for future students and parents? Are they at times that are convenient to all sections of the population (those who are in or out of work; men and women; those with or without families, and so forth)? How are they advertised or publicized (in which languages, by which media, in which towns and areas?)?

Each VET institution should provide some form of awareness training with its staff to help promote equality of access.

An important policy issue is whether or not the national training policy recognizes skills training as a right. Commonly, young people in pre-employment training are accorded this right more than employees or the unemployed. Procedures for implementing this right can determine national training demand and the way VET institutions should plan and deliver courses.

The principles of access to the publicly subsidized VET programmes is another issue related to equity. Some practical options include: competitive or merit-based entry to public training places; equity-based enrolment schemes intended to support the disadvantaged groups; and an open entry to training programmes. Experience suggests that competitive enrolment practices do not lead to equitable access to public training, since they tend to benefit urban rather than rural students, as well as students from wealthier families. Merit-based enrolment tends to be based on high entry-level requirements (marks acquired in general education), which could lead to elitist student groups.

One of the policies to make enrolments more equitable is to reserve training places, for instance, for students from rural areas, for girls and other groups which may be disadvantaged. Student fees should be income-tested, while education and training loans could be made available on an equal basis.

Government directives may also require VET authorities to identify the particular sectors of the workforce and the population that participate in education and training and the labour market below national averages or other benchmarks, and enact measures to improve such participation. Such population and workforce segments may typically include women, migrants and people who are not proficient in the main national language, people from indigenous communities, people with a disability, the unemployed and those with low levels of basic education.

Training policies may set up long-term national goals in relation to these segments in order to improve their vocational participation and labour market opportunities. These goals may be pursued through the requirements reflected in the performance and funding agreements with VET institutions. National equal opportunity legislation and policies (for example, for the disabled) should also apply to VET institutions.

(b) Efficiency

A national training policy generally contains provisions that encourage public VET providers to make more efficient use of public resources. Current options include placing a greater reliance on output- and outcome-based funding mechanisms by which public training providers are funded for the training that they deliver (output-based funding) or for the desirable outcomes of training. This approach differs radically from the method based on the cost of inputs (salaries, maintenance, and so forth). Incentives for good performance are greater when training providers are funded for what they do or achieve rather than for what they cost. However, performance-based funding requires a degree of institutional autonomy that enables the institution's management to take advantage of this approach by reducing its operational costs and increasing outputs.

(c) Responsiveness and accountability

A national training policy may also address matters of institutional responsiveness and flexibility. Responsiveness requires the training provider to become attuned to the requirements of its stakeholders and to be able to adjust its training delivery to meet changing needs. Policies may require the compulsory representation of major stakeholders on the institutions' governing councils and the carrying out of regular surveys on training demand and on the labour market success of graduates. The ability to respond to changing demands would be an indication of the flexibility achieved.

Policies may emphasize learner-centred approaches and the flexible delivery of programmes at times and in locations and using media that suit the needs of learners rather than institutions. Staff development programmes may be required to assist staff to identify and meet these needs.

Finally, a national training policy might contain provisions intended to ensure that training institutions are accountable for their use of public resources. Accountability is intrinsically linked to institutional autonomy. As autonomy is enhanced, so the accountability requirements will also require strengthening. Accountability regimes involve the systematic reporting and monitoring of institutions to ensure that the government's investment in education and training is being applied solely for the purpose of achieving the desired outputs and outcomes. The reporting and monitoring of autonomous VET institutions are also necessary to protect the government's ownership interest, since it is generally the government that bears the costs of institutional failure.

Inevitably, targets will be set for outputs, average unit costs and the flexible delivery of training services. VET institutions have to respond to these targets. National policies may also determine that there should be incentives and performance benchmarks established for VET institutions to operate cost-effectively, responsively and flexibly. These are dealt with in more detail in other sections of the handbook.

For more details on the policy requirements regarding equity, efficiency, responsiveness and accountability in different countries, consult **Unit 1.2: The regulatory role of national education and training policies** on your CD-ROM.

1.2.3 INTERNATIONAL EDUCATION
AND TRAINING POLICIES

VET institutions need to provide students with qualifications that are recognized in all parts of their own country as well as in other countries where jobs may be available or where students may wish to continue their education and training. Similarly, employers who trade with partners in other countries will sometimes need to have a labour force whose qualifications are widely recognized. International standards systems (such as the ISO 9000 family) often demand this for a wide range of jobs in manufacturing and, by derivation, by suppliers to those industries. Air transport and aircraft maintenance, for example, have truly international arrangements. Some other industries, such as the petrochemical and most chemical-production industries, may require plant maintenance and installation staff to hold qualifications to the standards of the American Society of Mechanical Engineering (ASME).

On the one hand, governments and employers are faced with a dilemma which is the more widely recognized the skills of their workforce are, the more opportunities the workers will have to migrate. This may lead to shortages of the skilled labour in the areas where employers consistently pay large bills for training. Striking a balance is not easy, particularly in developing countries. However, the ignorance of or non-compliance with the requirements of vocational qualifications systems in the countries where migrants go for work can result in most migrants being employed as non-skilled or, at best, as low-skilled workers. The remarkable rise in international labour migration, particularly in south Asia and south-east Asia, is clearly a case in point.

International arrangements and the EU

The international agreements and moves to establishing political or economic federations or trade and customs unions commonly reserve the responsibility for educational systems to the individual States. Most VET certificates are issued by governments or agencies on behalf of governments.

In the EU, although rights regarding education are reserved to the Member States, there are nevertheless attempts to establish joint policies. Each Member State accepts a clear obligation to enforce full equality between all citizens from within the Union, particularly in the labour market and concerning employment rights. The compromise has been to construct a series of agreements for the mutual recognition of qualifications or, at the very least, multilingual documents which make the situation transparent. For example, although the training programmes and qualifications for a hotel receptionist or plumber may differ between EU countries, each worker can obtain a document in the official languages that clarifies what their qualification includes. This document is sometime known as the "job passport".

Where there are specific agreements within the EU on the recognition of qualifications (usually at the professional level), each Member State must establish laws that prevent discrimination against other nationalities from the Union. In a few cases, such as the medical occupations, each Member State may make enforceable regulations demanding, in addition to the recognized medical qualification, that an employee must pass an appropriate language competence test.

For more details on international education and training policies, consult **Unit 1.2: The regulatory role of national education and training policies** on your CD-ROM.

Unit 1.3

THE CONFIGURATION
OF SUPERVISORY BODIES

1.3.1 GOVERNMENT ADMINISTRATIVE STRUCTURES

Autonomous public VET institutions will have a relationship with the machinery of government in order that they be held accountable for the public funding they receive and to protect the government's interests as owner. Various configurations of ministries, departments and agencies will, therefore, undertake regulatory and advisory roles on behalf of the government.

More that one government agency may influence or direct the work of VET institutions, but one single agency should have overall responsibility for their efficient and effective operation. This agency will be the direct link between the executive arm of the government and the provider, with its role depending on the level of devolution to and autonomy of the public VET institutions.

The organizational structure within the machinery of government may include a department or ministry of state. The distinction between department and ministry is, in part, semantic but customarily may reflect an operational (department) or policy (ministry) focus. The department or ministry may exert various degrees of control or direction of public VET institutions. It may also have relationships with broader elements of the vocational training system, or it may include other government interests, such as employment, and youth and sports affairs, for example.

Accordingly, the central government structure may, for example, be designated as a department (or ministry) of: vocational training; vocational education and training; vocational and higher education; education; education and employment; education, employment and youth affairs; and so forth.

In some countries, large groups of VET providers are commonly split between the ministry of education (vocational education institutions) and the ministry for labour (job-related and more short-term training in the training centres). Training for occupations in health, agriculture, transport or public services is often seen as separate from a main system of VET and may be implemented by or under the supervision of relevant line ministries.

The nature and scope of various functions of departments/ministries will expand and contract as the public VET providers are given greater autonomy. Policy advice and funding roles are likely to be unaffected, unless the funding role is divested to some other national organizations, such as a VET tertiary education commission or VET funding council. Technical support roles, including course approvals and institutional accreditations, may similarly remain with the department/ministry or they may be divested to a specialist agency set up for these purposes. In general terms, an enhancement of autonomy of public VET institutions should be balanced by a commensurate enhancement of accountability systems.

The roles performed by government administrative structures as well as by autonomous (or semi-autonomous) VET agencies commonly include:

☐ developing and maintaining legislation and regulations for government and parliamentary approval;

☐ developing national VET policies and strategies;

☐ establishing, disestablishing and accrediting institutions;

☐ building the capacity of VET institutions, enabling them to meet agreed objectives;

☐ developing regulations for institutions that establish the agreed rules and procedures for their operations;

☐ national or state level planning for the VET sector (determining the number and types of public institutions as well as the overall number of students that will be publicly funded);

☐ providing government funding to VET institutions through performance and funding agreements;

☐ supervising providers through guiding the implementation of service agreements and steering financial performance;

☐ implementing the overall performance and financial accountability for the VET system against its goals and targets;

☐ researching into VET policy issues and labour market needs;

☐ providing or funding various services (developing national VET qualifications, curricula, and learning resources; assisting in teacher and staff training; and so forth);

☐ determining the types of national vocational awards and requirements for achieving them;

☐ assuring the quality of VET delivery and of the qualifications that are issued;

☐ coordinating VET policies and operations with other relevant government agencies, such as employment, welfare, employment services, and so on;

□ consulting with industry and community bodies;

□ ensuring communication, promotion and improving the image of VET.

The government administrative structures and the autonomous agencies that oversee the public VET providers that have been given considerable autonomy do not:

□ directly involve themselves in the employment, transfer, and so on, of the institution's staff;

□ supervise and approve inputs, such as, for instance, the institutions' detailed budgets as well as their draft recurrent expenditures;

□ oversee the acquisition and disposal of less important assets, such as, for instance, training equipment;

□ determine the types of programmes to be delivered by individual providers as well as their course enrolments, and so forth.

For more details on government administrative structures in different countries, consult **Unit 1.3: The configuration of supervisory bodies** on your CD-ROM.

1.3.2 AUTONOMOUS GOVERNMENT AGENCIES

The reasons for establishing agencies

Many of the governing and operating functions in the VET sector may be devolved to autonomous or semi-autonomous government agencies, which are established under the enabling legislation and are sometimes referred to as non-departmental public bodies. A VET agency will generally operate at a distance from the government but will represent its own interests as well as those of other stakeholders. Its regulatory, advisory, technical or coordinating roles may include education and training policies and strategy development, resource allocation, accountability steering, and so on. In addition, it is also common for agencies to be established to regulate and implement certain technical functions, such as, for instance, developing vocational qualifications frameworks, training quality assurance, curriculum development, assessing skills and issuing awards, and so forth.

The distinction between government administrative structures and government agencies is that a department/ministry is accountable to its responsible minister, whereas an agency (national VET commission or funding council) is generally governed by a board representing a broad range of stakeholders and has a greater degree of independence from ministerial direction.

As a result, the ministry has responsibility for policy development and advising the government, while national VET agencies mostly have operational responsibilities. These might include funding, accountability and quality assurance systems that operate within the policy environment determined by government on the advice of the ministry. The roles and functions of VET agencies tend to become more significant as the institutional autonomy of public providers increases, and with it the need to balance accountability systems.

There are a number of reasons for moving government functions out of ministries into agencies, and they include the following:

- agencies are less subject to sudden changes of senior leadership than the political cadre of ministers;

- the agencies' governing councils represent a wide range of stakeholder interests;

- agencies are professional organizations with greater independence to analyse, provide advice and make decisions on VET policies and practices;

- agencies' research evidence, findings or conclusions are generally accepted as more accurate or objective by the community;

- agencies can establish a more permanent cadre of professional staff than is usual within a civil service.

Types of agencies

Government VET agencies with regulatory and advisory roles may commonly involve:

- umbrella-type VET agencies (a national tertiary education commission, funding council or board, and so on) that are assigned general supervisory and funding functions such as developing and implementing national training policy and strategy, financing public institutions and steering their performance, and so on;

- national vocational qualifications authority;

- national curriculum development authority;

- skills assessment and awarding bodies;

- employment promotion bodies that may be appointed by government in regions as tripartite organizations; they may have the power to advise on trends in local training demand and purchase training courses from autonomous VET institutions or other suppliers.

These agencies are usually established under enabling legislation and are governed by their boards appointed by the government. Given their type of activity, their boards are more likely to have professional representation than the tripartite representation of the general umbrella-type VET agencies.

There is always a risk that power tensions will arise between the government VET agency (council or commission) and the VET department of the ministry. Therefore, functions that are devolved to a VET agency should be clearly defined, with competent staff assigned to implement them. The different interests of stakeholders that are represented on a VET agency's board pose another risk. There is always a need to reach a compromise on these differing interests, which is something that takes time and can lead to considerable delays in operational activities. In maintaining the proper balance of interests, much depends on the position of the minister, who has the power to issue directions to the VET department, autonomous VET agency as well as to the VET providers.

For more details on autonomous government agencies in different countries, consult **Unit 1.3: The configuration of supervisory bodies** on your CD-ROM.

1.3.3 NON-GOVERNMENT VET BODIES

It is becoming increasingly common to have non-government VET bodies established, with the approval and financial support from the government, which are assigned the function of developing skills standards and industry qualifications (both national and those based on sectors of industry), advising on industry's future demand for skills, and so forth. Such autonomous regulatory and advisory bodies are set up by, and represent the interests of, particular industry stakeholders.

Industry training organizations (ITOs) are an example of such autonomous non-government regulatory and advisory bodies that may be established or recognized by government to undertake important functions in the VET sector. Through ITOs, governments are able to access and utilize industry networks and advice to support national policy-making, planning, priority setting and regulatory processes. These bodies may be established under enabling legislation but they differ from government agencies in that they are initially established by stakeholders who are external to government.

Membership of ITOs are likely to be industry associations, trade unions and individual companies. Although ITOs commonly operate on behalf of their industry stakeholders, they may also take into account the interests of other stakeholders, including the government, particularly if they receive public funding. Such ITOs frequently have governing councils drawn from pre-existing voluntary-membership industry, trade union and professional associations, with supplementary membership from ministries or related key agencies. Appointments are most likely to be made by ministers for fixed terms, with members eligible for reappointment. Members may receive remuneration

29

or so-called "sitting" fees. The ITO is governed by a board, with tasks and functions undertaken by paid staff of the organization.

ITOs are established for the same reasons as autonomous agencies. The usual activities of an ITO involve:

☐ advising training providers and companies on industry training needs, the number and types of programme, and who should provide them;

☐ determining or advising on content curriculum and standards in training programmes for the industry sector;

☐ determining, advising or participating in student/trainee assessment and certification;

☐ funding or managing the flow of government funds to industry;

☐ directly or jointly (with other providers) arranging on-the-job training;

☐ evaluating training providers;

☐ acting as the main decision-making bodies on VET policy, regulation and funding in industry.

The functions of ITOs may be determinative (that is, the authority sits with the body) or advisory (that is, advice must be approved by government) and may be subject to some direction by the government. Functions may be delegated to standing committees or subcommittees under formal delegation.

For their standing and credibility, it is important that ITOs are seen to be based in and owned by the industry they represent, and not seen as government agencies. Therefore, they should be incorporated as independent bodies, that is, as companies or associations, and not established under government statute.

For more details on non-government VET bodies in different countries, consult **Unit 1.3: The configuration of supervisory bodies** on your CD-ROM.

Unit 1.4

MAIN REGULATORY AREAS
OF PUBLIC VET INSTITUTIONS

1.4.1 REGULATIONS ON GOVERNMENT OWNERSHIP INTERESTS

The management of public VET institutions is commonly subject to regulation, the extent of which indicates the level of the autonomy that such an institution enjoys. The level of autonomy varies substantially between jurisdictions, from fully controlled, directed and advised, through to almost fully independent public VET providers.

In general, governments should influence the activities of autonomous institutions through contractual arrangements and performance and funding agreements rather than through statutory regulations, since the former can be negotiated and tailored to meet the circumstances of specific institutions.

A government's ownership interests regarding public autonomous institutions are commonly met through effective governance, which assumes compliance with rules and procedures for the establishment, composition and workings of their governing councils.

The government may also wish to regulate on the process by which the management of a public institution is established or disestablished. A government will pursue its ownership interests through the appointment of at least a minimum number of members of their governing bodies. VET institutions may be required to develop constitutions for governing bodies and to approve those constitutions. Guidelines may be set for the operation of governing bodies, including governance requirements, avoidance of conflict of interest and required standing committees (for example, an audit, which may require external members).

Institutional powers may be constrained where assets, particularly land, are owned by government, whose agreement may be required to dispose of or change the purpose of land usage. The latter may also be affected by covenants or legal restrictions based on the original purpose for which the land was acquired – usually educational.

Governments will want to ensure that, if the ownership of capital resources is fully transferred to the public VET institution, then those resources will be properly used and maintained and that capital assets will be used exclusively for the purposes for which they were established. They will wish to ensure that assets are not used to fund current or annual expenditure and that they are not disposed of recklessly.

An asset-owning VET institution will normally take the form of a corporation in which there are no shareholders to whom assets or profits can be distributed and which is unable to merge with such a corporation. Regulations will normally be put in place to ensure that the board of governors (or directors or trustees) is not able to benefit from the distribution of assets or profits and that any major disposals of land or capital must be approved of, in advance, by a senior government minister or by a major government agency. In addition, the minister (agency, and so forth) may require that the proceeds from any such disposals are used for the purposes of the public institution, some related and approved activity, or returned to the government.

Despite all these safeguards and hedges, the property may still be fully and legally owned by the VET institution, which may free the establishing authority, such as a government ministry, from the administration of any of the rights and obligations that go with the ownership of land or buildings usual in that community. In this situation the management of the VET provider will be more aware of the real running costs of the institution.

VET institutions will also face restrictions in asset disposal and utilization from local planning and zoning regulations, which may, for example, preclude the utilization of assets for different purposes, for example, the use of open spaces for car parking, the conversion of land from residential to commercial purposes, and so forth.

Institutions may be required to maintain accurate asset registers and develop long-term capital utilization and development strategies. Provision should also be made for assets, including buildings and equipment, information and communication technologies (ICTs) infrastructure, software, intellectual capital, financial management systems, and so on, to be re-invested.

Although autonomous institutions may be given legal powers to acquire, use and dispose of capital assets and/or borrow for the purposes of asset and capital development strategies, government regulations on the limits and procedures to do so are common. Borrowings by VET providers will form part of total public-sector debt and the risk will ultimately be carried by government. It is likely that governments will require approval of borrowings, at least over certain limits, and that they will also set debt/asset and working capital ratios for such institutions.

Risk assessment

Public autonomous institutions may be required to develop risk management strategies to guard against failure or underperformance in the areas of financial management, information systems, quality of training, governance, and so forth. These strategies need to identify and rate potential risks, and outline the ways in which they will be dealt. They should be developed and understood by staff at all levels and be endorsed by their governing councils.

VET providers may also be subject to external standards for registration as a training provider or for quality certification and may have to undergo an audit against these standards. To reduce risks, institutions should establish ongoing self-evaluation and audit programmes.

For more details on the regulations on VET institutions' management issues, consult **Module 3: The VET institution's management system**.

For more details on the regulations of government ownership interests in different countries, consult **Unit 1.4: Main regulatory areas of public VET institutions** on your CD-ROM.

1.4.2 REGULATIONS ON TRAINING FUNDING

Governments may decide to invest in training delivered by public and private providers in order to achieve economic and social policy goals. It could be argued that, without such investment, there would be under-investment in education and training for the economy as a whole (economic argument) or for particular sections of society (equity argument).

For more details, refer to **Unit 1.1: The legal environment for autonomous public VET institutions**.

Government funding interests in public VET institutions may be protected through appropriate regulation of their funding sources as well as their use of financial resources, whether derived from public or private sources. Accountability arrangements might include processes that determine how funding is to be utilized and accounted for.

These processes may include:

- regulating input funding intended for salaries, and so forth;

- regulating output-based funding, for example by prescribing the minimum requirements on how the institutions' objectives (outputs) must be met;

- regulating institutional performance, for example by prescribing the minimum requirements for acceptable performance indicators;

- regulating reporting obligations, for example by prescribing the minimum requirements for financial statements and annual reports.

In order to protect the interests of private funders, it might also be appropriate for governments to regulate the utilization of private resources used to finance the delivery of training by public providers. This would help protect the rights of trainees who pay tuition, given the often unequal relationship between training provider and trainee.

For various reasons, governments may decide to regulate the tuition fees charged by VET providers that are also receiving public funding. In particular, fee "ceilings" may be imposed to ensure that public funding is used as a subsidy to keep fees affordable rather than to increase institutional surpluses.

The government funding agencies may regulate how institutions handle, organize and receive funds. Costing and pricing at public institutions are notoriously difficult activities. The differences between "full-cost pricing", "full-cost pricing with surplus revenue" and the various degrees of "marginal costing" are all processes pertinent to public institutions. Inexperienced VET managers may find it extremely difficult to balance revenue and expenditure.

For more details on training funding regulations, consult **Module 5: Budgeting and financing**.

For more details on training funding regulations in different countries, go to **Unit 1.4: Main regulatory areas of public VET institutions** on your CD-ROM.

1.4.3 REGULATIONS ON TRAINING DELIVERY

Training programmes and enrolments

Public providers' training delivery may be regulated to support national education and training goals and priorities. Initiatives to ensure that the labour market demand for an adequately skilled workforce is met could include incentives or disincentives for student enrolment in particular occupational fields. A government's equity objectives could also be advanced through incentives for participation in training by particular target groups, which may include setting minimum enrolment quota.

Training quality

Governments commonly regulate to ensure the quality of VET delivery in order to protect the interests of trainees and taxpayers. This is often achieved by restricting the allocation of public funding to those courses that meet the minimum quality standards set and assessed by a government agency tasked with that function.

Regulations may extend from the processes by which the training curriculum is developed through the minimum standards of course delivery (its duration, use of instructional materials, minimum space allocations for class-rooms and workshops, minimum requirements for training equipment) to include the competencies of VET teachers and their preparation.

In the jurisdictions where autonomous VET institutions operate, their managers have the freedom to make decisions on training inputs, subject to an accountability regime that focuses mainly on assessing the outcomes of a training programme instead of regulating the inputs to it.

A further area for regulation is skills assessment and certification, which are often linked to procedures for training quality assurance, including course registrations and approvals. A central government agency is often established to carry out these functions. The autonomous VET providers may have del-egated powers of skills assessment and certification, subject to audit of their internal quality assurance processes by a central agency.

For more general details on training delivery regulations, consult **Module 8: Course development and evaluation** and **Module 9: The management of training delivery.**

For more details on regulations on training delivery in different countries, go to **Unit 1.4: Main regulatory areas of public VET institutions** on your CD-ROM.

1.4.4 REGULATIONS ON THE EMPLOYMENT OF STAFF

The staff of autonomous VET institutions are usually employed by their gov-erning councils. However, they may continue to have entitlements to public and private benefits, including membership of provident funds, pension funds, health insurance funds, and so forth. Employees transferred to autonomous institutions will be protected by the labour law of the country.

The employment protection offered to state employees is normally much higher than that offered to ordinary employees or employers (public autono-mous VET institutions), so there may be some resistance to the delegation of autonomy to public institutions. One way through this difficulty would be to establish some protection for all employees through a "transfer of undertak-ings" legislation. Whenever the former government institution is transferred from the government to the VET institution's governing council (from one owner to another), all the employees could be guaranteed that their conditions, salaries, pensions, and so forth, are "no less favourable".

At the point of the institution's incorporation as a public company, it is likely that the staff will be concerned about the status of their pension rights and other former entitlements. Countries introducing autonomous institutions will need to have an established pension fund that will continue to take care of the staff transferred to such institutions.

The staff of public institutions, whether employed by a central agency or the institution itself, will also be protected by common regulatory provisions of the employment laws of that country. This may, for example, include regulation of working hours, minimum entitlements to annual and sick leave, workplace minimum safety standards and a minimum wage.

Conditions of service such as sickness benefits, hours of work and annual leave can be left to be "no less favourable" for the transferred employees at the point of transfer, although in the longer run they may not improve in line with state improvements. Differentials may arise when new staff are hired on new or lower benefits structures.

It is also possible for the State to regulate the types or levels of qualifications of the staff to be employed in the VET institution, or even to continue to vary these conditions as time goes by. This can be done through annual regulations and conditions laid down within the funding regime and any associated quality assurance regime.

It is possible for the government to determine or merely give guidance on the salary grades to be used and the particular salary levels of those grades, while still giving institutions some autonomy. For example, it is possible to state clearly that there shall be certain grades of teachers (ordinary, higher, managerial) and to state what their respective salary scales shall be, but then give the institution an overall budget and the freedom to decide how many staff to hire at each grade.

The government intentions may be expressed in the following way: "We are increasing overall funding for autonomous VET institutions by 6 per cent. We hope to see an increase in student enrolment of 8 per cent and we suggest that teaching staff should be awarded an overall salary rise of 2.5 per cent, with some priority going to lower-paid grades."

Even where such broad guidance is given and institutions have the full legal authority to make their own decisions, they may be unwilling to do so, since their decisions may be seen as creating tensions between staff. In these circumstances, it is quite common to leave the detailed wage bargaining to a committee of the national association of VET institutions and the appropriate national trade union.

For more details on staff employment regulations, consult Module 7: Staff management.

For more details on staff employment regulations in different countries, go to Unit 1.4: Main regulatory areas of public VET institutions on your CD-ROM.

MODULE 2

The provision of services to VET institutions

Unit 2.1

SERVICE-PROVIDING AGENCIES

2.1.1 CORE AND NON-CORE ACTIVITIES

The core business of a VET institution is to provide learning opportunities for its students. All other activities are subservient to this goal: building maintenance, the planning of new buildings, cleaning, printing, staff recruitment, banking and finance, insurance, canteen and accommodation services, leisure facilities for students and staff are all non-core business activities.

The management of a VET institution has to decide whether the institution should provide any of these non-core businesses itself or whether it should purchase these services from specialist providers. Governments will also need to decide whether they think they should provide any of these services to the institutions, either directly (through specialized units within the ministry) or indirectly (through specialist organizations). A good deal of time can be taken up in managing the day-to-day provision of these services. Thus, at a time when resources are scarce and markets unpredictable, it is becoming increasingly common in modern business management for firms to create a lean management system that concentrates on the core business and buys in or outsources (contracts out) all other activities. Modern VET systems and institutions tend to do the same.

The more governments provide or subsidize the provision of any non-core activity, the harder it becomes to ascertain the true or full costs of the institutions and the services they deliver. This can create difficulties, particularly when a government increases the autonomy of VET institutions; there will be a tendency to underestimate the costs of provision and, as a result, the annual budget initially set for institutions in their first years of autonomy may prove to be insufficient.

The core activities of VET institutions take place in their classrooms, workshops, laboratories, resource and IT centres and libraries as well as in the premises of employers. Learning will also certainly take place in the homes of students, and in public libraries and IT centres. Yet there will be a core set of resources that must be controlled to guarantee the core provision, although some of these resources can be hired on a temporary or seasonal basis. None of these needs to be "owned". Similarly, there will have to be a core staff of professionals permanently attached to or employed by the institution to direct and assist students in their learning. However, there can also be a large number of peripheral or part-time staff, who are not permanently attached to or employed by the institution.

Between the central core business of a VET institution and the more peripheral activities of canteens, leisure facilities, and so on, lies an intermediate range of education and training support activities. These may sometimes be seen by governments as so important to the VET system that public providers are not given much freedom to purchase these services but are more or less compelled to take the services of national autonomous agencies, established by government for that purpose.

2.1.2 TYPES OF SERVICES

There exist many types of organizations that are external to public VET institutions and that can provide a wide range of support and other services. Without being prescriptive, this unit describes the support services that may be required by VET providers and the types of organizations that commonly supply these services.

In the countries that operate autonomous public VET institutions, some agencies may supply a broad range of services. Quality assurance is such an umbrella service that is assigned to a government or non-government agency and involves a number of functions. A more restricted role may be undertaken by a vocational qualifications authority that focuses on the development of VET qualifications as well as on the accreditation of training providers delivering these qualifications. There are other agencies that assist providers with the development of curricula for these qualifications. Skills assessment and certification and some other services may also be the responsibility of public agencies.

Policy advice and coordination services

Training and employment policy advice may be offered by a government's employment and education ministries. A national VET agency, such as a commission, vocational training council or board, may have a similar role to a central ministry. The VET agency, ministry, or association of VET institutions may also coordinate and liaise between training providers and industry stakeholders. Such coordination is particularly important when training programmes involve long-standing practical attachments to companies, which are often difficult to arrange for individual training providers.

Skills assessment and certification

Governments often will only fund programmes that lead to approved vocational qualifications. Students will naturally expect that their achievements in learning will be certificated by a qualifications authority that is widely recognized and accepted in the labour market in which they wish to find employment. Usually, this certification is provided by an authority established by central government for that purpose or by the government department itself. It is less common for an individual VET institution to have the right to certify skills.

In some countries, private associations or charities may be established for this purpose, and almost everywhere there are member-based professional associations that carry out these functions. These voluntary organizations may be largely integrated into a public system by being recognized by central government and given some sort of hallmark or other seal of approval by central government or a responsible agency. In some countries, groups of VET providers have banded themselves together for the purpose of awarding such certificates, although in practice such college-group certificates often operate more within a training market than a labour market, and are more credible as access routes to further VET than to substantial employment.

The certificating body needs to maintain credibility in society and in the labour market if the system is to work. Many students and employers prefer that the skills assessment is done by the national certificating body and often by a process of external written tests. This method of assessment is certainly cheap and can be considered reliable. However, others are aware that external written tests are a poor or invalid way of assessing actual skills in the workplace. The closer the tests come to an operating reality, the more expensive they are and the more likely they are to involve workplace supervisors.

The involvement of assessors who know the students personally is frequently seen as an unreliable system that is incapable of identifying poor performance.

Certificating bodies need to create good working patterns that use both systems. They also need to incorporate and train VET providers and workplace assessors to a sufficiently high standard in order to maintain the system's credibility. Generally, these decisions are the responsibility of an awarding body, although there is always some form of government monitoring of the systems being used.

Curriculum development services

Certificating bodies may or may not develop a course outline curriculum, which is needed to deliver a training programme leading to a national certificate. The knowledge and skills assessment schedule and the span of defined learning may be developed jointly by the assessing and awarding body and a leading industrial body or council.

Whatever course outline is agreed, it will need to be developed into a fuller curriculum and learning plan for the students. In cases where the industry is large and represented by many professional bodies and trade associations, the development of the curriculum may be undertaken by the certificating body by calling in a number of experts to initiate the work and/or validate it. In some countries, curriculum development is a function of teachers themselves; the teaching staff of VET institutions need to be properly trained in course and curriculum development.

Quality assurance services

Quality assurance systems are permanent and are commonly integrated into the funding regimes and are more or less imposed on VET providers as a condition of receiving public funds. Quality assurance services are frequently delivered through inspections and through regular reporting by VET providers.

One important quality assurance technique commonly used by certificating or awarding bodies involves assessment and validation (certification) of the institutions offering training. The validation may look at:

☐ the quantity and quality of the resources available at the institution (including its staff, workshops, training equipment, and so forth);

☐ the level of industry involvement in the VET institution;

☐ the systems and quality of decision-making at the institution;

☐ the overall management of the institution;

☐ the training courses or programmes that are to be assessed for "fitness of purpose";

☐ the capability of the institution to deliver the approved courses or programmes.

The accreditation of a course or institution is usually a one-off activity, which is undertaken prior to the start of a programme or course (although it may be repeated at some time in the future).

An autonomous institution may have the authority to provide its own internal quality assurance/accreditation, skills assessment and/or certification services, acting under the delegated authority of an external national quality assurance agency. In this case, the agency can then focus on assessing the autonomous VET institution's own internal quality assurance systems rather than undertake external quality assurance of the institution's service delivery.

Teacher training and staff development

VET providers need staff that are well qualified. Usually, this means that the teachers:

- possess appropriate VET qualifications (usually at least one level higher than the level of teaching);
- have worked for an appropriate period in the industry at which a programme is aimed;
- have a qualification in teaching.

The second of these requirements poses a problem for the acquisition of the third requirement. Once a suitably qualified worker has found employment in the industry and is earning good money, he or she may be reluctant to give up a salary and become a non-earning student again to obtain a teaching qualification. Teacher training has to be flexible, accessible on a part-time basis and possibly available at every VET institution. Placing VET teacher training in a small number of higher education institutions which have a predominance of school teachers is not always the best solution. Specialist institutions are considered by many to be the best way to deliver teacher training services.

The ongoing development of VET staff (training them in new industrial techniques and updating and upgrading their educational and assessment techniques) has the same problems as initial teacher training for VET teachers, only more so. Short development programmes that may be delivered by a number of supporting agencies can take place inside the institutions themselves. However, accessing the aforementioned external facilities and financing these services is a problem that VET providers need to deal with.

Labour market and training needs data

A crucial area of management decision-making is to determine the portfolio of training offerings that each autonomous VET institution makes. In which occupational sectors and at which levels should training programmes be expanded? Which courses should remain as they are and which need to be phased out? VET delivery planning will require access to quality research on labour market trends and training needs, since VET providers are not likely to have the internal resources for quality research, particularly on region-wide issues.

The data needed for management to reach such decisions may come from outside the institution, although internal data, particularly from follow-up studies (tracer studies) of graduates, are indispensable. For example, this information should at least cover whether course graduates are employed, where and in which sectors they are employed, which topics were useful to them and which were not.

Most of the external data for portfolio planning need to come from:

☐ ITOs rooted in the industry;

☐ government statistics from the ministry of education, labour ministry, or ministry of economics and from their regional agencies;

☐ local employment services.

Although some of these services and data may be available, VET providers need to have access to recent data, which should be produced in a user-friendly format. It is also important to ensure that the institutional management is prepared to interpret and incorporate the data into their training planning decisions.

Vocational guidance

The act of admitting a student onto a particular VET programme is one of vocational guidance, although the VET teachers may not be particularly qualified in this field. They may see themselves as enthusiasts for a particular vocation or simply that they need students to fill the following year's programme; they do not necessarily act impartially and in the best interests of the students themselves. Governments have to consider how to guide young people from school into working life, and decide which institutions can best do this. They will also need to consider how to move adult people up the vocational ladder and from declining into expanding trades. VET institutions are experienced in education and training but should be more modest about their assessment and guidance of possible students. Teachers have a role to play, but the management of VET institutions must make the best use of the other services that are available. Vocational guidance is usually provided within a general education system and may also be carried out by local employment services.

The promotion of VET

VET always needs to be promoted. Not only does every VET system have to compete for able students, but in many countries, academic, general and higher education all have a higher social and general status than VET does. Sector advocacy is required to promote VET and its standing in society, something which is best done jointly by VET providers rather than by individual institutions. A national association of VET institutions may undertake the two important roles of disseminating best practice and sector advocacy. Such sectoral organizations may also have other functions (which are outlined in more detail in Unit 2.2: Associations of public VET institutions).

The role of government in the provision of services

Every government needs to decide how much autonomy it wants to give to VET providers and what it wishes to retain in its own control. Full purchase of all the aforementioned services by the institution might not give the government the kinds of leverage it wants to have over the VET system. For example, leaving the promotion of VET to the uncoordinated activities of each provider acting separately would undoubtedly not work. The government might see the promotion of VET or initial training for vocational teachers as essential to its own vision and plans, and therefore prefer to retain control and funding over them. It might also be aware that these are two elements within the VET system that are likely to be cut by individual institutions in financial difficulties and so therefore wish to retain control over them in order to guarantee those services.

Conditions of access to services

Some services are by their very nature more "regulatory" than "support", for example, course accreditation. It is, therefore, difficult to envisage VET institutions "belonging" to an accreditation agency and receiving services free of charge. However, being charged for accreditation services would be quite normal for an autonomous provider and would not raise any issues of conflict of interest. Membership might be an appropriate basis for receiving services that are support rather than regulatory. These include the dissemination of best practice and sector advocacy undertaken by national associations of training institutions, for which membership is a customary and appropriate condition of access.

For more details on support services for VET institutions in different countries, consult **Unit 2.1: Service-providing agencies** on your CD-ROM.

Unit 2.2

ASSOCIATIONS
OF PUBLIC VET INSTITUTIONS

In each jurisdiction there may exist an association of public VET institutions, either through an initiative of central government, perhaps supported by enabling legislation, or arising from a collective decision of institutional governance/management, based on a recognition of the benefits that might accrue from such an association.

Associations can be established as independent legal entities with formal structures and constitutions. In this case, members should act as shareholders/owners and elect their governing councils. Professional staff, including the chief executive, should be appointed by and be accountable to the governing council. In this sense, VET institutions' associations should be distinguished from informal networks or groupings that may be formed from time to time.

An important issue that the association must resolve at the outset is exactly whose interests the association purports to represent, that is, whether they are the interests of the institution itself, raising further issues of what exactly constitutes an "institution": for instance, its governance, management, staff, students, or all of these as stakeholders? Clear objectives will be required to inform the decisions taken in respect of the roles and functions of the association and its *modus operandi*. Membership of associations may cover institutions as a whole, governing councils or chief executives, depending on function and purpose.

An association of public VET providers will require an agreed set of rules on how it is to operate and how it is to be resourced. The operational rules may include conditions for membership and termination of membership and for dealing with conflicts of interest. It is possible, for example, that an association might wish to promote a particular policy or course of action that, while beneficial to the sector as a whole, may be disadvantageous to a minority of members.

The rights, and possible restrictions, of those minority members to express their dissent may need to be codified in an agreed set of operational rules to protect the integrity of the association. Associations should establish clear criteria and processes for membership, including the ability to suspend or expel members who no longer meet membership eligibility criteria. By contrast, members should have the sanction of exit if they believe the association is not serving their interests. In principle, an association may be held more accountable to its constituent members if they provide the funding for operations through a levy or other device.

The purposes and functions of such VET associations may include:

□ representing the interests of members to government and the community;

□ performing an advocacy role on behalf of its constituent institutions; acting as their collective voice in dealings with other parties, including the government, other stakeholders and other interest groups; and maintaining links and dialogue with other organizations involved in tertiary education, both nationally and internationally;

□ acting as a focal point for advising the government on major policy issues and legislative change;

□ providing nominations for members of government VET committees and advisory bodies;

□ acting as a bargaining unit for system-wide negotiations. For example, an association of VET institutions would probably not be an appropriate forum to resolve particular industrial relations issues (for example setting staff remuneration levels), but the association could legitimately lobby the government as funder if, for example, systemic underfunding was perceived to be the case.

□ providing membership services to institutions, such as an information collection, research and professional development, accreditation and course approval services.

□ acting as a clearing house for information about institutions and for institutions; maintaining a communications network that facilitates cooperation and the dissemination of best practice among member institutions;

□ promoting the welfare of students, staff and graduates;

□ promoting member institutions as providers of quality education and training.

In exercising the functions listed above, individual members of the association may be inhibited by their status if they are public servants and, as such, have to comply with broader public service regulations – for example, their obligation to support the policy of the government of the day, not to criticize government policy, and so on. In the countries where the institutions' staff are civil servants, their associations may be quite limited in what they can say publicly. This can be in stark contrast to the situation that applies to institutions where the staff are not public servants and enjoy long-standing traditions of institutional and academic freedom.

For more details on associations of public VET institutions in different countries, consult **Unit 2.2: Associations of public VET institutions** on your CD-ROM.

MODULE 3

The **VET** institution's management system

Unit 3.1

THE GOVERNING COUNCIL
AND ITS PROCEDURES

3.1.1 THE COMPOSITION AND APPOINTMENT
OF THE GOVERNING COUNCIL

The most frequently used titles for the governing bodies of autonomous VET institutions are "board of governors", "governing board", or "governing council". These names clearly differentiate them from other boards, such as, for instance, the internal "academic board" of many VET institutions. In this module and throughout the handbook, the term "governing council" is used.

The composition and procedure for appointing the governing council of an autonomous VET institution is commonly prescribed in the legislation that establishes public VET institutions as separate corporate bodies (or in subsequent regulations issued by the minister as a result of powers given to the institutions in the legislation). Council members may be appointed for a fixed term of a specified number of years, often with a right of renewal.

The legislation or regulation may prescribe the size of the council or the upper and lower membership limits, allowing for variations in council size to accommodate variations in the size of institutions. The legislation or regulation may also state who may be appointed.

Usually, the regulations on membership attempt to reconcile or acknowledge three approaches to membership of the council:

□ the representation of various stakeholders, including national and local government, community groups, employers from a wide range of industrial sectors, trades unions from those sectors, staff and their unions, students, former graduates; secondary education and higher education professional bodies;

□ the representation of primarily the employers in the industrial sectors served;

□ a council composed of able, clear-thinking, business strategists.

The first of these approaches tends to result in larger, more representative councils, while the last tends to result in a smaller more business-oriented governing council. There are arguments for and against both of these approaches (and the last two are frequently not distinguished from each other). Examples of all forms of governing councils can be found in various national jurisdictions.

In the case of representational councils, the legislation or regulations may also prescribe the various constituencies that are to be represented on the council and the procedure(s) for their appointment, for example: by the minister; or by election from defined groups of individuals, such as alumni, current staff and/or students, professional groups, employers' and/or workers' organizations. In some situations the existing governing council will be encouraged to invite nominations or suggestions and then select members themselves, bearing in mind some general statement or understanding about constituencies. Legislation establishing governing councils may set out categories of membership, for example industry and the community, from which nominees are sought. External appointees must constitute a majority of the membership.

There may also be additional provisions that enable councils to:

☐ co-opt, elect and appoint additional members within any prescribed limits on membership;

☐ dismiss one of its members if that person's behaviour is unacceptable (for example is declared bankrupt; fails to attend meetings; fails to disclose conflicts of interest);

☐ elect a chairperson and deputy chairperson with prescribed terms of office;

☐ invite non-voting members or advisers to its meetings on a short- or long-term basis.

Although the composition of a governing council may reflect or be drawn from a range of stakeholders, the council must carry out its functions as an independent decision-making body acting in the interests of the institution as a whole. Appointments to and resignations from councils should be scheduled so as to provide continuity in expertise while ensuring that membership does not become entrenched and solely time-serving.

For more details on the composition and appointment of VET institutions' governing councils in different countries, consult Unit 3.1: The governing council and its procedures on your CD-ROM.

3.1.2 THE ROLES AND RESPONSIBILITIES OF THE GOVERNING COUNCIL

Governance versus management

Members of governing councils should see their responsibilities as broadly similar to those of directors of public companies: to oversee the good governance of the organization, for example to set and approve broad strategic directions; to ensure that financial viability is maintained through the approval of budgets and monitoring of financial performance; to appoint and review the performance of the chief executive (director/principal); to ensure that statutory obligations are discharged; to exercise due diligence in relation to commercial undertakings; to appoint auditors (unless appointed by the government or government auditors); to receive and act on audit reports and ensure that full and accurate information is available for informed decision-making; and finally to establish asset registers and risk management strategies.

A distinction needs to be drawn between the roles of governance and strategic planning, on the one hand, and the role of operational management, on the other. It is important that, in exercising their role, members of governing councils come to some agreement with the chief executive and the internal management structures (see table 3.1.2).

Table 3.1.2 suggests that the role of governance is one of deciding on the broad objectives of the VET institution. Effective governance is hands-off in the sense that it does not involve itself with the details of delivery. Management is about deciding how the outputs and outcomes are to be delivered by the institution.

Table 3.1.2 General distinctions between governance and management of VET institutions

VET institution's governance	VET institution's management
Governance is concerned with setting the overall direction for institutions through strategic planning and the development of clear goals, strategies and policies (that is, *what* to do).	Management is concerned with achieving the planned goals in accordance with the stated strategies and policies (that is, *how* things are to be done).
Governance is concerned with accountability, which is assured through appropriate reporting mechanisms that are specified and functioning.	Successful management requires that timely, accurate and accessible information is available for effective decision-making and accountability mechanisms.
Governance is about the *ends* of institutions' operations (outputs and outcomes).	Management is more about the *means* for achieving outputs and outcomes.

However, the distinction between strategy and operational management may be harder to maintain in practice. Strategy might state which industrial sectors the institution should be involved in, but then questions might arise about the number and levels of programmes, the number of students, part-time and full-time, and so forth, and the support necessary to implement such programmes. The level of detail on which the council governors may wish to decide may vary from that which the VET institution's director (chief executive) is willing to allow them. The chief executive might try to keep some detail of the decision within the institution. Certain matters will need to be negotiated.

Main functions of the institutional governing council

If legislation or regulation is silent on the matter, then legal systems commonly assume that a governing council has powers to delegate. The governors may delegate any of their functions or powers to the chief executive or to a council's committee; usually a council delegates many of its responsibilities to the chief executive. The formal roles and responsibilities of a governing council usually include the following activities:

☐ Strategic planning – customarily based on a mission statement or charter, strategic planning is, in effect, a long-term statement of the institution's roles, functions and characteristics (outlining the goals that the institution wishes to achieve). There may also be a three-, four- or five-year strategic plan, which outlines the sectors of activity, the levels of VET programmes (and the entry requirements for students) and the target growth areas (or reduction in provision) of programmes. It may also include statements about types of provision (full-time, part-time, distance learning, and so forth), gender or ethnic balance and accessibility. There may also be considerations regarding cooperation or competition with nearby or distant VET providers and some statements about regional planning with other authorities.

☐ Operational planning – usually involves the formulation of numeric objectives (outlining the services that the provider proposes to deliver to achieve its charter goals) and a corporate plan (outlining how these services are to be resourced and delivered), often on an annual basis. Operational planning may have four distinct phases: development (by management); approval (generally by both the council and the funding agency); achievement of objectives (service delivery by the management and staff); and monitoring (by the council and audit agencies responsible for service delivery).

☐ Financial planning and management – normally based on the preparation of a budget (by management), its approval and monitoring (by council), followed by the preparation of annual accounts (by management) and their approval (by council). While the council may delegate its authority in the case of minor contractual arrangements and expenditure to the institutional management, it will generally not delegate matters involving more substantive financial commitments. This element of control by the council can be seen as crucial. The more autonomous the institution, the more it should be keen to ensure its financial viability.

☐ Academic planning and management – the planning of proposed training courses and enrolments (delegated to management) and monitoring their delivery (by council), course and curriculum development, student progress, and course management (delegated to management). The development of courses and day-to-day supervision of academic aspects is usually seen as the responsibility of the academic board of the VET institution. But when course delivery and academic issues are aggregated together, they should be seen as aspects of management and planning.

☐ Determination of institutional policies – customarily developed by management for approval by council and subsequent monitoring by council of adherence by management to the agreed policies. Such policies may refer to ethnic and gender equality among the staff and students, general disciplinary policies, intellectual property rights, health and safety, public relations, or any other policies of the institution.

☐ Human resource management – may include the appointment of the chief executive and the monitoring of his or her performance (by council), and the appointment and monitoring of subordinate staff (customarily delegated to the chief executive or management).

☐ Land and site development, capital development (buildings and equipment) and maintenance – usually delegated to management by council. Councils may take a more detailed interest in the planning and approval of major capital developments to ensure compliance with the institution's charter and strategic plan.

☐ Accountability – customarily centred on the preparation of an annual report (by management) and its approval (by council) and audit (by an external agency). Accountability policies may be clearly specified in a governing council's "instrument of incorporation" or "articles of government".

☐ Entrepreneurial activities – activities proposed by management that are not closely aligned with the institution's charter and operational plans should be closely scrutinized by the governing council prior to implementation (by management) and subsequent monitoring (by council) to ensure consistency with the charter or other strategic planning documents.

☐ Representation and communications – managing public relations and the media.

The VET institution's charter (mission statement)

The strategic position of the charter (which may also be called a mission statement) is determined by the fact that it commonly involves high-level planning statements to meet the expectations of the relevant minister and other external funders and stakeholders. In a sense, the minister seeks reassurance through the charter that the public autonomous VET institution will be acting in general accordance with the government's broad objectives for the public education and training sector. A VET institution's charter should be developed by means of comprehensive consultations between all those concerned and contain details of the consultations to reassure the government that the objectives are supported by other stakeholders. Therefore, charters usually contain broad proactive statements, outlining what the institutions want to become and which services they intend to deliver in the long term.

By contrast, charters do not commonly propose long-term operational scenarios reflecting anticipated trends in the demand for services or the institution's possible responses to these trends. Such scenarios are often part of business plans and so are internal documents. Charters are generally easily accessible through the institution's web site and exist in published form. As they are public documents, they may intentionally be kept broad to avoid possible criticisms of having failed to achieve targets. On the other hand, governments or funding agencies frequently want the more precise operational targets to be lodged with them.

For more details on the roles and responsibilities of VET institutions' governing councils in different countries, consult **Unit 3.1: The governing council and its procedures** on your CD-ROM.

3.1.3 THE GOVERNING COUNCIL'S OPERATIONAL PROCEDURES

The foundation documents that set up the public VET institution as a corporate and autonomous body will usually establish and delimit some aspects of procedures that the institution may not thereafter change and which must be observed if their decisions are to be upheld in a court of law. The name for this document varies from country to country. It may be called an "instrument of government", a "memorandum of association", or a "constitution". This document may also be subject to government approval and must be consistent with legislation. It should reflect the objectives of the institution, the composition of the governing council and its appointment; the number, role and composition of subcommittees; meeting procedures and standing orders; rules for election of council members and other matters relevant to the internal governance of the institution. It should establish basic procedures for identifying the members of the council and for an annual general meeting at which annual reports are approved and at which the chief officials and auditors for the following year are decided on.

There will usually also be a second part to this foundation document or a separate document that sets out some of the procedures whereby the governing council will conduct its business between the annual general meetings. This will include business meetings of the governing council. The second document will also include what may be delegated to committees of the full council, what they may do, what decisions they may make and their procedures. This second document is sometimes called "articles of government", "articles of procedure" or occasionally "standing orders". The most important aspect of these two documents is that they are not something that the governing council can vary at will.

A governing council will often delegate many of its responsibilities to its committees or to the institution's chief executive. Committees may delegate to subcommittees. This process recognizes that council members cannot be expected to deal with an excessive level of detail. In the case that delegations, with appropriate accountabilities, have been made by a council, it is important that they be allowed to operate without council interference. Obviously, if there are evident problems or if accountability mechanisms are not working, the governing council may revoke a delegation.

Where the governing council creates committees or working parties, it may establish some procedures, membership and standing orders for them. As a general legal principle, any such statements, set by a higher authority, cannot be varied except by that higher authority. Where the higher authority is silent on such matters, the committee may make its own decisions.

Determining institutional policies

A key responsibility of the governing council is determining the institution's policies – defined as the general rules of principle or statements of intent or direction that provide guidance to management in reaching decisions on particular matters entrusted to their care.

Policies can be at any level, from general to very detailed. The purpose of the policies as determined by the governing council is to provide guidance to the chief executive and other managers on how to carry out their delegated functions. Accountability includes the determination by council of whether the management has followed their agreed policy.

Adopted policies are frequently documented in an internal policy manual and can be extremely detailed, including all the relevant decisions taken by the governing council and collated according to general themes. The policy manual then becomes a living archive of the governing council's policies. Particularly significant or contentious policy decisions may, of course, be disseminated separately in circulars and proceedings or protocols.

Legislation may allow governing councils to make statutes or by-laws on certain matters. These carry more force than simple policy announcements and give emphasis to the particularly significant decisions of a governing council; strict adherence to them is expected. These should be periodically reviewed to ensure their ongoing relevance. Subcommittees of the governing council may propose a policy that is relevant to a specific objective, and report back to the council with recommendations. Once a governing council has made a policy decision, the implementation of that policy lies with the chief executive. The governing council should monitor the way in which its policies are being administered and if concerns arise, then they should be dealt with as appropriate, whether this is by policy amendment or by reviewing the chief executive's implementation procedures.

Three stages in policy development and implementation can be identified:

☐ Determining policies – Who is responsible? On what basis is this responsibility determined?

☐ Revision and updating of policies – Who has the authority to amend policies? When can policies be reviewed and possible revisions made? How are revisions communicated?

☐ Monitoring implementation – Who is responsible for monitoring the policies? What are the appropriate monitoring procedures?

Some important areas for governing councils to monitor include: finance; academic matters; personnel; land and site development; capital development; advocacy; accountability; and public relations.

It is important for the council to evaluate how well the institution is performing. This can be done by referring to the performance indicators established for the institution. The performance of the chief executive should also be reviewed in relation to a mutually agreed set of criteria. Monitoring of performance will commonly be based on the institution's budget implementation recognizing that when the governing council adopts a budget it is endorsing the management's business plan for the forthcoming financial year.

Workings of governing councils

In certain jurisdictions, legislation provides for the:

☐ remuneration of council members within maximum rates fixed by the government;

☐ reimbursement of reasonable expenses for travel and other costs, in addition to meeting fees.

Legislation may also require council members to disclose any personal or family financial interest in the activities of the VET institution or in any aspect of its trading, buying or selling of supplies or property, or hiring of staff.

Such declarations may be required when a person becomes a member of the governing council. Subsequently, the member may be required to remind the council of this on any matter being considered by the council and be prevented from voting on the matter. A member may also be forbidden to vote or take part in the discussion of any matter before council in which the member has, directly or indirectly, any financial or pecuniary interest.

Council meetings require considerable resources and are expensive in terms of time and money, and a great deal of council and staff time can be spent preparing for and following up council meetings. The most effective form of meeting procedure is when decisions are made by consensus, after free discussion by all council members. In adopting the consensus approach, care must be taken to ensure that all legal requirements are met, particularly for record keeping (minutes), matters considered "in committee" and meeting closure. "In committee" means that the public (and the media) are excluded from the deliberations. The public's right to know has to be balanced against commercially sensitive or personal information, and so on, with the criteria strictly prescribed.

Where the goodwill required for consensus is absent or when meetings are adversarial, the chairperson should follow the governing council's own standing orders and these should be based on meeting procedures that are standard in the legal jurisdiction. Finally, the governing council of an autonomous public institution should regularly review its own performance with the goal of improving its own effectiveness, and at all times focus on the needs of its stakeholders – government, students, parents, employers, workers and the community.

Council subcommittees

The governing council of an autonomous institution should only form subcommittees and working parties to meet a real need, which may be either ongoing or related to a specific project. When this is the case, the governing council should consider establishing:

☐ the terms of reference of the subcommittee or working party;

☐ its decision-making powers;

☐ its length of life;

☐ a prescribed voting structure;

☐ arrangements for reporting back to the governing council;

☐ prescribed membership and the ability to co-opt additional members;

☐ any limitations on the use of expert witnesses in discussions, and so forth;

☐ expected outputs from the subcommittee or working party.

Each governing council must assess its own requirements for subcommittees and working parties. Some institutions may elect for the full council to deal with all matters and not to establish subcommittees other than those that may be required by legislation, for example an academic council. Others may decide to create subcommittees, such as "executive", "finance", or "works", while others may prefer to make extensive use of working parties on particular narrowly defined issues.

Committees and working parties can be important to the overall policy-setting role and may be able to consider situations in greater detail than the governing council itself. They can operate within terms of reference established by the council or set their own for council approval. Their membership may extend beyond the governing council itself and, for example, include sector or course advisory committees, whose main purpose is to serve industry or the community.

For more details on the operational procedures of governing councils in different countries, consult **Unit 3.1: The governing council and its procedures** on your CD-ROM.

Unit 3.2

THE ROLE
OF THE CHIEF EXECUTIVE

3.2.1 ROLES AND RESPONSIBILITIES

In general, the management structure of an autonomous VET institution includes the following elements (or their equivalents):

☐ a governing council;

☐ a clerk or secretary to the council members (or governors);

☐ a chief executive;

☐ a management team (involving chief executive and senior managers);

☐ an academic board;

☐ managers of departments, units and operational (cost) centres.

According to this configuration, the chief executive is in a position to manage the institution's academic and administrative affairs and to be the employer of its staff. The role of the governing council is to ensure that the chief executive manages the institution in accordance with its mission, objectives and required outputs. The council must ensure that the chief executive is given the authority needed to manage through appropriate delegations. A key aspect of any delegation is that, although the council can delegate authority for an action, the responsibility for that action remains with the council.

VET institutions' management structures can vary. In some structures, the chief executive is also the principal academic officer (or teacher). Although the role of chief administrative officer (also called registrar or bursar) may remain distinct, he or she may also act as the secretary (or clerk) to the governing council. In this way the governing council retains two avenues of approach into the academic and administrative affairs of the institution.

The council must also decide whether or not to merge the role of secretary to the council with the role of chief administrative officer. In commercial businesses, all administration is seen as the responsibility of the chief executive, while the secretary to the council is a clearly defined and separate role.

Once the governing council has made its decisions regarding the institution's mission and strategies, their implementation becomes the responsibility of the chief executive.

The chief executive of a public autonomous VET institution is customarily responsible for:

☐ preparing the corporate plan (an internal management document that describes how the institution will meet its objectives and deliver its expected outputs);

☐ developing the operating and capital budget; ensuring that internal controls are established to oversee expenditure and finance;

☐ managing the employment of other staff and maintaining industrial relations;

☐ ensuring that an internal reporting system is established to supervise the plan's implementation; preparing the annual report to enable the institution's performance to be measured against its objectives.

In some jurisdictions, autonomous public institutions are required by legislation or regulation to establish an academic board or equivalent to advise the council on matters relating to training courses, curricula, awards and other academic matters. The academic boards generally comprise the chief executive as chairperson and representatives of the staff and students. The relationships between governing council, academic board and the chief executive will vary between autonomous institutions, but it is important that each party has a clearly identified role. In some jurisdictions, academic boards are increasingly becoming involved in academic self-evaluations and internal audits.

The other crucial role is managing the so-called "boundaries", which are not always explicit. Someone has to deal with various stakeholders, such as funders, inspectors, employers, community and local government organizations, and so on. The chief executive of the public institution has either to do this directly or must delegate this function.

For more details on financial management in an autonomous VET institution, refer to **Module 5: Budgeting and financing**.

For more details on staff employment, management and industrial relations in the VET institutions, refer to **Module 7: Staff management**.

Performance monitoring and reporting

In normal circumstances, the chief executive is primarily responsible for any formal reporting to the stakeholders, including funding agencies. Although it is always the corporation itself that does this in a formal sense, the governing council normally delegates reporting to its chairperson, who then countersigns any documentation prepared by the chief executive and his or her team.

Responsibility for interacting with the media (and indirectly the stakeholders) is normally left to the governing council's chairperson or the chief executive and often depends on the matter of detailed knowledge or strength of concern with the community. Governing councils customarily decide who will be responsible for speaking to the media on issues of governance or management. However, usually it is a case of personal negotiations between the chief executive, the public relations director of the institution and the chairperson of the governing council. Precedents get established, but it is usually up to the chief executive to decide on whether it is necessary to consult with the governing council's chairperson on any new or particular issue before proceeding.

For more details on measuring and reporting performance, refer to **Module 11: Performance monitoring and reporting**.

For more details on the roles and responsibilities of VET institutions' chief executives (directors/principals) in different countries, consult **Unit 3.2: The role of the chief executive** on your CD-ROM.

3.2.2 CONDITIONS OF EMPLOYMENT

The role of the chief executive and the distinction between the VET institution's governance and management become more important as the institution gains more autonomy. Where autonomy is restricted, the government agencies assume the governance role and chief executives revert to being line managers. If the government relinquishes its governance role in favour of autonomous councils acting on behalf of government as a major (but not the only) stakeholder, the chief executive can expect to have conditions of employment and responsibilities more akin to a chief executive of a private company or corporation.

In the jurisdictions where institutions operate with substantial autonomy, chief executives are supposed to manage the academic and administrative affairs of institutions and are customarily the employer of all other institutional staff in lieu of the government. The governing council must ensure that the chief executive is given the authority needed to manage the employment of the staff and the institution.

In this case, the most important responsibility of the governing council is to select and appoint a competent chief executive, in accordance with the processes and conditions set out in legislation or other regulations and founding documents. The governing council will be the legal employer of not only the chief executive but also of all the staff. In practice, the governing council will only directly concern itself with the employment of the secretary to the council, the chief executive and occasionally a handful of senior staff. Even then, the council may choose to do this by subcommittee. It may also delegate the appointment of senior staff to the chief executive but ask to be represented by one or two governors.

The contents of a chief executive's employment contract are likely to include:

☐ a job (or position) description;

☐ details of remuneration and review procedures;

☐ details of tenure, right of extension and procedures for termination;

☐ arrangements for retirement and superannuation;

☐ procedures for a regular performance review;

☐ details of leave entitlements and hours of work;

☐ specified allowances, expenses and fringe benefits;

☐ training entitlements and arrangements and any sabbatical leave arrangements.

Clearly, it is not possible for members of a VET institution's governing council to know about every activity or transaction into which the institution enters, and it may be appropriate that a council delegates all responsibilities associated with management to the chief executive.

For more details on the roles and responsibilities of the chief executive in different countries, consult **Unit 3.2: The role of the chief executive** on your CD-ROM.

Unit 3.3

ALTERNATIVE ORGANIZATIONAL STRUCTURES OF AUTONOMOUS VET INSTITUTIONS

The organizational structures of autonomous VET institutions will vary considerably, in part reflecting the configuration of the external policy and organizational environment, the way demand for VET services is structured as well as the limits of their autonomy. However, in general a VET institution's structures will include some or all of the following elements:

- a governing council;
- a chief executive;
- a senior management team made up of the chief executive and other senior managers ("executive" or "senior management group", and so on);
- an academic board;
- a number of teaching departments (usually specified as operational units or cost centres);
- a number of academic, administrative and other support departments;
- campuses.

For details on the appointment, roles and responsibilities of governing councils, see **Unit 3.1: The governing council and its procedures**.

For details on the appointment, roles and responsibilities of chief executives, see **Unit 3.2: The role of the chief executive**.

The role of the academic board or equivalent is to advise the governing council on matters relating to training courses, their curricula, awards and other academic matters, and so forth. The relationship between a governing council, its academic board and a chief executive will vary between institutions, but it is important that each party has a clearly identified role. Internationally, academic boards are becoming increasingly involved in academic self-evaluations and internal audits. These functions are operated through internal academic quality management systems (QMSs), commonly approved by an external agency.

Education and training delivery structures

Most VET institutions are composed of two distinct groups of staff:

(1) those that directly teach the students or assist in their learning (training delivery structures);

(2) those that support the teaching and learning activity but may not normally deal with the students (support structures).

Usually, this means that the institutional structure is divided into two: an academic team and a support team, with each team often headed by a deputy chief executive or staff of similar rank. Each team may be divided into distinct departments that reflect their functions.

The organizational structure of an autonomous VET institution will, to varying degrees, be a matter for its chief executive to determine in coordination with the governing council. In general, the training delivery structure will include some form of breakdown into departments based on fairly broad vocational or academic areas. A designated "head of department" is customarily responsible to the chief executive for the activities and performance of his or her own department. What has to be determined is the size of these departments and the degree of spread or their specificity (as the opposite of spread).

There are two different approaches to establishing VET institutions. One is to keep them quite small, serving only a single industry or industrial sector or a group of occupations that are clearly related. The other approach resembles traditional polytechnics in that a single institution can serve a wide range of industries and occupations. The decisions about these matters are made usually before the VET institution is formed and are subsequently difficult to change.

In order to answer the basic questions of size and departmental specialization, it might be best to look for some guiding principles and purposes behind the organization of VET institutions. The following can be assumed:

☐ It is beneficial for students to be taught by a number of specialists in specific subdivisions of their vocational choices and that these teachers should coordinate their structuring of the learning and its assessment.

☐ The teachers of individual students should be able to communicate easily with each other and the industry they are indirectly serving as well as with any external curriculum and assessing bodies.

☐ Staff members should have a clearly identifiable line manager to whom they are directly responsible but they should also be able to communicate easily with other sections of the organization.

☐ Managers should have enough time and not too many people to supervise and coordinate. They should also have enough time to liaise with other managers in the organization to whom they are either internal customers or suppliers of services.

The following three examples of departments – a department of engineering, one of social welfare and childcare, and one of business studies – illustrate how these principles can work in practice. Few of the teachers attached to any of these departments would be able to offer much teaching in the other departments, although there might be some opportunities. The engineering department and the welfare and childcare department would probably not need to employ a specialist teacher of law on a full-time basis. It might be better to "borrow" a law teacher from business studies for a few hours a week. The engineering department might need a specialist in surface coatings of steel for only a few hours a week and would hire a freelance teacher or someone from a specialist enterprise. The same line of reasoning should be applied when deciding on other small blocks of time and teaching. In the above case, the three departments can be managed almost as separate entities. However, it is clear that:

☐ most teachers will have a single line manager for the bulk of their work and that that person will be known as the head of department;

☐ the head of department's role is to timetable, manage and control the staff;

☐ the head of department will have to manage the space and workshops and other resources allocated to this department;

☐ all team meetings for teaching planning and managing skills assessment can be convened and managed by a single head of department;

☐ the head of each department should be able to manage the course development and the staff development programmes, which should be determined by the demands of industry and students;

☐ for each larger course, if it involves various teachers, a course manager may need to be appointed;

☐ a wide range of costs can clearly be allocated either to the whole department (cost centre), or to subsections within it or to individual courses.

This is a traditional model of organization and it has its limitations. One key variation is whether or not the heads of departments are expected to teach and, if so, how much time they should set aside to teaching. A rough guide might be that where the head of department is expected to manage the equivalent of 24 full-time staff, or 40 courses or programmes of 600 or more students, he or she is unlikely to find the time to teach. When departments get larger, they might be split into two for similar reasons: namely, there are too many staff, programmes and students for one person to oversee. No clear guidance can be given; much depends on the degrees of similarity and differences contained and the pace of change required. However, as examples of divisions of the three aforementioned departments:

☐ the engineering department could be divided into mechanical and electrical;

☐ business studies could be divided into office management and legal studies, and accounting and professional studies;

☐ the social welfare and childcare department could easily be separated.

Some chief executives put a great deal of effort into making their departments roughly the same size, although the reason for doing so can be obscure. It may relate to salary structures, since it might be difficult to pay heads of department different salaries for different-sized departments, in which case it might be better to review the salary structures rather than to merge different sections of staff, courses and students into nominally the same department. However, the reverse could also happen; as industries or social priorities change, it might become necessary to merge and contract parts of the training delivery structures.

In larger institutions, a number of training departments may be aggregated into a few, larger units, commonly called faculties or schools. This may come about because of the "span of control" problems of the chief executive. If a chief executive has a deputy, he or she could be assigned to look after the support departments (see below) and many training departments as well as all the boundary relationships that can simply be too much for the chief executive. It might be better for the chief executive to look after only four deans or faculty heads, each of whom looks after four heads of department. A related problem is that of getting a workable academic board that can contribute to the effective management of the institution. One tradition is that each head of department must be on the board and that there also be an elected representative from the department's staff. Too many departments can become unworkable; it can sometimes be better to use just faculty representation.

Sometimes, departmental splits within these rather traditional structures may arise, which, for a number of reasons, follow a division between full-time and part-time students. In the examples given above, dividing business studies into office management and professional studies may effectively create two levels of programme: a Level 2&3 department and a Level 4&5 department. Splitting social welfare and childcare may, in effect, turn into a division of mature part-time students and younger full-time students. Departmental splits may be necessary in order to establish programmes of higher and lower status or simply to keep teaching teams more or less intact.

An additional delivery structure may be established when there is a need for a pre-vocational department, where all the students are either very young or are unemployed adults. Where significant blocks of the population do not have secondary education or have received it in another language, learning support units that specialize in providing basic language and literacy skills may be necessary. There may be some other specialized student-learning support units that do not have their "own" students but support students from many departments.

A key decision-maker in the structuring of a VET institution is the chief executive. Whatever general principles may exist, it might be better to acknowledge that much organization design and redesign comes about because a chief executive feels the need to remain in control. Such negotiations are usually triggered by an event such as the appointment of a new chief executive or by a major change in funding provisions, and so forth.

Whatever the situation, the chief executive will be held accountable for the institution's successes or failures by its governing council. The chief executive will want to ensure the complete control of the organization. Some reorganizations also take place simply to move certain individuals within the organization, to move some into the organization and to move some out. A characteristic of such situations is that the chief executive redesigns the structure, making some staff redundant. As some jobs have ceased to exist, staff must reapply for new jobs in the new structure or otherwise accept a redundancy package.

Support services structure

The administrative support staff, particularly in larger institutions, are commonly allocated at departmental level, where their day-to-day supervision takes place. They often remain in a more formal sense the responsibility of the chief executive's deputy for administrative affairs. A similar situation exists with technical, workshop and laboratory staff. For reasons of efficiency, most administrative support services are usually provided by a separate administrative section under a senior manager commonly called a "manager corporate services" or "director of administration". This person is usually a member of the senior management team reporting to the chief executive but may be equal in status to the director of academic affairs. Depending on the size of the institution, financial and information management support services may be separated from other more general technical and administrative support services.

The technical and administrative support services and staff required to support the training delivery functions of an autonomous VET provider will generally include the following separate departments or sections:

☐ human resources – staffing, payroll, recruitment, performance assessment, staff development, labour/employee relations;

☐ student management and the management of student records – courses and timetables, enrolments, academic records, student support and counselling;

- finance – accounting practices and systems, asset recording, insurance, purchasing, financial planning and control, internal audits;

- asset management – dealing with campus, buildings, equipment, facilities maintenance, cleaning, building security, canteens and related activities;

- libraries and IT centres and banks of computers – while essential for students, this section and its staff may be seen as attached to the academic structure rather than to technical support;

- information management – computerized systems, data integrity and security, communications, reporting;

- marketing and development – institutional profile, student enrolment, liaison with industry, market research;

- course and curriculum development – managing curriculum initiatives from inside and outside, relationships with external awarding or assessing bodies, quality assurance;

- staff development programmes – often linked to national curriculum and assessment initiatives, new educational or national promotional policies.

Not all the above departments or sections may exist. In the case of student enrolment, for example, where an institution and its departments have relied heavily on part-time students from industry, little student counselling will be needed, since the programmes required by employers are usually very clear. Recruitment and liaison with industry may be much the same thing and organized within departments. When the VET institution moves to full-time students, it may wish to centralize a good deal of its marketing into a professional marketing department or section (which may also use other professional firms). To ensure that students get onto a programme that is suitable for their needs, the institution might want to use a centralized student guidance and interview system that uses departmental staff. Student guidance may be a section within marketing or it could be seen as more academic and be moved across to the teaching side of the institution. The varieties of pattern can be large.

Implications of training policies to institutional structures

In some countries VET institutions have been subject to a wide variety of national initiatives, such as:

- adult literacy programmes;
- training programmes for the unemployed;
- IT programmes for those in work;
- IT development in all VET programmes;

☐ enhanced gender equality programmes;

☐ enhanced ethnic equality programmes;

☐ quality assurance systems and procedures;

☐ modularization of the learning and qualifications structures;
☐ competence-based training and skills assessment.

The above developments will certainly influence all departments and most teachers, and need to be supported by the VET institution's academic staff. The academic sections may be regrouped to reflect the aforementioned requirements; they will continue to report to the director of academic affairs (or deputy chief executive).

Multi-campus structures

The operation of larger institutions may also be conducted over two or more geographically separated campuses. Satellite campuses are usually the responsibility of a campus director or manager, who customarily is an ex officio member of the executive or senior management group. The managers of satellite campuses of a large multi-campus institution may enjoy a significant degree of autonomy from their parent institution.

In multi-sector campuses, a senior executive may be appointed at each campus to manage its day-to-day activities. In this case, the roles and responsibilities need to be made clear as the campus manager's roles can cut across the institution-wide responsibilities of deputies and heads of department. This can lead to a lack of consistency and integration across the institution.

Similarly, current practice is also to develop larger and broader academic departments (schools) in order to: capitalize on opportunities for teaching and learning across subject areas; ensure that programmes promote broad skills outcomes; and ensure effective interaction with industry.

Some multi-campus VET institutions do not appoint the campus managers; similar courses across all campuses are administered by the relevant "training school or faculty" managers from the institution's headquarters.

Institutions involved in fee-for-service and commercial activities commonly establish specialist units to promote and coordinate these activities, recruiting staff with commercial and business skills and experience to carry out these functions.

The identification of an optimal internal organizational structure is a matter for review by the institution's governing council and its management. Proposed changes to internal organizational structures are, understandably, matters of considerable interest for academic and support staff alike and will be achieved with the least disruption when governance and management ensure that there is full staff consultation.

For more details on alternative organizational structures of autonomous VET institutions in different countries, consult Unit 3.3: Alternative organizational structures of autonomous VET institutions on your CD-ROM.

Unit 3.4

INTERNAL OPERATIONAL PROCEDURES

3.4.1 DELEGATING AND REPORTING

The typical organizational structure of an autonomous VET institution will include the following elements:

- a governing council;
- a chief executive;
- a senior management team;
- an academic board;
- teaching, research and consultancy departments;
- operational units (cost centres). These units, depending on the size of the institution, will be organized into two or three tiers or hierarchies. The largest aggregations are usually called faculties, followed by departments and then schools or sections;
- administrative and support departments or sections (also cost centres).

At each level of the organization, individual section managers provide operational information to their relevant senior managers:

- the managers of operational units provide information to their respective heads of department;
- administrative sections will supply information both to the operational unit managers and to the senior management team;
- heads of departments report to the chief executive and the senior management team;
- the chief executive provides key information to the governing council to enable effective governance of the institution.

The complexity of the institution's operation will generally make it impossible for its governing council to know about every activity or transaction, and so it is appropriate for management responsibilities to be delegated to the chief executive. A key management decision is to determine at what levels of aggregation the data are routinely supplied. The chief executive may further delegate routine operational decisions to heads of departments or operational unit managers as appropriate. A key aspect of delegation is that, although authority can be delegated, the responsibility for it cannot.

For more details on governance, management and the delegation of responsibility in autonomous institutions, refer to **Unit 3.1: The governing council and its procedures**.

For more details on alternative organizational structures, refer to **Unit 3.3: Alternative organizational structures of autonomous VET institutions**.

A key responsibility of a governing council is to determine the institutional policies to provide guidance to the chief executive and managers. Governing councils may make statutes or by-laws or internal regulations that codify these policies (see below). Policies are usually introduced through the chief executive. The implementation of approved policy becomes the responsibility of the chief executive and the management.

The governing council should also establish rules and regulations governing the internal conduct of the institution. Rules and regulations should be regarded as an essential part of risk management and should be established in major areas of identified risk to protect the interests of the stakeholders – the government, students, staff and the community. Rules and regulations in some areas are likely to be influenced by government policies and legal requirements.

The scope for internal regulation

There is some merit in having all the policies, rules and regulations of an autonomous institution codified in a policy manual (or equivalent). Developing and codifying institutional policy in a manual generally involves three processes: establishing the policy; revising and updating the policy; and monitoring the policy.

The policy manual of an autonomous VET institution will normally include policies on:

☐ financial management;

☐ academic management (student management, student progress assessment, discipline and grievances; equal treatment, sexual harassment and privacy; research, consultancy and intellectual property issues);

☐ personnel management (staffing, discipline, capabilities and development);

☐ accountability management;

- managing land and site development;
- managing capital development (buildings and equipment, access to buildings, parking, library and information);
- managing advocacy, public relations and the media.

Public institutions that enjoy significant levels of financial autonomy are commonly subjected to rigorous financial accountability, often prescribed in legislation. Robust policies on financial accountability are essential to safeguard the VET institution's assets (intellectual, financial, physical as well as those of its reputation) and the government's ownership interests in them.

It is important that the governing council monitors the institution's financial performance. Because the governing council is not involved in routine operational matters, it normally uses the institution's budget for this monitoring role. Having agreed to the budget, the governing council is, in effect, endorsing the management's plan for the financial year.

The governing council is only able to monitor an institution's financial performance effectively when there is effective management reporting, which should be clear, understandable and in a format that enables the governing council to be aware of the present and likely future financial health of the institution. In essence, the institution's management is required to perform in accordance with the agreed budget and to be held accountable to the governing body for any divergencies from it.

The chief executive is responsible for the development of the operating and capital budgets. Final approval of a budget by the governing council should be on the basis of whether it accomplishes its priorities and whether it is realistic.

An autonomous institution may control substantial resources, and its governing council should ensure that the best possible use is made of them. A strong internal control is necessary to manage expenditure and financial information properly, and a treasury policy is necessary to ensure reasonable security over cash assets while still obtaining a reasonable return for them. The chief executive is responsible for ensuring that appropriate internal control systems are established, generally through explicit delegations to designated individual staff.

Flexible organizations do not establish all operational procedures but only those relating to the first two or three levels. Heads of operational and support departments may then establish their own control systems below that. Anything that a head of department may properly do, they may delegate by clear and explicit methods. To reiterate, a key aspect of delegation is that, although authority can be delegated, the responsibility for it cannot.

For more details on financial management in autonomous institutions, refer to **Module 5: Budgeting and financing**.

The chief executive normally manages the academic and administrative affairs of an autonomous VET provider and may be the employer, either directly or by delegated authority, of other staff of the institution. In the capacity of employer, the chief executive will be responsible for implementing the policy on personnel management and for industrial relations within the institution.

For more details on staff management in autonomous VET institutions, refer to Module 7: Staff management.

Policy on training matters will normally originate from within an academic board (or equivalent), consisting of the chief executive and staff and student representatives. The function of a VET institution's academic board is generally to advise its governing council on all matters relating to training courses, curricula, awards and other academic matters, such as research, consultancy and intellectual property.

For more details on delegating and reporting in autonomous VET institutions in different countries, consult Unit 3.4: Internal operational procedures on your CD-ROM.

3.4.2 PLANNING AND ACCOUNTABILITY MECHANISMS

Autonomous institutions will require a number of planning and accountability mechanisms that operate at various levels within the institution. Some of the mechanisms may be prescribed by legislation. These planning and accountability mechanisms normally follow an annual cycle, which is linked with the institutional budget process. They generally include four elements:

(1) a charter (or equivalent) that sets out long-term goals and purposes appropriate for the institution and provides a long-term view of its future direction, and that has been prepared, after appropriate consultation, with the stakeholders;

(2) a statement of objectives (or equivalent) expressed in the form of outputs (deliverables), that describes *which* services the institution expects to deliver;

(3) a corporate plan (or equivalent) that describes *how* the institution will deliver its outputs as set out in its statements of objectives;

(4) an annual report that provides a qualitative and quantitative measure of the institution's actual performance against its statement of objectives.

Usually each department, section or faculty within the institution will have its own annual plan that is cross-referenced to its corporate plan. This link serves as an important communications tool – each department, section or faculty is able to identify how it contributes to the outputs of the institution as a whole – and it facilitates broader acceptance of the institution's goals, objectives and future direction.

A common problem of all VET providers is handling the interaction of the length of the academic and planning cycles with the relative brevity of the annual financial cycles that governments prefer. Routinely, it takes a year to plan a programme, two to three years before the first graduates emerge, a further year before any community and industrial evaluation is possible and yet another year for evaluation to affect planning: five to six years in total. Most governments will only commit themselves to a single year, with a very broad "indicative plan" beyond that. For this reason governments need to be urged to turn at least part of their indicative plan into a commitment, while institutions need to acquire flexible institutional management systems.

For more details on the planning cycle in autonomous VET institutions, including examples of charters, statements of objectives and corporate plans (or equivalents), refer to **Module 4: The planning of training delivery**.

For more details on the accountability cycle including examples of annual reports, refer to **Module 11: Performance monitoring and reporting**.

The governing councils of autonomous VET institutions are also responsible for the maintenance of fixed assets and the capital investment base, and must deal with issues of acquisitions, construction and facilities management. Before any development is embarked on, a governing council should consider the requirements for future facilities and how these are to be funded. In this regard, governing councils should be proactive. The greater the level of the VET institution's autonomy, the more its governing council should be proactive rather than simply monitor situations. A facilities management plan (or equivalent) will address these issues and will document the timing and action required.

For more details on the internal operational procedures in public VET institutions followed in different countries, go to **Unit 3.4: Internal operational procedures** on your CD-ROM.

Communicating internal regulations

Codifying the policies of an autonomous VET institution in a policy manual (or equivalent) makes it easier for interested parties (staff, students, external stakeholders) to access approved policy. A policy manual needs to be updated regularly and the updated manual may exist only on the intranet of the institution; staff will be advised that printed copies may be outdated. This would facilitate the update of regulations and their use in the induction process of students and staff.

Certain sections of manuals may only draw attention to the existence of policies that are easily accessible through a library or Internet. As the cost of updating such manuals tends to be high, it is not unusual for different sections to have different levels of detail. For example, students need to know about their assessment and discipline procedures as well as their rights and procedures of complaints about staff. However, they may not need to know all the procedures for staff discipline or the regulations governing the procurement of equipment.

A national association of training institutions is well placed to act as the collective voice for institutions, and to develop, confirm and promulgate agreed policy advice on behalf of its members as well as to provide an effective communications framework and support service for its members.

Autonomy means that an institution will have to make some sort of legal declaration that its own terms and conditions follow exactly the advice of a national association of VET providers or show where it departs from the advice. Some attention may have to be paid to the precision with which this operates.

A useful support service that a national association of VET institutions can provide for its members is a country handbook that contains relevant information and advice on the country's legal and regulatory environment, governance and management processes, and best-practice institutional management, including planning, financial management and accountability.

Sections of a country handbook can be further customized to the needs of middle-level management (heads of department, cost centre managers, and so forth) as appropriate. Less formal measures for communicating internal policy and regulations can include in-house publications, such as newsletters, memoranda and circulars, which can be distributed in print form or by email.

For more details on the role of national associations of VET institutions, refer to **Unit 2.2: Associations of public VET institutions.**

For more details on the planning and accountability mechanisms in the VET sector in different countries, consult **Unit 3.4: Internal operational procedures** on your CD-ROM.

Unit 3.5

THE VET INSTITUTION'S
MANAGEMENT INFORMATION SYSTEM

3.5.1 ORGANIZATIONAL DESIGN
OF THE MANAGEMENT INFORMATION SYSTEM

A modern VET institution requires a management information system (MIS) to support the effective governance of the institution and to assist in external reporting and accountability. The government needs information about the performance of the VET system in order to respond to the problems experienced by institutions and stakeholders. It also needs up-to-date information on enrolments and quality-assured courses to deliver its public resources effectively. Providers need information on student participation and learning progress to plan effectively and to respond quickly to changing patterns of demand. Providers also need information to support internal financial and quality assurance processes. Students need easy access to comprehensive information about what training programmes have on offer and their likely outcomes.

A comprehensive MIS that supports an efficient and effective VET system will generally include a national data collection mechanism through which training providers furnish data on their courses and students. This national data collection system can be used to support a number of useful databases, for example:

□ lists of quality assured providers, qualifications, training packages and courses across the national training system to support quality assurance;

□ information on training courses and training outcomes to support informed decision-making by both students and training providers.

National databases may be maintained by central agencies charged with collecting, storing, analysing, collating and making available useful information on the national VET system. The collection of information is substantially facilitated by introducing a national student identifier system which will utilize the agreed descriptors assigned to previous and current students. The use of a national student descriptor system does, however, raise some privacy issues for students that should (and can) be adequately addressed. There is an important difference between the commonly used descriptors of a student and a unique student, for it is the latter that raises issues of privacy. However, even where it is decided, nationally, to use a unique student identifier that they carry throughout life, the issues of confidentiality can still be met.

The useful descriptor data that are collected, stored, analysed, collated and made available may include some or all of the following information:

☐ student participation – for example enrolments, full-time/part-time status and whether study is contact or distance;

☐ student characteristics – basic demographic information (age, gender, ethnicity, nationality, location of residence);

☐ student outcomes – for example exam passes, learning credits achieved, qualifications awarded, labour market destinations and employer satisfaction;

☐ course programmes offered – described by occupational sector, industrial sector and level;

☐ quality approvals/accreditations, quality audits, compliance, complaints;

☐ research activities – for example areas of activity, cost and outputs;

☐ course costs – for example costs per equivalent full-time student (EFTS);

☐ student fees and other charges;

☐ uptake of any assistance provided directly to students, for example loans and grants;

☐ provider performance – for example viability reports.

The information collected by national agencies may be made available for quite different purposes. For example, a central agency may collect information on a national vocational training system to:

☐ inform the allocation of public funding to training providers, that is, information on participation, course costs, course quality, provider performance, and so on;

☐ inform decision-making by prospective students, that is, information on learning outcomes, graduates' employability, course costs and quality, fees, and so on.

In addition, databases are often maintained locally by the training institutions themselves to inform decision-making by their governing councils and senior management.

A new requirement to report information to one or more external agencies in categories or descriptors as required by the agency may be a challenge for the MIS of an autonomous VET institution, particularly if public funding is made conditional on the provision of such information. However, it may also enable more effective local decision-making because the governing council and senior management of the institution will then have access to better information, held locally in institutional databases and/or nationally by the responsible external agencies.

It is necessary to distinguish between, on the one hand, essential and minimal operational information required to run an organization effectively and, on the other hand, management information. Examples of operational information might include:

☐ an explicit accounting for the money the VET institution disburses;

☐ a record of student progress (for instance a record of every student's work-based assessment).

Clearly, the VET provider cannot run effectively on a day-to-day basis without this kind of operational data. However, some elements of operational information can become management information when, after some form of aggregation, comparison and analysis, it can inform management decisions.

In addition, there are many pieces of information that are analysed in management decisions, which are not "operational information" essential to the immediate day-to-day needs of the institution. These include:

☐ policy statements from governments and their agencies;

☐ basic demographic data from the community;

☐ relevant labour market data, for instance, occupational structures of the local industries;

☐ local economic and development data.

As a hypothetical example of the use of operational data as management data, one could take as a typical government policy the wish to raise the take-up of vocational qualifications among those aged 25 to 45, particularly at Level 4. An institution then needs to review its database to see how many such students it had over the past four or five years, see the size of that demographic group in the general population in the catchment area, develop policies to see how it can expand recruitment in that group and monitor, with some care, the growth (or otherwise) of such groups in its student population.

This will not only need to be done at the level of the whole institution's student population, but also at various levels of disaggregation to evaluate which faculties, departments and schools are doing well and which are doing less well. At this point, the basic operational data of the institution becomes management information.

It is clear that the general descriptors or descriptive categories used in the databases of VET institutions must be the same as those used in the policy, operation or funding documents of the government or its agencies. In addition, these basic descriptors will have to conform to the categories used in the wider demographic, economic, and labour market data to which the institution has access.

VET providers commonly develop their own MISs to suit their own particular requirements and purposes. In general, MISs will be based on commercially available software packages or, less commonly, will have been developed for particular objectives by consortia or associations of VET institutions, sometimes working collaboratively with a private-sector software development company.

Business systems should, where possible, be integrated (although care must be taken not to make systems too complicated and difficult to integrate) or allow for easy translation of information between systems. For example, human resources information may need to be used for the purpose of financial management; tracking of student performance can be useful for budget monitoring where payments levels depend on levels of completion; the teaching staff information can be processed together with the student information for timetabling and the allocation of staff.

Best practice in data and information management pinpoints seven critical success factors:

(1) Quality of information – institutions should ensure that systems are in place to manage effectively the accuracy, accessibility, processing, timeliness, completeness and relevance of the information within the organization, as well as providing staff with the appropriate training and support.

(2) Physical attributes of information – institutions need to have systems in place to ensure ease of collection, storage, processing and distribution of information within all the units or departments of the organization.

(3) Customer satisfaction information – institutions should ensure that systems are in place to manage effectively the identification and reporting of client needs, the comparison of client needs to actual performance, and the data of clients or potential clients and markets.

(4) Organizational infrastructure – institution administration is committed to nurturing effective information management system.

(5) Management information – institutions should ensure that systems are in place to manage strategic information which allows for the effective forecasting, planning, scheduling, measuring, controlling and reporting of organizational goals and objectives, and their implementation into operational and/or business plans.

(6) Organizational information – institutions should ensure that systems are in place to manage human resources, contractors and subcontractors, staff

education and training needs, financial performance, assets, equipment and consumables and processes for effective product and service delivery.

(7) Staff ownership – institutions should have systems in place to ensure maximum communication across all levels of the organization, high levels of staff ownership of the information and high levels of confidence in the information used.

For more details on the organizational design of MISs in different countries, go to **Unit 3.5: The VET institution's management information system** on your CD-ROM.

3.5.2 MAJOR SUBSYSTEMS OF THE MANAGEMENT INFORMATION SYSTEM

MISs operating in autonomous VET institutions generally include several standard components, normally based on commercially available software packages that have been customized where necessary.

Financial management systems

These should support: budget preparation based on cost centre and programme structures; financial reporting against cost centres and programmes/projects in terms of year-to-date income and expenditures and variances; cash flow monitoring; regular performance reporting against performance and funding agreement requirements; year-end trial balance and financial reconciliation and reporting against government standards; and preparations for annual reporting and audits. The system should also include monitoring of contract performance, invoicing and payment.

Human resource management systems

These should include all the relevant information on staff, support salary payments, payment of entitlements, accrued liabilities for individual staff, staff qualifications and staff access to and engagement in training and development.

Student records and tracking systems

These should record all student enrolments, demographic information, progress against enrolled subjects/modules and student outcomes, to be compliant with and capable of being uploaded to national or state data systems.

Student activity monitoring

Modern systems use smart card technology to aggregate a range of possible options, including library borrowing, printing from network computers, access to extended hours learning facilities, class attendance, payment of fees, access to online systems, assessments and results, and so on. Some activities may be charged while others are considered part of the enrolment fee. In both cases, activity is tracked. Students pay into their smart card account, which is automatically debited when undertaking designated activities.

Quality assurance systems

These should contain relevant compliance and quality assurance standards and performance benchmarks, and allow for the tracking of performance and compliance against those benchmarks (for example student outcomes, employer and student satisfaction). The schedule should include review protocols and processes.

Assets and facilities systems

These systems should maintain records of the capital infrastructure, including buildings, furniture, hardware, machinery used in training, classroom equipment and vehicles. The records should include cost, depreciation and a schedule for the maintenance and replacement of assets.

Internal and external information systems

A web-based communications and information system should offer consistent, current and readily accessible information to a range of internal and external stakeholders. Content and activity options should respond to the needs of the interested public, potential students, current students and staff. It should include corporate information, course and enrolment information, learning and library resources related to courses and staff support resources. The issues to be considered include:

☐ the choice of the platform for the web presence, using common web site or portal technology;

☐ security considerations to protect from hackers and Internet vandals;

☐ security protocols for authorized users to restricted-access parts of the site, such as staff and students;

- □ the use of templates, logo or style sheets to reinforce and protect corporate branding;

- □ the incorporation of W3C's Web Content Accessibility Guidelines 1.0 to support access to users with disabilities;

- □ integrity of information to ensure use of single authoritative sources of information in the database;

- □ cost-effective and efficient development and maintenance regimes;

- □ complementary roles of the web site for marketing and promotion, student access and information and communications by the institute's community.

Critical in all the above is the notion of cost centres or management control centres. Effective management requires that all operational costs are attributed to a cost centre where a known manager (or group of managers) takes decisions that have cost implications. Some costs must be regarded as central (or as overhead costs). However, even for these, there must be some mechanisms in place to attribute or distribute them to the management centres (schools, faculties, departments, and so on). Central to the way the management system is conceived are the conclusions reached about how many levels of cost centres there should be in order to make managers aware of the costs and implications of their decisions.

With the notable exception of the student management package, most if not all of the packages listed above will also have applications outside VET institutions and accordingly are likely to be commercially available. Although the education and training market is often large enough to encourage private-sector software developers to offer packages applicable to student management (for example PeopleSoft), autonomous VET institutions (or associations/consortia of them) may elect to develop their own customized student management systems – perhaps working collaboratively with a private-sector software developer.

It is important that such customized student management systems be designed from the outset to comply with the reporting requirements of central agencies that have responsibilities for public funding and/or external quality assurance. They should also be compatible with information industry standards, including Microsoft Windows and UNIX, make full use of the Windows graphical user interface and, where possible, be designed to resemble commonly used PC software packages. These customized student management software packages are likely to comprise a number of functional modules and utilities (see table 3.5.2).

For more information on procedures and information systems based on commercially available software packages used for financial management in autonomous VET institutions, refer to Module 5: Budgeting and financing.

Table 3.5.2 Functional modules and utilities
for a student management package

What makes an effective student management package?

- A teaching structures module – manages the structure and planning of programmes and courses;
- A finance module – manages student fees and debtor records;
- An admissions and enrolments module – admits, registers and enrols students, and administers their study contracts;
- A student support module – manages student loan applications;
- An academic records module – contains details of each student's academic record and the results of each learning assessment, including marks and grades attained;
- A resource assignment module – manages classroom scheduling and teaching resources;
- A practical experience module – manages the placement of students with supervisors in workplaces to enable the students to gain practical experience;
- A reporting module – allows the user to standardize and customize reports using a third-party reporting tool;
- An archiving module – allows the user to store data and records that are no longer current;
- A system manager utility – allows information to be configured according to the parameters defined by the institution's administration based on their own set of business policies and rules;
- A security system utility – operates at both client and server levels and imposes access limitations on users, such as "read only", "read/write", "disabled" and "invisible";
- A system tools utility – includes dashboards, electronic notes and dynamic browsing to assist users in the administration and management of student data.

For more information on procedures and information systems based on commercially available software packages used for quality assurance management in autonomous VET institutions, refer to **Module 11: Performance monitoring and reporting**.

For more details on major subsystems of VET institutions' MISs in different countries, consult **Unit 3.5: The VET institution's management information system** on your CD-ROM.

3.5.3 THE DEVELOPMENT AND MAINTENANCE
OF THE MANAGEMENT INFORMATION SYSTEM

The implementation of a new student data collection system by a government can severely test the MIS of an autonomous VET institution already in place, particularly in respect of data compatibility. Even if a system of autonomous VET institutions had, up to that point, been developing their own MISs, operations would have been far smoother if a general consensus on standardized data protocols had existed. Such agreement does not carry significant costs, and would be facilitated by sustained consultations between government officials and representatives of the autonomous VET institutions. A national association of VET institutions could play a significant role in achieving a national consensus on standardized data protocols.

Many of the standard components of MISs operating in autonomous VET institutions are normally based on commercially available software packages (refer to **Section 3.5.2** above). In some jurisdictions, institutions have chosen to develop and use collaboratively a cross-sectional system for student management as an alternative to using commercial software packages. User groups that represented such institutions were able to pool their resources and experiences and interactively drive the ongoing development of a customized student management system.

A key development in the implementation of a comprehensive national student data collection system has been the introduction of a national student identifier system, that is, a system of unique identifiers assigned to previous and current students enrolled in a national training system. The introduction of a national student descriptor system requires the intervention of a central agency (for example the ministry of education or equivalent national funding body), which assumes responsibility for designing, developing and piloting the national system of student descriptors, usually in association with vendors of student management systems.

Contingent on the introduction of a national student identifier system, VET institutions could then be expected, as a condition of public funding, to access this system through an interface option that suited their particular circumstances. These circumstances would be dictated by the number of students, how student enrolments were processed and the sophistication of the institution's own student management processes and systems.

Particularly for its awards and certification system, each institution will need its own system of unique student identifiers. However, national naming customs may result in large numbers of students with the same name. To avoid confusion, the VET institution could develop its own identifiers for its students. A national authority might also insist on creating unique identifiers that students (citizens) carry throughout their lives. Many object to this on the grounds of confidentiality or privacy. And many object to it because of the tradition that exists in institutions of giving students a second chance, allowing them to start again with no negative records following them through life. Whatever the situation, the database in any VET provider will need unique identifiers for students – numeric or alpha-numeric codes that should not be re-used for at least five to six years.

Ongoing responsibility for the day-to-day operations of the national student identifier system should lie with the central agency and involve maintaining access protocols for training providers, the distribution of documentation and the provision of technical and operational guidance.

For more details on the development and maintenance of MISs in different countries, consult **Unit 3.5: The VET institution's management information system** on your CD-ROM.

MODULE 4

The planning
of training delivery

Unit 4.1

SUPPLY AND DEMAND FACTORS IN PLANNING FOR TRAINING DELIVERY

4.1.1 SUPPLY AND DEMAND FACTORS

Stakeholders in planning

A VET system should aim to meet the current, emerging or anticipated needs for education and skills training within an increasingly complex and volatile local, national and global environment to the satisfaction of the stakeholders.

Planning for training delivery is effective when it is assured that the risks of a mismatch between supply and demand are minimized. These mismatches may be quantitative (an undersupply or oversupply of a particular kind of enrolled students/trained graduates) or qualitative (the delivery of inadequate training content that does not meet the job requirements or personal needs of the stakeholders).

Effective planning is not a straightforward management task, for several reasons:

☐ There are many stakeholders (students, industries, VET institutions, communities, government) whose interests and demands for training do not necessarily coincide.

☐ Stakeholders (particularly students) may make imperfect decisions based on incorrect or incomplete information or on peer group pressure.

☐ Student learning priorities and demand for training do not perfectly match the needs of the economic sectors.

☐ Local supply and demand for training may be influenced by complex external factors, including government intervention and labour market volatility.

☐ Supply and demand may be interrelated in complex ways while changing over time at different rates.

☐ Different areas of industry experience growth, contraction and change factors at different rates and in response to a range of external stimuli.

☐ Difficulties may arise in defining the boundaries of national, state and local interests in terms of the demand for and supply of training resources.

☐ Community preferences may not match the current and future employment and skills shortages resulting in supply/demand mismatches.

☐ As training is a protracted process, there is a potential mismatch between current enrolments and future demand for skills.

☐ There may be many public and private providers, including service and manufacturing companies, capable of operating in similar training areas and of serving the same clientele.

In addressing the issue of who should determine enrolments and which programmes to deliver, it is useful to consider the interests of the various stakeholders. In addressing the issue of who is best placed to make the right planning choices, it is useful to consider where choice and access to information actually reside.

The interests of students

Many students make a substantial time commitment, and may forgo income, to undertake training with the aim of improving their future employment or income prospects in the labour market. Both the oversupply or undersupply of training courses or inadequate training content can diminish their future employment or income prospects. Students clearly have vested interests in making sound decisions about the training they choose to undertake, particularly if they are also required to meet part or all of the costs through the tuition fees.

Students arguably have a particular incentive to make sound decisions concerning their training if they have to pay tuition fees. Nevertheless, students do not always make the right decisions: they can be unduly influenced by peer pressure; make decisions based on incorrect or incomplete information; or miscalculate the costs and benefits of training (for example the opportunity cost of income forgone compared with the enhanced lifetime earning potential).

The extent to which students are able to exercise choice may also be problematic. In general, students are only able to enrol in those courses that VET institutions choose to offer and in which unallocated places are available.

The skills needs of the economic sectors and the student learning interests can differ to a considerable extent. First, some of the faster growing economic sectors may offer jobs that are low paid and precarious and, as a result, students may be unwilling to undertake training even if courses are offered free of charge. Second, some occupations are commonly more prestigious than others and the number of young people willing to enrol in related courses is far and away greater than the number of graduates that the labour market can absorb.

VET providers must have considerable autonomy and flexibility in shifting government resources between courses if they are to balance the needs of industry and the demands of students. This is often more easily accomplished in a large institution. Smaller public training providers tend to be less flexible, since their resources are more likely to be fixed in terms of staffing and facilities and, therefore, be more difficult to re-orient.

The interests of industries and communities

Employers are clearly interested in having a regular supply of suitably trained graduates that meets their industries' current and future requirements for skills: an undersupply of training can lead to skills shortages and eventually to reduced productivity, and so forth. On the other hand, an oversupply of certain skills could conceivably distort the labour markets by, for example, dampening employees' wage demands. Accordingly, employers may be less concerned about the oversupply of skills, unless they are also required to contribute to training costs through, for example, industry training levies, or in cases where an oversupply of training in some areas causes an undersupply of training in other areas.

Industries are arguably better placed than students and VET institutions to assess their own needs for particular skills and competencies. Their requirements for general and particular skills may be customarily translated by institutions into courses designed to provide such skills. Success in translating the skills needs of industries into training courses delivered by VET providers depends on the incentives to respond to the skills needs of industries, the expertise of both parties in identifying such needs and VET providers' expertise in course and curriculum development.

Communities may have an interest in the delivery of VET to the extent that it meets local development needs by enhancing local employment prospects.

The demand for education and skills may reflect short-term fluctuations of economic activities, while rapid technological change may create pressing needs for new skills or make current skills obsolete or redundant. Assessing future qualitative and quantitative requirements for occupational skills is often problematic.

Government concerns and powers

Governments have an interest in the delivery of training as it may fulfil their broader economic and social policy objectives; the supply of training could reasonably be expected to meet the broader needs of the economy and address unemployment. They may also be concerned about the use of public resources allocated to public VET institutions, to industries and to those students who receive training subsidies or other means of public training support.

Governments are arguably least well placed to make training planning decisions, because such decisions would inevitably be made by officers who lack the incentives that students have to make sound private decisions. Furthermore, government departments are remote from the workplace and, accordingly, their staff may lack first-hand knowledge of industries' current and future needs for skills as well as the learning interests of students.

On the other hand, governments are better placed to take a broader view across the economy – of employment, education and training matters at large – and (through their VET agencies) can arguably synthesize information relating to VET provision and the labour markets more proficiently.

Governments are also uniquely placed to intervene in training delivery because they, alone, have the powers to do so. In exercising these powers, governments are more likely to bring training supply closer to demand through enabling the various stakeholders (VET institutions, students, industries, and communities) to make sound decisions. They are less likely to achieve success if they resort to micromanaging the institutions through determining training courses and enrolments.

Public VET providers may be caught between centralized planning imperatives at national and state levels and the need to respond to local conditions and markets. Centralized planning may be too inflexible to respond dynamically to the complexity inherent in today's innovation and knowledge economy. The optimum point for planning decisions may well be at the local level.

The planning role of the VET institution

By definition an autonomous VET institution will have considerable responsibility for the planning of training delivery. In order to succeed in their primary role of providing learning opportunities for students, VET institutions must first get students to enrol. The incentives to attract students will depend on the funding mechanism, which should be linked to enrolments.

Second, the incentives for VET institutions to offer courses that students want will depend to a substantial degree on supply/demand considerations. A provider will have less reason to respect student choice if there are more applicants than available funded places, and a greater reason to respect student choice if an institution competes with other training providers, such as public and private institutions or industry, for enrolments.

VET institutions are arguably better placed to make sound decisions on training planning and delivery because they are more likely to be aware of the choices of students and the skills needs of local industries. These capabilities should, however, be supported by national VET governance and funding arrangements, which provide incentives for institutions to respond to local and national training needs and to help their graduates achieve high employability.

The jurisdictions that promote autonomous VET institutions commonly opt for enhanced student and industry choices as the predominant driver of training delivery planning. The role of institutions in understanding and interpreting local conditions and markets is, therefore, paramount. They will focus their service provision on specific outreach areas (districts, regions, and related industries and communities) and therefore play a vital part in informing and fine-tuning government priorities. Each provider may choose a combination of local, state and national sources to underpin their judgement of the training markets.

VET institutions' ongoing relationships with regional and local bodies and with key industries may exist at both strategic and operational levels. Their knowledge and experience are important factors in understanding and managing the supply and demand equation. VET institutions, therefore, need to develop and maintain robust and continual relationships with local government and regional bodies, with community groups as well as with industry bodies at local and regional levels.

Autonomous VET institutions should also remain in touch with trends and developments in industry at the national level. Although this can be maintained in a centralized way through the national education and training sector, a successful institution will also develop independent sources of knowledge through research and analysis from important bodies in sectors of industry and the community.

The government body in charge of VET funding will eventually negotiate and approve the quantum of services at the entry, development or advanced skills levels that can be purchased from a training institution. This decision will determine the current delivery plan of the VET provider as well as the amount of revenue that it will be able to generate.

The VET institution with a good knowledge of the local training markets may also deliver training services to companies, organizations and individuals on a contractual basis.

For more details on supply and demand factors, interrelationships and issues in different countries, consult **Unit 4.1: Supply and demand factors in planning for training delivery** on your CD-ROM.

4.1.2 GOVERNMENT INTERVENTIONS
IN SUPPLY AND DEMAND

The role of training policy

Governments have a number of "levers" that allow them to intervene in the planning of training delivery. A government is more likely to achieve success (that is, a closer match of training supply and demand) through setting the appropriate policy environment than by micromanaging institutions through directly determining courses and enrolments.

A government is able to articulate its expectations of the contribution of VET to its economic and social policy objectives through a national training policy. A national training policy may state that some degree of training is becoming increasingly necessary for an individual to participate fully in a country's workforce and economy. It may also present VET as part of the lifelong learning process. It will acknowledge the ownership interest that the government retains in public VET institutions.

A national training policy may express the strategic purpose of the planning of training by:

☐ ensuring a sufficient flow of new entrants to the labour market to address skills needs resulting from structural change and an ageing workforce;

☐ overcoming skills gaps and upgrading the skills of the existing workforce in order to boost productivity and support industry restructuring;

☐ providing for future skills needs in the identified key areas of economic and employment growth, such as, for instance, advanced manufacturing, design or environmental technologies;

☐ identifying and providing the skills needed for developing emerging industries and for innovation and knowledge creation;

☐ meeting the skills needs of vulnerable groups, including young people, the unemployed and underemployed, people with a disability, displaced workers, indigenous people and those living in communities that have been hard hit by structural change.

For more details on the content of a national training policy statement, consult **Unit 1.2: The regulatory role of national education and training policies**.

National training priorities

Government interventions that are intended to influence training supply and demand often determine the national VET priorities regarding:

□ target groups, such as disadvantaged people, workers without skills certificates, and so on, which are entitled to priority services;

□ industries in special need of the training services that the government decided to support;

□ training programmes or trades that will have acquired considerable national importance.

National target groups are usually identified to meet a government's social policy objective, for example to address perceived social disadvantage associated with underachievement or under-representation in VET. Targeting may be on the basis of ethnicity, income, locality, or some other appropriate indicator of social disadvantage.

Intervention mechanisms supporting national target groups may involve:

□ a funding mechanism – to encourage disadvantaged groups to participate, funding is made available either to relevant students or allocated to VET institutions;

□ an accountability framework – a requirement that institutions enrol specified quotas of target students out of general non-specified public funding.

Priority sectors in industry may be identified if their further development and expansion are considered vital (for example that of biotechnology). Targeting may involve providing publicly funded places in order to encourage VET institutions to offer training programmes that are particularly relevant for priority sectors, or providing enhanced levels of funding (or other kinds of student support) to encourage students to enrol in identified priority programmes.

National priority trades may be identified by the government if skills shortages in certain trades are having an adverse economic impact or if skills shortages are likely to arise because of economic and employment growth in priority sectors.

Strategic planning mechanisms

A government's strategic planning mechanism will attempt to balance demand for training and its supply across a diverse range of stakeholders. The government should provide a strategic view of overall needs and relative priorities, ensuring the responsible use of national resources.

A dynamic and responsible government operating autonomous VET institutions will govern the process of training planning through:

☐ a research and evaluation programme that gathers data and intelligence from a range of government and industry sources; industry training organizations may be contracted out by the government to produce reports on demand for occupational skills in the sectors;

☐ a strategic priority setting process by means of developing relationships across the various stakeholders (industry and community organizations, and government departments);

☐ establishing dialogue with VET providers on local training demand, taking account of their knowledge of local conditions and linking the ambitions of individual providers to government priorities;

☐ negotiating training delivery targets and funding plans with individual providers and outlining frameworks to verify that delivery targets have been met.

VET institutions' training targets

Training delivery targets must lie with the government agency and be clearly expressed in the performance and funding agreements. They may:

☐ establish the delivery floors (minimum delivery) and the delivery ceilings (maximum delivery);

☐ be expressed in EFTSs (equivalent full-time students) or in SCHs (student contact/guided hours);

☐ be established separately for apprenticeship training and for classroom-based courses;

☐ be specified for each type of certificated programmes (for instance Certificate IV in health nursing) as well as non-certificated programmes;

☐ be established for the training of priority target groups, such as disadvantaged people.

An EFTS is a planning measure of training "volume". It is the workload undertaken by a VET institution to train a student in a full-time course for a full year. Obviously, a full-year course will require more resources than a one-week course. Accordingly, an output of 1.00 EFTS delivered for courses in particular training fields and at different qualification levels will require different resources. Therefore, 1.00 EFTS is also a "funding category" on which basis the budgeting and resource allocation for VET institutions is arranged. The planning indicators and definitions of full-time and full-year training are determined by the national government/funding agencies.

The calculation of SCHs for planning and funding purposes is based on the following. Each training package or curriculum nominates the number of hours that an average student under normal conditions might be expected to take to demonstrate a particular competency or set of learning outcomes in a module or course. The calculation of SCHs takes the predicted hours of training for a course within a year and multiples it by the benchmark class size.

For more details on government interventions in supply and demand in different countries, consult **Unit 4.1: Supply and demand factors in planning for training delivery** on your CD-ROM.

ASSESSING INDUSTRY DEMAND
FOR VET COURSES

4.2.1 INDUSTRY DEMAND FOR VET COURSES

The planning of training delivery by a VET institution will be effective when all the possible (known) risks of the training supply/demand mismatches have been assessed and minimized to the satisfaction of the various stakeholders. Entry-level students and industries are a VET provider's most important training clientele.

Students will decide to enrol in a course if they believe that the training will improve their employment prospects. Employers, or their employees, will commonly choose in-service training that provides or improves skills and competencies.

Some employers may be looking for quite explicit job-related skills and competencies in trained graduates, while others prefer more generic skills and competencies to build on through further in-service training. The difference between these two approaches comes down to the employer's preferred recruitment strategy. A VET institution needs to be aware of the preferred recruitment strategies of the employers who, at the very least, are in its catchment area and should adjust courses accordingly.

Structuring industry demand

By definition, the planning of pre-employment education and training should focus on future employment opportunities and offer competencies that meet the expectations of prospective employers. In both cases, it is important that a VET institution has the capability to assess industry's demand for graduates and their competencies.

Generally, industry demand falls into the following categories:

☐ demand for trained graduates in certain occupations or occupational areas (for example carpentry, plumbing, electronic engineering) and at certain qualification levels;

□ demand for the further education and training of people in employment, provision being usually of shorter duration;

□ demand for a school-based component of apprenticeship training;

□ demand for retraining from companies that are about to retrench workers as well as from agencies that finance the retraining of the unemployed.

Basic factors influencing training planning

Certain basic factors should be taken into account as they influence the VET institution's planning of training delivery for industry. They are:

□ the existing workforce's occupational and qualifications structures in the VET institution's catchment area;

□ the directions of technological change in the sectors of industry, which might create pressing needs for new skills or make current skills obsolete or redundant;

□ the short-term fluctuations in economic activity, mostly at regional and local levels;

□ the levels of investment in local employment promotion and industry development projects that might enhance demand for training;

□ the government funding priorities for specified industry sectors (in some countries, governments allocate training funding by industry sector);

□ incentives or disincentives for training, such as training subsidies paid either to students, industries and/or training providers, which make training an attractive proposition.

Understanding labour market signals

Various national, regional and local factors can determine an industry's demand for graduates. In most cases the VET institutions will study national or regional advice on the training needs and economic trends, which is usually produced by the VET agency. Information can also be obtained from national and local industry bodies or individual enterprises.

Sometimes, the particular industry or individual enterprises are unable to formulate clearly their current and future demand for occupations, skills and competencies. When this is the case, VET institutions have no choice but to arrange the detailed assessments of industry demand on their own.

A number of signals from the local labour and training markets can be easily collected and interpreted by VET institutions. Such signals include:

☐ data on the graduation of young people from general education and their labour market destinations;

☐ data on applicants per VET course and per occupation;

☐ the labour market success of graduates, and so on.

Precautions need to be taken when interpreting the signals from the labour and training markets. On the one hand, the demand for highly skilled workers by industry is not always satisfied by newly qualified graduates, that is, employers looking for skilled workers will not necessarily employ young graduates. On the other hand, large numbers of job vacancies in certain occupations do not necessarily mean that graduates will apply for these jobs; vacancies in certain occupations may continue to exist when the jobs advertised are precarious and badly paid.

Need for understanding training supply

When the demand for skills is known, the VET institution needs to examine the local training supply of individual occupations, since many other providers might have carried out the same assessment and draw the same planning decisions. If all training providers, including the industry itself, react to the local skills shortages in the same way, then an oversupply of graduates is likely to be the result. To avoid this situation, government agencies need to ensure that a reasonable amount of coordination of the service delivery exists among the VET providers.

For more details on the demand for VET courses by industry in different countries, go to **Unit 4.2: Assessing industry demand for VET courses** on your CD-ROM.

4.2.2 METHODOLOGIES AND TECHNIQUES FOR ASSESSING INDUSTRY DEMAND FOR VET COURSES

The role of stakeholders

The assessment of industry demand for VET courses may be undertaken jointly or separately by the key stakeholders:

☐ Government agencies may undertake the assessment, which may be used to inform interventions in the labour market and to inform decision-making by training providers (VET institutions, industry) and prospective students;

☐ ITOs set up by industry groups to ensure that the training needs of their industries are met have an interest in the assessment of industry demand for training; alternatively, the government might request or contract out the assessment to ITOs;

☐ VET institutions have considerable potential to examine the industry demand for training; they can gather information on their own or through a national association of VET institutions, and so on.

Various techniques for information gathering may be used in this process:

☐ conducting (mapping) surveys of occupational qualifications structures in local industries by way of company visits and administering question-naires;

☐ conducting surveys of industry-based training practices and the opportuni-ties that may then arise for VET providers to deliver off-the-job components of industry-based training;

☐ conducting surveys of graduate destinations (so-called "tracer studies") that determine where a sample of VET graduates end up after graduation (for example in employment, in unemployment, or in further training);

☐ conducting a survey of the current workforce to find out the principal ways of entry into major occupations, either through institution-based training, on-the-job training, retraining, and so on (so-called "reverse tracer studies");

☐ collecting data on current job vacancies as reported in the advertising media or as obtained from employers;

☐ collecting data on the extent of unemployment and underemployment in the region served by the provider with the focus on trades and skills that are offered in the VET courses;

☐ collecting information on future local industrial and/or developmental projects and other interventions that may create incentives or disincen-tives for skills acquisition;

☐ collecting data on employment opportunities that may exist in small and micro-enterprises in the region served by the VET provider.

Advice from industry on training needs

An advice from industry on the skills and training needs across the VET institution's target area (local, regional) is required. The industry advisory reports may be commissioned to ITOs by the government and forwarded to VET institutions. The information may also be obtained through direct link-ages between training providers and the staff in companies where graduates used to find employment.

A VET institution's planning and funding systems now need to be:

☐ flexible to accommodate emerging skills needs of the industry through the uptake of relevant training courses;

☐ better able to cope with cross-industry skills issues such as generic and employability skills;

☐ prepared to balance the industry training needs and the student learning interests in their course offerings.

Although there may be substantial differences in the perspectives on training needs determined by industry training bodies and individual enterprises, reconciling the differing perspectives is the task of the government VET planning and purchasing agencies rather than individual providers. The agencies will receive information from all major industry sectors as well as from VET institutions which should be able to gather and articulate the trends and needs of the local consumers of education and training services. A robust consultation process will provide institutions with the opportunity to comment on and influence the training planning and funding arrangements.

National training agendas will also be influenced by the industrial relations environment. Where pay increases for workers are linked to training and qualification levels, demand from industry may be stimulated. Government may also stimulate demand by introducing subsidies to the cost of training in priority industries, skills or qualifications. Initiatives may target language, literacy and numeracy courses for low-educated workers, as well as occupational health and safety programmes, and so forth. Occupational regulation and licensing may also require higher skills standards, which in turn will increase demand for skills.

The data that influence training priorities will be gathered from a range of sources. Typically, government agencies with responsibility in relevant areas, such as employment, economic development, workplace and industrial relations, education and training, will publish an analysis of issues of interest to their stakeholders. Similarly, these agencies will use the demographic data collected by the statistical office to inform their conclusions and policy directions.

This broad approach may operate at the state and regional levels, with each layer of information advising both the VET providers and the users of the information. The sophisticated user of the information will distinguish between national trends and local observations that conform or are contrary to the data. If local variances are observed, a VET institution should question the local data to determine the underlying causes, the longevity and the extent of the variance.

Communication can be enhanced if the major industries and enterprises served by the VET provider are represented on its governing council. Such representation may help to ensure that the institution's management is fully accountable to its major stakeholders in industry.

Advice from industry on skills shortages and prospective training needs should be region specific, industry sub-sector specific and occupational qualifications specific. For instance, training needs in the industrial construction industry may differ from civil construction and housing. While in industrial construction enterprises, the principal skills shortages may be in trained concreters and scaffolders, particularly at the highest qualification levels, in civil construction there could be an urgent need to train people in environmental and quality management and in road construction and maintenance activities.

For more details on the methodologies and techniques for assessing industry demand for VET courses in different countries, consult **Unit 4.2: Assessing industry demand for VET courses** on your CD-ROM.

4.2.3 RESPONDING TO INDUSTRY TRAINING NEEDS

Once a VET institution has completed an assessment of industry demand for training, the information has to be interpreted and translated into the training planning and funding proposal by the provider. The training delivery plan will need to be finalized through negotiations with a government agency in charge of VET planning and funding.

The agreed training delivery plan may involve a global allocation for a public provider in EFTSs or in SCHs. The provision of apprentices recruited by enterprises with a school-based education and training component is a common priority endorsed by government-funding schemes.

For definitions of EFTS and SCH, refer to **Unit 4.1: Supply and demand factors in planning for training delivery**.

Autonomous VET institutions will also exercise a degree of freedom in responding to local industry needs by the packaging of courses or through the combination of content, delivery and assessment mechanisms.

The development and delivery of new courses packaged at the request of industry can take a considerable amount of time. Therefore, it may be impossible to respond immediately to the identified demand for training.

For more details on course and curriculum development, consult **Module 8: Course development and evaluation**.

For more details on practices of responding to industry training needs in different countries, consult **Unit 4.2: Assessing industry demand for VET courses** on your CD-ROM.

Unit 4.3

ASSESSING STUDENT DEMAND
FOR VET COURSES

4.3.1 STUDENT DEMAND FOR COURSES

Government regulation of student access to training

The planning of training delivery by an autonomous VET institution will be effective when all the possible (known) risks of the training supply/demand mismatches are assessed and minimized to the satisfaction of the various stakeholders. These stakeholders include the students and the industries served by the provider but may also extend to the local communities and to the government as funder and regulator.

A cyclical approach across governments over time tends to result in the regulation and deregulation of the provision and accessibility of training places for students. The outcome may be designed to improve training supply, meet demand or stimulate demand. Government interventions may involve:

☐ the application of subsidies or fee concessions for students in priority occupational or geographic areas;

☐ the allocation of increased resources for the institution's infrastructure or for the provision of extra training places;

☐ the restriction of training places in areas of declining employment opportunities;

☐ the setting of delivery targets for providers with regard to particular cohorts of students (priority target groups) and occupational areas;

☐ the allocation of funding for projects that support the development of skills, expertise and resources in priority areas.

Autonomous VET institutions may be largely constrained in the publicly funded courses they offer through the national system of purchasing courses with national accreditation. Such a supply is determined by government through analysing regular national census data and from the advice received from industry and VET institutions themselves.

VET institutions will also use data collection mechanisms (such as applications from school leavers and adults, the analysis of phone enquiries, waiting lists and market intelligence) to monitor course demand and preferences on a continuous basis.

Student demand for VET generally falls into two main categories:

(1) demand for pre-employment training, from students seeking (among other things) skills and competencies that may enhance their future employment and remuneration;

(2) demand from adult learners (including the unemployed), who wish to acquire new trades or upgrade their current qualifications.

Students' choices

Students commonly base their choice of course by assessing whether it will improve their employment prospects as well as future income. If well informed, students tend to choose vocational courses that meet the employers' expectations. Students may bear the risks of a possible oversupply of graduates, while industry mostly bears the risk of an undersupply of sufficiently qualified workers.

For more details on the interplay of interests of the various stakeholders in the supply/demand of vocational training services, see **Unit 4.1: Supply and demand factors in the planning of training delivery**.

In VET courses, student demand is commonly structured by occupation (for example carpentry, plumbing, electronic engineering, and so on) and by the level of vocational award (for instance, Welder General, Level 2, or CAD/CAM Operator, Level 3). However, public funding may also be made available for tailor-made courses that are not registered on the national qualifications frameworks but are quality assured.

Autonomous VET institutions develop their delivery plans on the basis of data collected from their catchment areas where the majority of their prospective students live. To acquire an accurate definition of the catchment area, assumptions need to be made about student mobility, that is, willingness (and ability) to travel for study purposes to a VET provider or to undertake distance learning as an alternative to travelling.

Other considerations affecting demand may include the level of support that prospective students receive from their families, for example, whether they will be able to study full-time or whether they will have to mix part-time study or distance learning with employment. Support may also be available from other sources, including, for example:

□ government tuition subsidies, loans to cover tuition fees (if any), grants to cover travel and living expenses and course costs, or perhaps targeted assistance to priority groups;

□ industry traineeships and apprenticeships, and so forth.

In addition to tuition subsidies and other forms of support, there are other interventions by government agencies that can lead to a rise in training demand. Agencies may, for instance, address problems of local unemployment or under-employment through fostering the development of small and micro-enterprises or of local development projects.

The promotion of training by the government or ITOs may change a student's perspective of the value of training, and also increase student demand. So, too, may marketing by a VET provider, either of training courses on offer or, more commonly, of the institution as an attractive place to study. Students themselves can also access information that is (arguably) more objective than the self-promotional material provided by the institutions. The information sources available to potential students may include the following:

□ careers advisors at school;

□ labour market information provided by government agencies and industry via labour market reports, other publications and web sites, and so forth;

□ information on employment opportunities, job vacancies, and so on, in the media;

□ the prospective student's peer group (likely to be influential but not always a source of reliable information).

VET institutions may provide information on training opportunities to careers advisors for promotional purposes. They are also able to access, perhaps more comprehensively, the information available to students from government agencies and industry via publications and web sites, and so forth.

Adult learners

Adult learners wishing to acquire qualifications for the first time (second-chance learners) or wishing to update or enhance their current qualifications can also represent a significant component of student demand. Adult learners may certainly be more driven and committed to undertaking training than younger students. VET institutions' publicly funded training component for priority adult learners will need to be negotiated with the national VET agency or the government department. Various training courses may also be fee-financed.

For more details on student demand for VET courses in different countries, go to **Unit 4.3: Assessing student demand for VET courses** on your CD-ROM.

4.3.2 METHODOLOGIES AND ASSESSMENT TECHNIQUES FOR STUDENT TRAINING DEMAND

Comprehensive demographic information on the school leaver cohort is customarily gathered, collated and disseminated by the government agency (department or ministry) responsible for the compulsory education sector. This information, and particularly any long-term trends that are apparent, may be particularly relevant for assessing future student demand by the VET institutions.

Statistical information on at least enrolments – and ideally on throughput, retention and graduation rates as well – may be available from the government agency responsible for regulating and funding public providers. In some jurisdictions, public institutions are required to furnish such information as a condition of public funding allocation. The government agency may also need statistical data to inform its funding decisions, and to hold the VET institutions accountable for the use of public resources.

Graduations do not necessarily lead to employment. Students, the government, industry and VET providers all need to understand the links between training and employment. Such understanding can be developed through two surveying techniques:

(1) tracer studies of graduates, which explore their post-training behaviour in the labour market and further education;

(2) reverse tracer studies of employees, which explore how they entered certain occupations and the role therein of training providers and enterprises.

Well informed students will generally choose to enrol in pre-employment vocational courses that maximize their prospects for future employment and income. The information derived from tracer studies may be of considerable interest for students and their advisers (school counsellors).

Tracer studies are usually carried out by the VET institutions themselves or sometimes by their national association or by government agencies in charge of VET. The tracer studies conducted on the national scale are commonly based on samples and are less useful for training providers to advise their planning and student enrolment process.

Interpreting data on the student demand for VET courses may be problematic. Although statistical information about supply should be readily available from the demographics of the school leaver cohort, outcomes are uncertain, for a number or reasons:

☐ Students often have many choices (for example between employment and training; between competing providers; between various modes of education and training, including full-time and part-time, distance and on-the-job training, and so forth).

□ Defining a VET provider's catchment area requires making judgements about student mobility.

□ The impact of marketing on student demand needs to be assessed; marketing may have to be used to modify demand.

□ The effect of external interventions on student demand needs to be assessed (see Section 4.3.1 above).

□ The quality of information available to students and their advisers and the effect of peer pressure on the enrolment decisions need to be assessed.

For more details on the methodologies and assessment techniques for student demand in different countries, consult **Unit 4.3: Assessing student demand for VET courses** on your CD-ROM.

4.3.3 STEERING LOCAL TRAINING SUPPLY

Each VET institution is not delivering its training programmes in isolation but is likely to be operating in an environment influenced by other players. In particular, these include other (public and private) training providers that may be offering similar institution-based courses as well as industries that may offer industry-based training and apprenticeships.

The relationship between a particular VET provider and other training providers in the local labour markets may be cooperative or competitive, depending partly on the regulatory and funding environment in which they operate and partly on the strategy of the VET institutions themselves. In its assessment of student demand for its own courses, a provider will need to understand the supply of training from its potential or actual competitors and assess its own role in the local training markets.

A VET institution should also do an assessment of the industry's ability to offer occupational training. Such an assessment may also identify opportunities that may then arise for the institution to deliver, cooperatively, off-the-job components of industry-based training and apprenticeship programmes.

An institution may also elect to negotiate arrangements with potentially competing VET providers on course rationalization (to minimize duplication, for example) and on the joint promotion of training (to avoid wasteful advertising). It may prove helpful for providers to differentiate clearly between areas of competition (for enrolments) and areas of cooperation (on delivery).

Marketing can also have an important role in steering local training supply. It could, for example, be used to foster competition for enrolments. Alternatively, it could be used to emphasize cooperative arrangements among providers and to promote the generic value of training. Promotion, however, always carries with it the risk of encouraging oversupply.

VET institutions should monitor student learning progress, completion rates and the graduate post-training destinations. Courses that are regularly undersubscribed, or involve high dropout rates, or do not lead to employment in the trades in which students had been trained warrant attention with regard to level and content. Such courses may become cost-inefficient to deliver and need to be rationalized or replaced by the more popular programmes.

Further analysis, however, may be useful to determine the underlying preferences of students for subjects or competencies as opposed to courses. The nature of the changing world of work may result in students who prefer to select a set of subjects/competencies that are aligned to their needs rather than to a nationally accredited content of a course.

Similarly, the analysis of student enrolments over time may reflect that a significant number of students prefer to spread their studying over several years of intermittent and discontinuous activity. The successful VET institution will ensure that these preferences are recognized and accommodated.

The planning of a new course needs to be carried out about three years ahead of delivery. This time frame may be necessary to confirm and detail industry demand and preferences as well as to ensure that all the appropriate facilities, learning resources and teaching staff are in place to run the new course.

For more details on steering local training supply in different countries, go to **Unit 4.3: Assessing student demand for VET courses** on your CD-ROM.

THE METHODOLOGY
AND TECHNIQUES OF PLANNING
FOR TRAINING DELIVERY

4.4.1 STRATEGIC PLANNING FOR VET DELIVERY

The planning of training delivery by an autonomous VET institution will be effective when all the possible (known) risks of the training supply/demand mismatches are assessed and minimized to the satisfaction of the various stakeholders. These stakeholders include students and industries served by the provider but may extend to the local communities and to the government as funder and regulator.

Effective planning takes place over two different time scales:

☐ long-term strategic planning, which gives effect to the governing council's vision for the VET institution, its agreed mission, and its long-term strategic development;

☐ short-term (annual) business planning, which determines the provider's training delivery for the forthcoming academic and financial year (outlined in Section 4.4.2).

A VET institution's strategic plan is developed by a small group of people with the requisite skills, commonly a subcommittee of the governing council, which may be strengthened by secondees from management staff. A customary starting point for developing a strategic plan is to reach consensus on:

☐ the vision (that is, what the VET institution is – its core values, perceived role, and so on); and

☐ the mission (what the VET institution's major task is).

Although vision and mission may seem fuzzy concepts, without any basic agreement on them among the members of the governing council, the development of a strategic plan may become problematic (since it may otherwise lack essential purpose).

Various techniques will then be utilized by the planning group to develop a strategic plan. These techniques may include some or all of the following:

☐ analysis of the institution's strengths, weaknesses, opportunities and threats (a SWOT analysis);

☐ production of alternative scenarios that are narrative descriptions of the institution's possible future development. These scenarios may then be ranked for their compliance with the agreed vision and mission statements of the VET institution;

☐ structured consultation with the stakeholders, which may be valuable as a source of useful information and as a way of achieving greater acceptance ("buy-in") of the strategic plan once it has been finalized by the governing council;

☐ development of performance indicators and milestones by which the compliance of the operations of the VET institution with its strategic plan can be readily assessed.

The strategic planning group will also need to take into account various external inputs to the planning process, including some or all of the following:

☐ factors within the government's training policy that provide opportunities (or disincentives) for particular development strategies under consideration;

☐ labour market forecasts and their implications for future demand for VET;

☐ long-term economic and demographic factors and their implications for future demand for VET;

☐ an assessment of the VET provider's current capacities (financial, physical, human and intellectual resources) to implement the strategic scenario as well as an analysis of deficiencies or surpluses in these capacities (for example a shortage of competent teachers in certain skills areas, demand for which is expected to expand, and so forth).

Successful VET institutions need to oversee and monitor trends in the external and internal environments. The role of their planners is to interpret and predict the future training market. Their research and expertise lie in detailing emerging trends and, as importantly, forecasting trend breaks. They examine regional and national research data and liaise with the major VET funding (purchasing) body. Institutional planners work with senior management to shape the training delivery profile in order to ensure its sustainability and financial return. Their challenge is also to work with teaching department managers to translate plans into action.

113

A high-level strategic plan provides long-term guidance (usually for a period of three to five years) on training delivery to the autonomous VET institution's governing council and its staff. In particular, the plan may specify the delivery of training services and identify the areas that are to be expanded or reduced over the period. A strategic plan will set an objective of the number of EFTSs or SCHs to be delivered over the planning period (definitions are given in **Section 4.4.2**).

A special section of the strategic plan will indicate the implications of delivering the proposed volume of training for budgeting and financing, staffing, and site and building development, and so forth.

Strategic planning is a routine governance/management function and is commonly funded on the same basis as all other governance/management functions. Some strategic plans may have separate budgets for capital expansion. When strategic planning is compulsory for autonomous VET institutions, the government may insist that the plans should follow a uniform format.

The strategic plan may also specify the inherent risks for the VET provider and for its students, including contingencies (events that could have a negative impact on the institution but cannot be predicted with certainty) and uncertainties in the assumptions and forecasts on which the plan has been based. Sensitivity analyses that examine the predicted consequences of a range of input assumptions can identify the inherent risks to which a VET institution is likely to be most vulnerable (see **Section 4.4.3**).

For more details on strategic planning for training delivery in different countries, go to **Unit 4.4: The methodology and techniques of planning for training delivery** on your CD-ROM.

4.4.2 SHORT-TERM PLANNING FOR TRAINING DELIVERY

Autonomous VET institutions base their operational delivery plans on the projections and plans developed by national VET agencies at the regional or national levels. VET institutions generally operate within an annual cycle of academic and financial years (not always congruent), a cycle of substantially shorter duration than the period covered by the strategic plan. Necessarily, the strategic plan will lack the details required for day-to-day operations. These details (covering the annual academic and budget cycles) are usually contained within the VET institution's annual business plan.

The processes for developing long-term strategic and annual business plans although similar in many ways also differ in important respects. In particular, the business plan tends to be:

☐ more focused on the training outputs and outcomes;

☐ short-term (that is, it should cover annual training and budget cycles);

□ carried out by lower-level managerial staff within the institution (for example by heads of departments reporting to a senior management group);

□ explicitly linked to the VET institution's annual budget (or, more strictly, the annual budget is an important component of the business plan).

Performance indicators and milestones defined within the business plan may often be used as part of the national accountability regime that determines whether an institution is delivering its expected outputs and is operating within its approved budget. Commonly, the principal training output indicator is the delivered EFTSs which is based on the number of students who are enrolled in approved courses. The EFTS is used as a proxy for graduates' skills and competencies (which are the actual outputs that governments want). The placement of graduates in employment is not usually an indicator formally used for reporting purposes.

An EFTS is a measure of training volume. It is the workload undertaken by a VET institution to train a student enrolled in a full-time course for a full year. Obviously, a full-year course will require more resources than a one-week course. The funding category for a particular training field (discipline, area and level of study, and so forth) is the amount of funding allocated to 1.00 EFTS. The planning indicators and definitions of full-time and full-year training are determined by the government/funding agencies.

For more details, see **Section 4.1.2.**

A major factor in developing the institution's operational capabilities is the availability of appropriate resources when significant changes to infrastructure must be made to meet emerging skills needs. This may include negotiating capital infrastructure funding and liaising with leading enterprises in an industry sector for access to new technology or partnerships with industry. Similar strategies may also be used to ensure that the teaching staff are equipped with the new skills to train students or that qualified staff from industry have been recruited. Robust and enduring local networks with industry are a key factor in interpreting and responding to emerging demands.

An additional component of the annual plan is ensuring that existing students will be allowed to complete the courses in which they are enrolled. Although demand may change, students who have enrolled in a government-funded course have the right to complete their course under the same conditions.

In case of unexpected demand for training, a provider will try to shift resources internally. Unfortunately, in the case of courses that run for more than one year, resources may be tied up for a longer period. A provider may also contact other providers and refer students to those competitors. The government may also release funds under special allocations or competitive tender arrangements to support the provision of extra training places in specific areas.

Even if a public VET institution's operational planning is flexible, delivery may remain constrained if the institution relies fully on public funding. Many

VET providers seek opportunities to deliver services to industry. More planning and operational freedom is indispensable when VET institutions implement training through commercial contracts with enterprises.

Contracts may include training for industry specific processes, the development of staff training strategies and associated learning and skills assessment resources. This market may be highly competitive, with both public institutions and private providers seeking out industry contracts. Issues such as infrastructure costs, training facilities, learner support strategies and the availability of training offerings may be deciding factors in the package that is presented to an enterprise wanting training for its staff.

For more details on short-term annual planning for training delivery in different countries, go to **Unit 4.4: The methodology and techniques of planning for training delivery** on your CD-ROM.

4.4.3 RISK ASSESSMENT

The student's risks

The delivery of training is not without risk, both for the student receiving training and for the VET institutions delivering it. For the student, the greatest risk may be the opportunity cost of undertaking training instead of doing something else (for example working and earning an income). There is always an opportunity cost but this should, in principle, be more than offset by the benefit that the training provides (for example through enhanced employment or earning potentials). However, if the training is not relevant to the student's intended employment or is of inadequate quality, the student will have to take responsibility for the whole of the opportunity cost as well as the costs of tuition fees and other expenditure incurred during training.

The benefit of training generally accrues over a sustained period. A cost-benefit analysis of training is able to take into account this extended benefit through a "discounted rate of return" analysis. When this approach is taken, all future benefits are converted to "present value" currency and are expressed as a "rate of return" on the opportunity and other costs incurred while undertaking training. A positive rate of return indicates that training is financially advantageous for a student undertaking it.

In practice, estimating rates of return on training courses is problematic. Furthermore, few students have the ability or the inclination to undertake such estimations. However, students may be able to reduce their risks by ensuring that they are well informed on the quality and relevance of the training that they are considering. Relevant information may be available from careers advisors in schools and from publications and web sites provided by government agencies, industry and the VET institutions.

The training institution's risks

VET institutions also face risks, irrespective of their level of autonomy. Differences in autonomy only shift the balance of risk between institutions and the agencies to which they are accountable.

Some of the significant risks that VET institutions face may be ethical. Delivering training courses that do not meet the needs of students could be argued as being unethical; they certainly are not in the best interests of students or other stakeholders – industry and employers, the government as funder and regulator, and the community.

In practical terms, their most significant risk is arguably political, either as the result of policy changes (often following a change of government or minister) or as the result of political interference (particularly in funding allocations). These risks may be reduced if there are clear statements of national training policies and there are transparent and objective funding and accountability systems in place.

Autonomous VET institutions, like other businesses, may also face financial risk from a number of sources. A common challenge facing all VET institutions is that of handling the interaction between the length of the academic and planning cycles and the relative brevity of the annual financial cycles that governments generally prefer. Routinely, it may take up to one year to plan and launch a new training course, one to three years before the first students graduate, and a further year for the course to be evaluated by industry and for concomitant adjustments to be made. Thus the planning cycle may extend over five years, yet most governments will only commit to annual funding, possibly with a very broad indicative funding commitment beyond that period.

Over a five-year or more planning cycle, the current demand for skills that is used to guide a new programme may have little relevance for its graduates. This risk may be reduced if the providers can flexibly respond to changes in the type and volume of the training demand.

A further determinant of risk is the financial and regulatory environment in which autonomous VET institutions are operating. If they are competing for enrolments and their funding is enrolment-based, then providers that do not achieve their estimated enrolments may fail financially. As noted in **Section 4.4.1** above, sensitivity analyses that examine the predicted consequences of a range of input assumptions during the strategic planning exercise can identify the inherent risks to which an institution is likely to be most vulnerable. Assumptions about future enrolments are critical inputs that sensitivity studies can assess.

On the other hand, if funding is input based (that is, determined by salaries and other input costs) and/or there is no competition for enrolments among providers, there is likely to be a greater risk for the government of insufficient, inefficient or irrelevant VET delivery. Competition also tends to lead to fewer

117

low-quality courses, since students can exercise choice in deciding where to undertake their training.

For more details on the risk assessment of training courses in different countries, go to **Unit 4.4: The methodology and techniques of planning for training delivery** on your CD-ROM.

MODULE

Budgeting
and financing

Unit 5.1

EFFICIENT, EFFECTIVE AND EQUITABLE FUNDING MECHANISMS

5.1.1 THE MEANING OF EFFICIENT, EFFECTIVE AND EQUITABLE FUNDING

Governments finance VET institutions because they contribute to desired national economic and social equity objectives. For VET institutions, these outcomes may include a skilled workforce, enhanced economic competitiveness, an informed population, improved social equity and cohesiveness, and cultural enhancement.

It is generally accepted that participating in VET conveys substantial private benefits to individuals through higher lifetime incomes, better employment prospects and enhanced job satisfaction. However, vocational participation also conveys substantial public benefits to society as a whole. These public benefits are sometimes called externalities or spillovers (that is, they cannot be entirely appropriated by the individual graduates).

Governments finance public VET institutions for essentially two reasons:

(1) Without public financing, investment in education and training is likely to be insufficient, principally because of the market's failure to provide sufficient financial resources. Investment usually takes place when an investor can capture the benefit of the investment. In a number of respects, benefits from investment in VET cannot be entirely captured by the employer of the trained person. For example:

☐ A bank may be reluctant to finance a prospective student's pre-employment training because the skills and expertise gained through it are not readily redeemable as collateral for a loan and, accordingly, the bank may charge high interest rates, reflecting the riskiness of its investment.

☐ An employer who invests in an employee's training is not able to recover that investment if the employee leaves to work for someone else.

☐ Private education providers may be unwilling to invest in more expensive training courses (for example science and engineering) and may focus on cheaper courses, which may result in an undersupply of certain skills.

(2) Government investment in VET is justified because a society in general can benefit from the externalities of education and training, which contribute to the desired national objectives. This is particularly the case for the non-economic benefits involved, which include improvements in social equity and cohesiveness.

In essence, governments purchase (or finance) the outputs of VET institutions. For vocational training courses, these outputs include the graduates of the courses (or, more accurately, the skills and knowledge acquired by graduates). Governments typically fund entry-level training to facilitate the transition from school to work.

A VET funding system is *efficient* to the extent that it maximizes outputs that contribute to desired national economic and social equity objectives for the minimum input costs. An efficient funding system is characterized by:

☐ incentives or sanctions that encourage public VET institutions to be efficient in their service delivery by maximizing outputs for a given input of public funding;

☐ minimum transactional costs (incurred in the allocation of funding by both the funding agency and the training provider);

☐ minimum compliance costs (incurred in ensuring that training providers are accountable for their use of public resources).

A VET funding system is *effective* to the extent that it encourages training providers to deliver courses that give graduates the skills to enable them to become employable and so contribute to desired national economic and social equity objectives.

An effective system should also provide the government with the information to ascertain what return it is receiving from its investment, that is, what the VET system is achieving rather than what it is costing. Currently, there are a number of countries where public VET is funded by meeting the costs of provision, so that governments have little notion of what value they are receiving for the investment of public resources.

An effective funding system should also protect the government's ownership interest in the assets of public institutions. Generally, a government has two distinct interests in public VET institutions:

(1) a purchase interest – in which the government finances the education and training outputs of public VET institutions that support the desired national objectives;

(2) an ownership interest – in which the government, as the owner of VET institutions, finances the expansion and maintenance of the institutional

capital assets (buildings and equipment) and bears the risk of their financial failure.

An *equitable* public VET funding system should enable students from families with different levels of income and of different backgrounds to have equal access to education and training courses.

Requirements for designing funding mechanisms

VET funding mechanisms should aim at contributing to the current and future national priorities for skills development in industry and the community. The mechanisms used for funding VET institutions should take account of: labour market trends; the distribution of wealth across the population; the size and demographics of the population and workforce and the location of urban and rural areas; the balance between supply and demand for VET; and the maturity of the infrastructure available in VET institutions.

VET funding mechanisms and their accountability requirements must be designed to:

□ implement the government's identified priorities;

□ maintain critical skills in key industries and address skills shortage areas;

□ provide equal access to training across geographic regions and industry sectors;

□ balance the public and private benefits of training;

□ address the needs of disadvantaged groups of the population;

□ support providers through the generation of sufficient revenues so that they can remain financially viable;

□ ensure the maintenance of a robust institutional infrastructure;

□ provide incentives and encourage innovation and entrepreneurship in VET institutions.

For more details on the meaning of efficient, effective and equitable funding in different countries, consult **Unit 5.1: Efficient, effective and equitable funding mechanisms** on your CD-ROM.

5.1.2 ALTERNATIVE FUNDING SOURCES
FOR PUBLIC VET INSTITUTIONS

A public VET institution has customarily three principal sources of finance to support its operations:

(1) public funding allocated by a funding agent (for example a government department or ministry, or a funding council);

(2) private funding (tuition fees, endowments);

(3) revenue-based financing (cost-recovery, sales of services, and so forth).

Students who pay tuition fees recognize the private benefits that education and training convey. They have to choose their courses carefully and be diligent, since they are paying for part or all of the cost of training (even though the major cost may, in fact, be the income forgone while in training). Tuition fees also provide incentives for the VET institutions to respond to students' expectations of their training courses, since the provider is dependent in part (or in whole) on tuition fees for its income. An argument against tuition fees is that they may discourage participation in VET by students from poorer families.

Endowment funding may be received from charitable and philanthropic trusts or from former students or alumni, and is generally not recurrent. This feature may represent a financial risk for VET institutions that are strongly dependent on this form of funding as a source of revenue.

Care may be required to avoid unfair competition between public institutions and private VET providers. A public institution that uses its public funding to cross-subsidize its service delivery to undercut the fees charged by a private provider is an example of unfair competition.

Cost-recovery mechanisms may involve:

□ training and/or consultancy arrangements with individual enterprises and industries outside government-subsidized training. These contracts are usually negotiated on an individual basis and meet specific needs at market value rates. They may relate to both accredited and enterprise-initiated courses or target specialized enterprise requirements, such as the development of learning resources;

□ education and training for individuals in the community or region that lie outside government-subsidized priorities. The courses may be accredited or target the development of specific skills or interests, including hobby or recreational courses. They are charged at market value rates;

□ partnership projects with government agencies at local and national levels where training and associated services are part of a wider project or initiative;

☐ project funding from government agencies for the delivery of specified outcomes in research, training, resource development or community development.

☐ facilities and equipment being hired out to external bodies at market value rates.

For more details on alternative funding sources for public VET institutions in different countries, consult **Unit: 5.1: Efficient, effective and equitable funding mechanisms** on your CD-ROM.

5.1.3 ALTERNATIVE FUNDING MECHANISMS

A government can fund its public VET institutions using a number of options, which fall into three sets of financing methodologies:

(1) input- and output-based funding;

(2) negotiated and normative funding;

(3) absolute and relative funding.

Input and output funding

If a government uses the methodology of input funding, it may elect to purchase training outputs by funding the input costs of an institution directly (teachers' salaries, the cost of materials, utilities, and so forth). With this approach, the provider is funded for its costs. Consequently, the government has little idea of the value it is receiving for its investment, so it bears the risks of inefficient delivery, and so on.

Alternatively, if the methodology of output funding is used, a government may decide to purchase the VET institution's outputs directly. These might include the:

☐ skills and expertise of vocational graduates produced by a VET institution (or, as a proxy, the volume of its graduates derived from the number of enrolments or EFTSs, and so on);

☐ volume of courses delivered, which is derived from course weeks, student weeks, student contact/guided hours (SCHs) of curriculum delivered, and so forth.

With this approach, the government has a better idea of what its investment is producing, but the VET institution bears the risk that its output-based funding may not be sufficient to meet its input (operating costs). This risk is exacerbated if the VET institution's management does not have the autonomy to match its input costs to its output funding (for example by divesting surplus staff). True output funding may be problematic when the provider's staff are public servants with permanent tenure rather than employees of the institution under a fixed-term contract.

Funding for capital development and expansion, and recurrent (operational) funding for training delivery are often treated differently. The former may be based on actual costs (input funding) or related to training outputs (output funding). Another option is that capital and operational funding are lumped together as bulk funding and that the VET institutions make their own decisions on the most effective balance between capital and operational expenditure (an example of maximized autonomy). Some jurisdictions distinguish between recurrent operational funding and the additional resources required to fund growth (that is, increasing enrolments) in the VET sector.

Negotiated and normative funding

A second set of alternatives can be applied to both input and output funding.

Negotiated funding involves a budgeting process to assess the resource requirements of each institution in a VET system, usually based on negotiations between each institution and a central financing agency. It can be:

☐ incremental – the budget's starting point is the previous year's (historical) budget for each institution, adjusted by negotiation for any changes to costs and revenues anticipated in the coming year; or

☐ zero-based – the budget for each institution is negotiated anew every year from a "first principles" consideration of costs and revenues.

Normative funding involves the application of financing norms/standards/averages, financing formulae and other quantitative factors. The process includes formulating a conceptual model of a VET institution in terms of various parameters (for example the number of enrolments by vocational field). The funding entitlement for each institution is calculated by applying a formula that includes the funding standards or norms for the training system as a whole.

An example of such a funding model is one that allocates resources to a VET institution on the basis of its student enrolments expressed in EFTSs, with each EFTS financed by a standard allocation.

Absolute and relative funding

Irrespective of whether negotiated or normative financing is used, the allocation of resources can never be completely objective or free from contention.
Negotiated financing usually reaches a conclusion by an interactive negotiation
process that reconciles:

☐ absolute (bottom-up) budgeting – each VET institution submits its own
resource requirements; the overall budget is the sum of the VET institution's
bids, inevitably substantially in excess of the national financial resources
available; and

☐ relative (top-down) budgeting – the available resources are allocated centrally to VET institutions in relative proportion to assessed needs.

The application of an absolute (bottom-up) funding approach to normative
financing is generally impracticable as national VET resources are usually limited. Moreover, there is no notion of the "right" amount to be spent on VET
as the return on education investment is generally accepted by economists to
be non-linear, that is, the benefits of increased expenditure reach a notional
maximum, however much is invested in education.

Hence, normative financing systems usually adopt a relative (top-down)
funding approach. The starting point is a politically determined budget appro-
priation for education (and its subsectors) at the national level, which is then
allocated to VET providers by a normative financing methodology according
to relative need.

Comparisons between alternative funding mechanisms

In VET, there has been a gradual move in direction from input to output
financing, based on the belief that desired outcomes are more likely to be
achieved by the latter methodology. This is because governments will have
better information on, and control of, the services that they are actually purchasing from VET institutions. Output funding is likely to increase efficiency,
effectiveness, responsiveness and flexibility, provided that the public VET sector
has sufficient flexibility to operate this funding model.

Normative financing is more transparent and is potentially fairer and more
equitable than negotiated financing. The financing process is open to scrutiny
and the allocations are predictable. VET institutions are financed for their outputs, not according to their negotiating skills or access to political patronage.
This stability allows sensible business and financial planning to take place. An
important condition is that the financing formula is fair and equitable. Normative financing enables national consistency in funding allocations, without
precluding targeted assistance to particular regions.

The implementation of a particular funding system generally takes place over an annual budgetary cycle, although it is more advantageous for VET institutions to operate according to a longer term budget cycle. Thus, a common challenge facing all VET institutions is handling the interaction of the length of the academic, planning and funding cycles with the relative brevity of the annual financial cycles that governments generally prefer.

For more details on this challenge, refer to **Unit 4.4: The methodology and techniques of planning for training delivery**.

For more details on alternative funding mechanisms in different countries, consult **Unit 5.1: Efficient, effective and equitable funding mechanisms** on your CD-ROM.

Unit 5.2

INSTITUTIONAL
BUDGETING PROCESSES

5.2.1 BUSINESS PLANNING IN A VET INSTITUTION

Business planning in an autonomous VET institution relates to the legislative and regulatory framework within which it operates, accepted national accounting standards, the strategic directions of the institution and its current state of financial health and viability.

A measure of the autonomy of a public VET institution is the extent to which its managers are permitted to make decisions on how the public and private resources available to it are allocated to support the delivery of education and training and other outputs.

Where resources are allocated through a funding mechanism designed to meet the input costs of the institution (salaries, course materials, equipment, maintenance, site and building development, and so forth), managers are often constrained from diverting funding allocated to a particular input cost (for example salaries) to meet a different input cost (for example the purchase of new equipment). In this case, decisions on the effective use of public resources are essentially made by the funding agency, and institutional managers consequently have restricted financial autonomy. Planning, in as much as there is planning, is centrally driven.

Output-based funding, in which VET institutions are funded on the basis of the outputs that they deliver, generally offers enhanced autonomy. Institutional managers are free (usually within prescribed limits) to determine the institution's outputs and to allocate resources to their various competing input costs. Decisions on the most effective use of public resources are essentially made by institutional managers rather than by the central funding agency.

A worldwide move from input to output-based funding is being driven by the belief that VET managers are better placed than central funding agencies to decide on the best use of public and private resources for delivering their outputs. The planning of training delivery in this environment of enhanced institutional autonomy becomes an important function of institutional governance and management.

A key component of business planning is the development of a business plan. Effective planning takes place over two different time scales:

(1) long-term strategic planning, which gives effect to the governing council's strategic plan for the VET institution;

(2) short-term (annual) business planning, which determines the VET institution's outputs for the forthcoming academic and financial year(s).

The outcome of the strategic planning process is generally a high-level strategic development plan for the institution that provides long-term guidance to its governing council and management staff (usually for a period of three to ten years). In particular, the plan may specify the training services that are to be delivered over the period, and the implications of delivering the proposed training for budgeting and financing, staffing, and site and building development, and so forth.

For more details on strategic planning, refer to **Unit 4.4: The methodology and techniques of planning for training delivery**.

Autonomous VET institutions generally operate within an annual cycle of academic and financial years (not always congruent), a cycle of substantially shorter duration than the period covered by the strategic plan. The details required for day-to-day operations (covering the annual training and budget cycles) are usually contained within the VET institution's annual business plan. The business plan tends to be more focused on the detail of actual training outputs.

The governing council is responsible for examining and endorsing the business plan on an annual basis, as well as for the ongoing monitoring of progress against that plan and the endorsement of any adjustments that may be made in response to emerging circumstances.

Training delivery indicators

Training delivery indicators may include:

☐ measures of anticipated enrolments;

☐ measures of training quality;

☐ measures of performance outcomes for trainees and staff;

☐ the costs of delivering specific services;

☐ other non-financial indicators of the institution's core direction and capabilities.

Financial indicators

The VET institution's annual budget is an important component of its business plan. The plan will project income and expenditure and forecast revenue. The financial indicators applied to different types of activities, such as the delivery of government-funded accredited courses and fee-for-service contracts, may differ. The financial performance indicators to be considered when developing a business plan include:

☐ recurrent infrastructure expenses, such as insurance, facilities maintenance, equipment replacement schedules, telecommunication expenses;

☐ staffing levels, which are aligned with income forecasts and contract requirements;

☐ staff employment rates;

☐ the projected income from government-funded activities and from fee-for-service activities;

☐ cash-flow considerations;

☐ creditor and debtor conditions;

☐ profit rates to be derived from income;

☐ infrastructure funding rates to be derived from income;

☐ departmental targets for generating income.

The financial planning indicators of a VET institution may include:

☐ projected operating surpluses;

☐ returns on income and assets;

☐ operating cash flows; and

☐ measures of liquid assets, working capital and debt ratio.

Performance indicators and milestones defined within the business plan may often be used as part of an accountability regime that determines whether an institution is delivering its expected outputs and is operating within its approved budget.

For more details on short-term planning for training delivery in different countries, consult **Unit 4.4: The methodology and techniques of planning for training delivery** and **Unit 5.2: Institutional budgeting processes** on your CD-ROM.

5.2.2 APPLYING FOR EXTERNAL FUNDING

Funding may be allocated to a VET institution by means of:

☐ An application to a government funding body regarding the services that will be delivered and the price that is to be paid for those services. The services may be expressed as objectives, performance indicators and performance targets. The price per equivalent full-time student (EFTS) or student contact/guided hour (SCH) may be set at a common level across VET institutions or may be modified for individual institutions in relation to specific circumstances. This information is generally contained within a business plan, which the institution is expected to disclose (refer to Section 5.2.1 above).

☐ An application to a funding body regarding the funding for infrastructure improvements. In this case, the institution will be required to demonstrate that the funds be used to advance government priorities and that it has the capacity and capability to manage the expenditure of the funds.

☐ Competitive tendering, which will require interested VET institutions to submit proposals against defined criteria for the expenditure of funds or the delivery of services. This may include applications for the development of learning resources or supply of additional education and training services. VET institutions will need to support their proposal with data related to their capability to deliver the required outcomes to the required standard.

The funding-for-services application process is, to a great extent, determined by the funding mechanism operated by the government funding agency. Where resources are allocated through a funding mechanism designed to meet the input costs of the institution, managers are often constrained from diverting funding from one input to another, and decisions on the most effective use of public resources are essentially being made by the funding agency. Under these circumstances, planning is centrally driven, and VET managers have restricted financial autonomy. There is generally little need (or opportunity) for institutional managers to apply for external funding, since their resources are already determined by the funding agency.

However, with output-based funding, VET institutions are resourced on the basis of the outputs they deliver. Managers are then free (usually within prescribed limits) to determine their outputs and to apply and allocate public and private resources to their competing input costs.

Where public VET institutions have significant autonomy, output-based funding is preferred for the reasons outlined above; this funding may be negotiated or (more commonly) is normative.

For more details on the alternative funding methodologies, consult **Unit 5.1: Efficient, effective and equitable funding mechanisms**.

For more details on the application process for external funding in different countries, go to **Unit 5.2: Institutional budgeting processes** on your CD-ROM.

5.2.3 THE INTERNAL ALLOCATION OF REVENUE

Internal budgets are derived from a VET institution's business plan and aim to support its operation. Budgets should have realistic income and expenditure targets. The budget allocation should be done in consultation with teaching and support departments but against clear guidelines to ensure that all the responsible staff understand their accountability requirements. These staff, generally at the manager level, need to have daily access to their devolved accounts in order to track income and expenditure.

Where resources are allocated to institutions as output-based funding, the funding can, in principle, be undifferentiated, that is, managers are free to decide how to allocate the revenue from government subsidies, tuition fees and fee-for-service income. These decisions are internal and may include allocating resources to capital expenditure and overhead costs.

With this funding mechanism, the public resources can be directly linked to each cost centre and unit of the institution (for example department/school/ service) in terms of a unit's actual contribution to outputs. For instance, with normative financing, an institution's public revenue could, in principle, be allocated to each unit, in proportion to the unit's number of enrolments, to meet the costs incurred at the level of each cost centre.

If managers separate budgets into accounts that reflect income from contracted public training and accounts that derive their funding from private sources, they may also be able to align salary and non-salary costs against specific income. This strategy also provides a clear view of the viability of each activity and allows for the nature of expenditure to be closely tracked. It also makes it possible for senior-level staff to analyse the overall viability of income streams and of associated expenditure against budget line items.

The prudent institution will establish formal mechanisms to ensure that all budgets and accounts are monitored at regular, perhaps monthly, intervals, so that progress can be made regarding the business plan and remedial action taken where necessary.

Funding capital expenditure

Major cost items, such as capital expenditure on new buildings and equipment that provide benefits for more than one cost centre, and on units that indirectly support rather than deliver training outputs (such as the library), are normally dealt with by the chief executive/senior managers, subject to approval by the institution's governing council. By way of illustration, the financing of a major capital expenditure item could be achieved by:

☐ deducting a proportion of the institution's public funding prior to its allocation to the various cost centres (the so-called "slice-off-the-top" approach);

☐ debt financing (borrowing).

Major capital expenditure on buildings and equipment and on service units could be regarded as an overhead cost shared by all the cost centres within the institution, irrespective of whether the costs are met from operational cash surpluses or by debt financing.

Financing management and support services

The costs of supporting the governing council and of employing and supporting the chief executive are customarily treated as overhead costs met by a slice off the top. Services that benefit the entire institution, including the library, IT networks, and so forth, may also be treated as overhead costs, and funded centrally by this process.

Technical and administrative services may be organized and delivered at departmental level, particularly in larger institutions. However, for reasons of efficiency, many services of this nature are usually provided by a separate administrative section, headed by a senior manager (commonly designated "manager corporate services" or "director of administration"), who is often a member of the senior management team. Depending on the size of the VET institution, financial services may be separated from other general technical and administrative services.

In many VET institutions, there will be some degree of cross-subsidization between units. This may be necessary to ensure that the institution offers an acceptable range of courses, even those that may be uneconomic because of low enrolments.

New courses often have developmental and start-up costs initially met by cross-subsidization. Some courses may be kept going only because they enhance the institution's standing and reputation, even though they consume resources disproportionate to their contribution to the institution's revenue. Other courses may be underfunded because the relativities established for the normative funding methodology are inaccurate. Indeed, it is for this reason that normative funding may be delivered as undifferentiated funding explicitly to allow cross-subsidization to occur when it becomes necessary.

For more details on the internal allocation of public and private revenue, consult **Unit 5.2: Institutional budgeting processes** on your CD-ROM.

5.2.4 PROCEDURES FOR THE COSTING OF SERVICE DELIVERY

The costing of service delivery may be undertaken by specialist staff within the finance unit or it may be devolved to department staff. The costing of service delivery requires a clear and consistent approach across all areas of operation. It includes:

☐ costing for staff at all classifications, including adjustments for expected salary increases;

☐ staffing costs, including annual leave, workers' compensation levy, sick leave, and so on;

☐ infrastructure costs, such as insurance, facilities and equipment maintenance, utilities, IT, and so on;

☐ arrangements for costs of operational services, such as telephone charges, postage, use of vehicles, out of hours opening of facilities, photocopying, and so on;

☐ non-salary costs, such as catering, student materials, small ancillary items.

It is common practice for all institutional overheads to be allocated to all cost centres (for example departments/schools/services). The method used will depend on the nature of the overhead, as follows:

☐ The institution's administration may be allocated a fixed portion of the total public and private revenue. Some may be distributed to the administration of each cost centre (department/school/faculty), calculated on the basis of that unit's contribution to institutional revenue from public and private sources of income.

☐ The administrative costs of human resource management may be allocated according to the number of full-time equivalent (FTE) staff in each teaching or service unit (department/school/library).

☐ Property services costs may be allocated according to the actual space occupied by each cost centre (department/school/library). With this approach, accommodation is not regarded as a "free good", and each teaching and service unit is charged an occupancy charge based on the area occupied.

Most jurisdictions will have some form of standardized external reporting requirements for state-owned entities, including their VET institutions. These requirements provide a codified basis for GAAP within each jurisdiction, and usually are the basis for institutional accounting and audit practices.

A common requirement is that state-owned entities match their costs in a prescribed period with the income derived during that period (usually a financial year). The matching of costs and income leads to a need to accrue for income not yet received from debtors and expenses not yet paid to creditors (that is, accrual accounting). This approach to costing recognizes all income and expenditure, whether or not receipt or payment has occurred.

Depreciation of fixed assets expenditure

It is necessary to distinguish between recurrent operational income/expenditure (for example tuition fee income, expenditure on staff salaries) and capital expenditure, because only then can the depreciation of fixed assets (an overhead cost) be obtained as an important component of the costs of providing VET services (that is, building and equipment cannot be regarded as free goods in an assessment of the true costs of public training delivery).

Building and equipment will inevitably require replacement in due course, and replacement costs are customarily incorporated into the costing of service delivery. Assets may be assigned an initial valuation (for example the cost of construction or purchase), which is then depreciated at rates based on their expected lifetime (for example 50 years for buildings, five years for computer equipment).

Departmental interests

The budgeting procedures for cost allocation assume that senior managers are accountable to their colleagues both for the efficient operation of their respective departments and (collegially) for the efficient operation of the institution as a whole. They are in a position to see how their departments contribute to the operation of the whole institution, whether it accrues revenue through service delivery (for example a teaching department) or not (for example the library).

It is in an institution's best interests to provide incentives to encourage efficiency. Good managers will endeavour to do this by ensuring that cost centres are able to benefit from savings (cash surpluses). Revenue-raising departments generally do not have direct access to their own revenue. Funding allocations and tuition fees are generally processed through a central finance department and are available to the whole institution as its management decides. Savings from underspending usually accrue to the institution as a whole and may be redistributed according to priorities negotiated by senior managers. Redistribution may include bonuses for staff whose work has led to savings.

However, all departments, whether revenue raising or not, may try to inflate their costs; any attempts to do so need to be detected during the internal budget allocation process. Cost centres are expected to operate closely to their budget and they mainly report on exceptions through disclosing overspending or underspending.

For more details on the procedures for costing service delivery, consult **Unit 5.2: Institutional budgeting processes** on your CD-ROM.

5.2.5 FINANCIAL RULES

Ownership and purchase interests

The State retains a strong ownership interest in the financial viability of autonomous VET institutions, reinforced by its financial support to public institutions. The State customarily provides VET institutions with their major source of funding through purchasing services from them.

Accordingly, governments will impose financial rules on public institutions to protect their "purchase interest" (that is, they hold the institutions accountable for their use of public resources) and their ownership interest (that is, to minimize the State's ownership risk).

The funding agency will normally apply the financial rules covering the purchase interest, often as a component of the funding mechanism designed to ensure accountability for the use of public resources. In some jurisdictions, the financial rules that protect the State's ownership interest may be operated by a risk-monitoring agency established for that purpose; in others the responsibility lies with the funding agency.

Governments are tending to move from a system of central control of inputs to an approach where the VET institutions' governing councils have enhanced autonomy but are also held accountable for the training delivery. Governing councils may have full use of the institution's assets, which are subject only to ownership monitoring and the financial rules that are intended to limit financial risks.

In jurisdictions where a formal ownership-monitoring regime has not been established, the government will generally impose input controls to protect its interests. These usually include limitations on the sale of institutional assets deemed surplus, on the investment of cash surpluses and on borrowing and leasing powers.

Financial rules are also likely to encompass: the keeping of accounts and reporting of standards; authority for expenditure and the rules and procedures for delegating authority; reporting requirements (monthly, quarterly, and so on); and benchmarks for financial performance, for example working capital ratios.

Regulating asset disposal and investment

In many jurisdictions, legislation or regulations will impose restrictions on the ability of a public VET institution to dispose of surplus assets. For example, a public institution may be required to obtain the consent of the minister or the director of the relevant department or funding agency before selling or otherwise disposing of surplus institutional assets of value above a prescribed limit.

Similarly, legislation or regulations will generally impose conditions on the investment of cash surpluses held by public VET institutions. Customarily, an institution may be empowered to establish, maintain and operate a bank account at an approved bank, and all moneys received by the institution are required to be immediately paid into that (audited) account.

From time to time, public VET institutions may control substantial cash surpluses and it is reasonable to assume that governing councils will try to ensure the best use of that money. In some jurisdictions, money that belongs to a public institution and is surplus to its immediate cash-flow requirements may be invested prudently, as prescribed by legislation or regulation, for example deposited with an approved bank, in public securities or in such other securities as the government may determine. Such securities may include loans, bonds, debentures, Treasury bills and government stock or other securities that have a low risk profile.

Rules for borrowing

In many jurisdictions, legislation or regulations will impose restrictions on the ability of a public VET institution to borrow, issue debentures or otherwise raise money without the consent of the minister or chief executive of the funding agency. It is customary for any public VET institution wishing to receive approval for borrowing to submit a business case to the relevant agency.

The business case should justify the purpose of the loan, include an analysis of alternatives to borrowing, fit in with the institution's strategic direction and disclose the loan's financial implications. It is important that risk be assessed, including the consequences of:

- delays in completion;
- cost overruns;
- technical failure;
- change of government policy;
- uninsured losses;
- price increases;
- failure to meet enrolment targets;
- loss of competitive position;
- management failure.

Approval to borrow is usually subject to standard conditions (financial rules) that relate to the terms of the loan, the institution's liquidity, the government's fiscal position and the ongoing role of the risk-monitoring agency.

Tax regulations

Provided their activities are educational in focus, public VET institutions in many jurisdictions are exempt from paying income tax. However, there may be other taxation requirements with which public institutions have to comply. These may include:

□ tax on consumption (for example goods and services tax (GST), value-added tax (VAT)) applied to taxable activities that may include the provision of services (public VET institutions are often liable for consumption tax but may be compensated for it through their public funding);

□ tax on interest and dividend receipts (public institutions may often qualify for exemption if such interest or dividends are earned for the sole purpose of the institution's advancement);

□ local body land tax (public VET institutions are often exempt from paying this tax);

□ income tax deducted at source from the salaries of employees (pay as you earn (PAYE) or equivalent);

□ provisional tax on fees paid by VET institutions (for example to members of governing councils).

For more details on financial rules in different countries, consult **Unit 5.2: Institutional budgeting processes** on your **CD-ROM**.

Unit 5.3

FINANCING
THROUGH COST RECOVERY

5.3.1 COST RECOVERY THROUGH TUITION FEES

The rationale behind public and private funding

A public VET institution usually has three principal sources of finance to support its training delivery:

(1) public funding allocated by a funding agent (for example a government department or funding council);

(2) private funding (tuition fees, endowments);

(3) revenue-based financing (cost recovery, sale of services, and so on).

Public funding is commonly allocated to (or invested in) a VET institution by a government because: (a) without it an investment in the government's desired national economic and social objectives is likely to be insufficient; and (b) the society in general can gain from the benefits of education and skills training.

For more details on the rationale for public funding and on alternative funding mechanisms, refer to **Unit 5.1: Efficient, effective and equitable funding mechanisms**.

Fee-charging policies

Students who pay tuition fees recognize the private benefits that VET conveys to individual graduates through higher lifetime incomes, better employment prospects and enhanced job satisfaction. Tuition fees also encourage students to choose their courses carefully and to be diligent, because they are paying for part or all of the cost of training (even though the major cost may be the student's income forgone while in training). A further benefit of tuition fees is that they provide incentives for the training provider to respond to students' expectations of their training courses, since the provider is dependent in part (or in whole) on tuition fees for its income, and dissatisfied students may exercise their right to exit.

It may be appropriate to charge full-cost fees to those students enrolled in courses that are perceived to have low public benefit, such as hobby courses that amuse but do not provide the skills necessary for a trained workforce.

In some jurisdictions, public VET institutions are constrained from charging any tuition fees at all, and are required to undertake their training delivery within the limitations of the revenue solely derived from public funding. In other jurisdictions, the government determines a standard tuition fee (or a set of tuition fees) that depends on the particular field of training.

There are a number of principles that should underpin the fees and charges policy. These principles are often competing and involve balancing individual, employer and community-wide benefits as well as providing access and equity, while ensuring providers are able to generate sufficient revenue to remain viable. Alongside these issues are those of targeting training delivery to priority areas, interacting with higher education and managing provider issues.

The more detailed considerations are as follows:

☐ It is vital that fees do not present a barrier to student access and participation, particularly for young people and disadvantaged groups. Even government-subsidized fees may be a barrier to the enrolment of students, particularly in entry-level groups.

☐ Although VET students may later benefit from their education, they need to access funds for it immediately. This may not be a concern for those students who are employed and whose employer may be financing their studies, but it may be a barrier for students enrolling in entry-level courses.

☐ A deferred payment system could prove more equitable for lengthy courses as students could pay fees via smaller instalments or possibly defer paying fees until their income reaches a certain level.

☐ Both current and potential students as well as service providers must be able to understand and apply the fees and charges policy, which needs to be practical and consistent. It also needs to be open to minimal interpretation and should be able to be audited.

☐ A simple fee-charging model that consists of a set rate per hour regardless of course may be desirable. However, the simple model may be waived in favour of supporting government priorities for training and development, which might suggest that some courses should be charged to students at preferential rates to ensure maximum uptake.

☐ There need to be a clear concessions policy, calendar-year charging practices and withdrawals and refund policies. As far as a concessions policy is concerned, the key issue is how to determine eligibility. Public VET providers might grant concessionary fee status to those classified under specified government living or study conditions, such as apprentices and disadvantaged groups. With regard to equity and access through a set concessionary rate, institutions might also have the discretion to reduce or waive fees in cases of extreme hardship.

☐ Situations need to be interpreted in a consistent manner, whether a programme is in a priority or skills shortage area, where and how the training is delivered, and the perceived private and public benefits of the training course.

☐ The relationship between government-funded and fee-for-service activities must be taken into consideration.

Practical issues

Matters to be considered with regard to tuition fees include:

☐ the means by which the tuition fee is calculated, such as: differential fees by industry/occupation or qualification; parity of fees across public VET providers; the need for minimum and maximum fee levels, including caps related to hours of study in a year or a course;

☐ the level of tuition fees in comparison to government funding of the institution and with regard to the viability of the institution;

☐ the option of a concessions policy, including reimbursement to public VET providers for students who may receive government living benefits related to social conditions, disadvantage or government priorities;

☐ supporting the costs of non-tuition fees, such as equipment costs and student services fees, library support, counselling and other non-infrastructure costs;

☐ considering the issues related to educating full fee-paying students alongside government-subsidized students.

A tuition fees policy may specify restrictions on what providers may charge. In this case, a VET institution may charge fees in relation to an enrolment in a government-funded course for:

☐ student tuition. However, it should be decided whether there should be a set charge for fees across all VET providers for the same course, regardless of geographic location or specialization;

☐ the recovery of no more than the actual cost of providing goods or materials that will be retained by a student as his or her personal property;

- □ the recovery of the actual cost of an excursion or field trip that is a requirement of the accredited course;

- □ ancillary services and support;

- □ the recovery of no more than the actual cost of assessing a student's prior learning for the purposes of the course, but only if the assessment is conducted at the request, or with the consent, of the student.

VET providers should also consider whether:

- □ all fees and charges are built into the advertised charge rate to give students a more accurate indication of course cost;

- □ all fees are included as part of course information to enable students to make comparisons between courses and institutions;

- □ there should be set materials and ancillary fees for identical courses across different institutions;

- □ a concession rate should apply to materials, ancillary fees and services and amenities fees;

- □ a cap should be applied to the charges for materials and ancillary fees.

Student fees and charges may generate only a comparatively small but important source of revenue for the VET system. Revenue generation through student fees may be particularly important for providers in rural and remote areas, which may have less capacity to engage in fee-for-service activities. Students tend to feel more comfortable when it is the government or its funding agent that sets (that is, limits) tuition fees rather than the institution.

To the extent that a VET provider is free to set and charge tuition fees to supplement its public funding, enhanced autonomy gives greater flexibility. This enables the provider to determine its own delivery costs (minus any surpluses). In turn, this enhanced autonomy/flexibility should enable a VET provider to compete with other institutions on the basis of price (that is, tuition fees charged) and quality. In principle, choice of higher fees should allow choice of a higher quality of training delivery. It should also encourage greater efficiency.

There are arguments for and against the setting of tuition fees. An argument against tuition fees is that they may discourage students from poorer families from engaging in VET. Equitable access to VET requires that tuition fees not be a barrier to participation. However, equitable access can be facilitated by a number of strategies, including:

- □ the introduction of tuition fee rebates/discounts, usually targeted on income or some other appropriate indicator of social deprivation;

- □ the provision of scholarships or equivalent assistance for students from priority target groups;

143

☐ the provision of non-discriminatory loans available to all students irrespective of their family or personal income and assets (a bank may be reluctant to finance participation in training by a student lacking collateral because skills cannot be redeemed as collateral. Alternatively, the bank may charge very high interest rates, reflecting the riskiness of its investment in the student's education and training);

☐ the provision of income-contingent loans, that is, repayment is expected only if the graduate student's income exceeds a specified threshold, thereby demonstrating that the graduate student has indeed derived private benefit from the training course.

For more details on cost recovery through tuition fees in different countries, consult **Unit 5.3: Financing through cost recovery** on your CD-ROM.

5.3.2 COST RECOVERY THROUGH SERVICE DELIVERY

Fee-for-service revenue

A public VET institution's fee-for-service engagements may include training, assessment and certification services, consultancy services related to a range of learning and development functions, learning resource development and maintenance projects.

Fee-for-service-financed delivery of training and allied services may be considered an important component of a VET institution's income and revenue. A successful institution that has good links with its local and regional industries may be in a position to attract contracts and projects outside its government-funded training delivery.

The costing of such initiatives will include a complex interplay of employment conditions for a range of staff, an estimate of staff time, projected non-salary expenses and a levy for infrastructure expenses. For simplicity's sake, a VET institution will calculate salary oncosts and infrastructural expenses in general terms and derive an indicative rate for a range of planned projects.

In general, salary costs, which are related to employment conditions such as sick leave, long service leave, annual leave and workers' compensation, and the infrastructure costs, which are related to electricity, gas, land and capital costs, may be standardized across all sources of income. The profit margin associated with each source of income, however, will vary according to the funding source. This may be allied to the perceived downstream benefit to the public institution and its core business, the potential for further income from the client, the ability of the client to bear the price charged, the ability of the market to bear the charge, the strength of competition in the market and economies of scale in the resale of similar and associated products.

The fee-for-service delivery by public VET institutions may be encouraged by government policies and targets. The intent is twofold:

(1) to encourage increasing levels of self-sufficiency;

(2) to promote close links with public institutions' directions and expertise and the needs of industry.

The government may, however, need to balance an overall policy direction with the level of opportunities that are realistically available to metropolitan, regional, rural and remote public VET institutions. Targets for individual institutions need to be realistic.

Other sources of revenue

Public VET institutions may also generate fees by charging external parties for the use of their premises, for example as conference venues. Such arrangements could be expanded to include charging rental fees for the sustained use of buildings (deemed surplus to the requirements of training delivery) for other purposes, for example storage, commercial premises, and so on.

Selling services or products generated within the public institution as a consequence of its training delivery, for example saleable items produced by students, and so on, may also generate revenue. In principle, the income derived from saleable items produced by students (or staff) could be shared between the VET institution and its students (or staff) by agreement. Some care may be required to avoid unfair competition between a publicly funded institution that is selling its services or products and another private-sector company that provides equivalent services or products. A public VET provider that used its public funding to cross-subsidize its service delivery in order to undercut the price charged by a private provider for an equivalent service or product would be an example of unfair competition.

The issue of unfair competition between a public VET institution and a local private provider of a similar service or product is usually addressed by setting up a "business arm" of the public institution to provide the service or product that is explicitly self-funded. Funding transparency should ensure there is no perception of unfair cross-subsidization within the public VET institution to the detriment of a competing private-sector provider.

An example is the delivery of chiropody services to a local community as part of the public VET institution's provision of clinical experience for its trainees. In this instance, the public institution should take care not to undercut the fees charged by a private-sector chiropodist by fully costing its student "free" labour. The "chiropody business arm" should be required to reflect the (market) cost of the service.

This could be ensured by:

☐ requiring the business arm to pay an equivalent amount to the institution (as a contribution to its service delivery revenue); and

☐ charging clients an appropriate fee for the chiropody services delivered by students while gaining their necessary clinical experience.

For more details on cost recovery through service delivery, consult **Unit 5.3: Financing through cost recovery** on your CD-ROM.

Unit 5.4

MANAGING ASSETS
AND REVENUE

5.4.1 BORROWING AND LEASING

Autonomous public VET institutions that are largely or entirely publicly funded will be guided by government legislation and regulations. They will also be subject to annual and longer term performance measures that include financial indicators. The governing council of an autonomous public VET institution is responsible for ensuring the viability and sustainability of the institution, and its task is to balance opportunity with risk.

From time to time, the management of an autonomous institution may determine that the institution lacks the resources it requires for some particular aspect of its operations. The deficiencies may be:

☐ financial – accumulated cash surpluses are insufficient, for example, to meet the costs of a proposed capital works programme or the purchase of new equipment; prudent borrowing may be an appropriate response; and

☐ physical – the public institution lacks sufficient buildings to accommodate its staff and students adequately; prudent leasing may be an appropriate response.

Borrowing

Capital may need to be borrowed to cover deficits or to fund expansion and development. In the former case, an autonomous public VET institution may be in breach of its legislative and regulatory responsibilities. If its operating expenses exceed revenue to the extent that its working capital ratio is put at risk, then management practices, processes and structures will all have to be reviewed and improved in order to return the institution to a healthy financial state.

A short-term fix in the form of borrowed funds may be more appropriately dealt with by the funding body, that is, the government, rather than by commercial lending institutions. Resorting to a commercial entity could compromise the future and autonomy of the institution in terms of the solutions it needs to use to repay the loan and re-establish financial health. A loan through the funding body, on the other hand, would be underpinned by government policy and so ensure continuing attention to the core business.

If a VET provider wishes to fund expansion or development, there may be a similar risk if the capital is provided by a commercial entity. Any diversion from the core business and the introduction of an additional key stakeholder may complicate the operating environment of the institution.

Although borrowing provides additional resources for a proposed capital works programme or the purchase of new equipment, there is still an element of risk involved for the public VET institution and for the government as a principal funder, owner and regulator. A government has a legitimate interest in a proposal for borrowing by an autonomous institution, and generally will regulate the ability of an institution to borrow in order to protect its ownership interest.

The degree of regulation is determined by the VET institution's degree of autonomy, which may range from an outright ban on borrowing to light-handed regulation that includes a requirement on the part of the public VET institution to produce a business plan that demonstrates that borrowing is a prudent (minimal risk) course of action to follow. The level of regulation may also depend on the proposed magnitude of borrowing, since this will affect the financial risk. For example, a VET institution may be permitted to borrow sums up to a prescribed limit without being subjected to regulation.

Leasing

Leasing may be an appropriate response to a shortage of accommodation or equipment. It may, in principal, offer enhanced short-term flexibility over a substantial building programme because it may be easier for a public VET institution to terminate a lease (of premises no longer required) than to dispose of a surplus building. However, leasing, like borrowing, is not without risk for the institution nor for the government as owner, and for similar reasons is often regulated by governments.

Leasing may involve general equipment, ICT equipment, machinery, vehicles or buildings. The case for the lease of each will be made against established criteria determining financial benefit for the institution. This will include the terms of the lease, the cost to the VET provider at the end of the lease, the status of the institution at the end of the lease with regard to the leased property, and any attendant conditions such as maintenance or the updating/upgrading of contracts or options.

For more details on borrowing and leasing in different countries, consult **Unit 5.4: Managing assets and revenue** on your CD-ROM.

5.4.2 CAPITAL EXPENDITURE
(BUILDINGS AND EQUIPMENT)

From time to time, the management of an autonomous public VET institution may determine that the institution lacks sufficient accommodation for its staff and students and/or adequate equipment to support its training delivery. An appropriate response may be to undertake (often substantial) capital expenditure on buildings and equipment.

Decisions on major capital expenditure are determined by the public institution's degree of autonomy, and so will either be taken by its governing council and management (in the case that institutions have such an autonomy) or centrally, by a ministry or funding agent. In jurisdictions where public VET institutions are financed through the input-based funding system, decisions on capital expenditure are customarily made centrally.

On the other hand, in jurisdictions where public institutions are resourced through output-based funding mechanisms, decisions on capital expenditure are customarily delegated to the institutions themselves, since it is believed that the managers of VET institutions are better placed than government officials to prioritize capital expenditure against other input costs.

Capital expenditure exposes a public VET institution and the government (as owner) to arguably greater financial risk than borrowing and leasing do. Consequently, governments have a legitimate interest in any proposals for significant capital expenditure, and will generally regulate to protect their ownership interest.

The degree of regulation is determined by the VET institution's degree of autonomy, and may range from a capital works programme operated centrally, usually by an agent of the government, to a requirement on the part of the public institution to produce a business plan which demonstrates that the proposed capital expenditure is a prudent (minimal risk) investment. The level of regulation may also depend on the proposed magnitude of capital expenditure. For example, an institution may be authorized to undertake capital expenditure up to a prescribed monetary limit without being subjected to regulation.

Decisions on major capital expenditure by an autonomous VET institution generally need the approval of its governing council. The financing of major capital expenditure may be achieved by:

☐ deducting a proportion of the VET institution's public funding prior to its allocation to training delivery (the slice-off-the-top approach, but unlikely to be sufficient for larger projects);

☐ using accumulated cash surpluses;

☐ debt financing (borrowing).

In effect, capital expenditure on building and equipment can be regarded as an overhead cost that should be shared across the institution, irrespective of whether the costs are met by cash reserves accumulated from operational surpluses or by debt financing.

Although a common (and fiscally prudent) approach would be to limit capital expenditure to the value of the VET institution's cash reserves accumulated from operational surpluses, there are equity arguments for borrowing if students are required to make a significant contribution through tuition fees. When capital works are paid for from operational surpluses derived in part from tuition fees, the capital costs are borne by current students, who are unlikely to derive any benefit from future buildings. With debt financing (borrowing), the debt-servicing costs will be borne by future students, who are more likely to derive benefit from the capital investment. A counter-argument is that current students are benefiting from tuition fees paid by previous students. Nonetheless, debt financing may address the equity issues of intergenerational transfers more cogently than financing via operational surpluses.

The maintenance of assets and resources is very important in realizing the maximum benefit from buildings and equipment. Estimating the useful life of an asset is necessary to set its depreciation rate and to determine its replacement schedule.

It is important to balance short-term gain and longer-term strategy in order to maintain a depreciation schedule and eventual write-off. Autonomous public VET institutions will also need to review facilities and equipment on an annual basis in order to determine that they align with the institution's strategy and future plans. The divestment of an asset or resource may be affected by property values and industry trends, and also by forecasts of growth and initiatives undertaken by both the public VET institution and the funding body.

In all cases capital expenditure will need to be aligned with planning priorities over a long time frame and contribute to the viability and growth of the institution. A key criterion in the planning phase will be its overall contribution to meeting the needs of the core business of the VET provider. The clear commitment, agreement and engagement of the whole institution are critical. Any significant changes after the start of a project are costly and time consuming. A further consideration will be the maintenance schedule of the new establishment/equipment; over the useful life of a building or machine, maintenance costs will contribute to the cost, viability and value of the investment.

VET institutions would be well advised to employ specialist contractors to develop specifications and manage the design and building/installation of new buildings/equipment.

For more details on capital expenditure in the VET institutions of different countries, consult **Unit 5.4: Managing assets and revenue** on your CD-ROM.

5.4.3 DISPOSAL OF ASSETS AND WRITE-OFFS

From time to time, the management of an autonomous public VET institution may determine that a particular asset (land, building, or piece of equipment) is surplus to the requirements of the institution's principal role of training delivery or, in the case of a building and/or equipment, has become unserviceable or obsolete.

Decisions on getting rid of surplus assets or write-offs in respect of unserviceable or obsolete buildings and equipment are determined by the institution's degree of autonomy, and may be made by the governing council and management. The government as owner has a legitimate interest in divestments and write-offs and may reasonably regulate to protect this interest. For example a government may:

☐ determine that the proceeds from any divestments be returned to the government or a nominated agent;

☐ permit divestment or write-offs only of assets of a monetary value below a prescribed maximum;

☐ require that a public institution obtain the consent of a nominated agent (for example ministry official) before disposing of any asset of monetary value above a prescribed minimum.

For more details on the disposal of assets by VET institutions in different countries, consult **Unit 5.4: Managing assets and revenue**.

5.4.4 THE UTILIZATION OF OPERATIONAL SURPLUSES

Sources of surpluses

The monetary difference between revenue and expenditure is the public VET institution's operational surplus or deficit. To be meaningful in the long term, the operational surplus or deficit should take into account the depreciation of the institution's fixed assets as a component of the real costs of delivery. This is necessary to ensure that provision is made for the replacement of such assets as may become necessary.

Any recurrent deficit should be of concern to the institution's governing council and management as well as to the government as owner, since it potentially increases the risk of financial failure.

A significant surplus raises the issue of who should benefit from it. In situations where a public VET institution is financed through input-based funding, a surplus would indicate that the input costs have been overestimated or that the VET institution has been unexpectedly efficient. If a system of normative output-based funding is used, a surplus is an indication that:

☐ the funding norms in the funding model (average costs of outputs) may have been overestimated;

☐ tuition fees have been set excessively high;

☐ the public institution is unusually efficient compared with the VET sector averages.

A government may elect to reclaim all surpluses and require that they be remitted to the government funding agent as a way of recovering its costs associated with training delivery. Although doing so may reduce VET funding costs to the State in the short term, it would also remove:

☐ a strong incentive for public VET institutions to be efficient;

☐ the VET provider's capacity to accumulate reserves as buffers against financial contingencies, and/or finance future capital expenditure.

A policy that requires public VET institutions to remit operational surpluses seems inconsistent with a policy of maximizing institutional autonomy, although some regulation may be justifiable, particularly if students are being charged excessive tuition fees.

The use of surpluses

Before considering how to use operational surpluses, a prudent VET institution will ensure that there is an adequate cash flow in current assets to take advantage of opportunities and minimize risks.

Operational surpluses may be invested in two ways: investment to support cash flows, and reinvestment in the business. A successful institution may choose to adopt both courses simultaneously.

Investments in property, short-term and longer-term secure cash management funds or bonds will contribute to the financial health of the institution and provide future sources of cash. A clear plan approved by the governing council will ensure the viability of the strategy.

The reinvestment of surpluses in the business may include: making improvements to buildings, infrastructure and staff/student facilities; introducing initiatives that engage the local community; initiating professional development and support strategies for staff; undertaking market research and promotion; targeting support for programmes and activities that provide long-term stable income; establishing research programmes in areas of strategic importance; and funding scholarships and awards that benefit current and potential students.

For more details on the utilization of operational surpluses in different countries, consult **Unit 5.4: Managing assets and revenue** on your CD-ROM.

Unit 5.5

STANDARD FINANCIAL STATEMENTS AND THE FINANCIAL AUDIT

5.5.1 THE SET OF FINANCIAL STATEMENTS FOR AN AUTONOMOUS VET INSTITUTION

For a public VET institution to have a level of financial autonomy it is necessary that its governance and management are accountable, and are seen to be accountable, for the use of the public and private resources allocated to it. Public VET providers are to be accountable for the public funding provided by the government as owner, principal funder and regulator. They should also be accountable to other stakeholders, including industry, local communities and, in particular, to students for the tuition fees and other costs that they are required to pay and for their time committed to training (as well as for income forgone). The government has a legitimate interest in ensuring that public institutions are also accountable to these other stakeholders.

Although financial accountability (that is, accountability for inputs) is paramount, other important aspects of accountability include the quality and relevance of training (that is, accountability for outputs). These can be assured by a number of processes.

For more details on accountability arrangements for institutional outputs, refer to **Module 10: Quality assurance in education and training** and **Module 11: Performance monitoring and reporting**.

Financial accountability is generally achieved by requiring a public institution to prepare a standard set of financial statements for a financial year. Usually, the set of standard financial statements will include corresponding sets of data for previous financial years to allow trends (over time scales longer than one financial year) to be identified.

A standard set of financial statements is generally required to be prepared in accordance with the generally accepted accounting practice (GAAP) that pertains to each jurisdiction. Professional bodies representing accountants and auditors within each jurisdiction have often codified this practice. Accounting requirements may be made more explicit through specific (education and training) legislation or generic (public finance) legislation or by government regulation.

Although details of GAAP may differ between jurisdictions, a standard set of financial statements will often include the following:

- ☐ a Statement of Financial Performance: allows a comparison between the total operating income (from government funding, tuition fees, and contract, investment and trading incomes, and so on) and the total cost of operations (staff salaries, administration costs, depreciation allowance and the costs of property, equipment, teaching materials, other sundries, and so on); the difference will be the net operating result (surplus or deficit) of the institution;

- ☐ a Statement of Financial Position: allows a determination of the VET institution's total public equity (net assets), being total assets (cash, receivables, investments, fixed assets, and so on) minus total liabilities (payables, loans, entitlements, and so on);

- ☐ a Statement of Movement in Equity: allows a comparison of movement in public equity (net assets) from initial public equity after adjustments for revaluation, and so on, plus (minus) operating surplus (deficit);

- ☐ a Statement of Cash Flows: provides summaries of operational cash income (funding, fees, operating revenue, and so on) and expenditure (salaries, suppliers, and so on), investment cash income (asset sales, and so on), expenditure (buildings, equipment, and so on) and financing activities (borrowing, loan repayments, and so on);

- ☐ a Statement of Commitments and Contingent Liabilities: provides summaries of future commitments to capital expenditure, leases, and so on, and of payments that the VET institution may become liable for at some future date;

- ☐ a Statement of Revenues and Expenditure: provides summaries of actual and budgeted income and expenditure by cost centre (for example faculty or service unit).

True accountability raises the issue of who is to be actually held accountable. In some jurisdictions, the required set of standard financial statements also includes a Statement of Responsibility (or equivalent). This statement, often jointly signed by the chairperson of the governing council and the chief executive, incorporates declarations that the VET institution's governance and management:

- ☐ accept responsibility for the accuracy of the annual set of standard financial statements;

- ☐ accept responsibility for maintaining a system of internal financial control that provides assurance of the integrity and accuracy of financial reporting;

□ believe that the annual financial statements give a fair reflection of the financial position and operations of the VET institution.

To enhance the credibility of the annual standard financial statements, a statement from a qualified auditor should accompany them, certifying that the statements give a fair reflection of the financial position and operations of the VET institution (see also **Section 5.5.2** below).

For more details on the standard set of financial statements for autonomous VET institutions in different countries, consult **Unit 5.5: Standard financial statements and the financial audit** on your CD-ROM.

5.5.2 ORGANIZATION OF THE FINANCIAL AUDIT

Internal audit

The public institution will be required to have effective financial management procedures in place. To give substance to the Statement of Responsibility (or equivalent) and to strengthen its system of internal financial control, an autonomous institution should have a system for the (internal) audit of all of its financial transactions. In larger institutions, the position of chief internal auditor (or equivalent) may be created to carry out this function. Usually the auditor will be a member of the senior management team but with additional safeguards to ensure the appointee's necessary level of independence.

The internal auditor will be designated by the public VET institution's governing council and will have direct access to the chief executive. Reports from the internal auditor may indicate areas for further investigation and action to be taken by the governing council and management.

The internal auditor has defined responsibility and the authority to:

□ ensure that the institution complies with its financial management policies. Important policies would, for instance, involve a documented system for protecting fees paid in advance and for fair and reasonable refund policies;

□ monitor and report on compliance with the established financial management policies and procedures, for review and as a basis for improvement;

□ investigate and report on matters of interest and/or concern according to a schedule set annually by the governing council as part of a risk management framework;

□ provide, when requested, a statement of assurance that the institution has sound financial management standards for matters related to the scope of registration and scale of operations.

External audit

For the public VET institution's annual financial statements to be credible, they need to be accompanied by an independent audit report carried out by a qualified external auditor. This external audit report should certify that the statements give a fair reflection of the financial position and operations of the institution (with appropriate qualifications as necessary) on at least an annual basis. This report must be made available, on request, to the registering body.

In some jurisdictions, the accounts of public entities, including public VET institutions, are subject to external audit by a state entity established for this function. In others, it is permissible for a public provider to tender for independent external auditing services provided by a qualified private-sector auditor and subject to the terms, conditions and procedures that may be required by the government.

For more details on the organization of the financial audit of public VET institutions in different countries, consult **Unit 5.5: Standard financial statements and the financial audit** on your CD-ROM.

MODULE 6

Student management

Unit 6.1

THE STUDENT ENROLMENT PROCESS

6.1.1 ENROLMENT POLICIES

Enrolment as a service agreement

Enrolment in a course constitutes an agreement between an individual and an organization in which the organization undertakes to provide educational services over an agreed time frame and for an agreed cost for the purposes of passing on specific skills/competence and knowledge. As such, the enrolment form or contract of study should identify the personal details of the student, and also specify the course and subjects or competencies that the student wishes to study. The student should be making an informed choice, based on clear and accurate information, regarding the course in which he or she enrols, its structure and outcomes. The student commits him- or herself to the contract by signing it and paying the agreed fees, while the public VET institution commits to the contract by providing the enrolment form and registering the student as a client in its system.

To ensure that enrolment decisions are based on informed choice, potential students should be given information and support to make them aware of the requirements for attendance, assessment and participation and also of the opportunities to progress once the course has been successfully completed.

Open-entry policy

A publicly funded VET institution operating within a particular jurisdiction is required to attract, select and enrol its trainees in accordance with an enrolment policy determined by the government or its funding agent. The enrolment policy usually aims to bring about the government's economic and social objectives, and may be influenced by the government's ability to finance training. The greater the autonomy granted to the institution, the more likely it is that the VET institution will set its own enrolment conditions.

In principle, the enrolment policy is usually one of open entry, that is, any prospective student who wishes to enrol in a training course may do so without restriction. This policy is usually subject to the student meeting certain minimum entry standards. These standards are introduced to ensure that a prospective student has the prerequisite knowledge to cope with the requirements of the course. To the extent that public funding fully meets the costs of training delivery, an enrolment policy based on open entry removes most barriers to participation: any student who wishes to enrol is able to do so.

Where public funding is limited and the balance of costs is met through tuition fees, access to training may be limited by the ability of the students, their families or their employers to pay these fees, that is, rationing by price. Tuition fees can be an impediment to equitable training delivery as students from middle-income families may be able to afford fees and take advantage of a public tuition subsidy, whereas students from poorer families may be excluded from this possibility. Employers have a clear interest in vocational training, and they are usually expected to contribute to the costs of training in the VET institution for their employed apprentices and other staff.

Restricted entry

In other jurisdictions, the enrolment policies may operate restricted entry to publicly funded education and training places. By capping the number of places which the government is prepared to finance, it can minimize its financial risk of investing in skills which may not be demanded in the labour markets. Restricted access does, however, have serious consequences for equity.

The restricted entry systems are commonly based on competition-based enrolment principles and are equitable to the extent that competition is based on merit. So students of equal merit have an equal chance of participating in the publicly funded education and training.

"Merit" in this context is based on the training provider's assessments of the candidate's academic ability, recognition of prior learning, or competencies and skills achieved, and so forth. Such a policy ensures that the most able prospective students are successful in gaining enrolment. However, it also assumes that the most able students will derive the greatest private benefit from publicly funded further education and training.

For further discussion on why governments fund VET, refer to Unit 5.1: Efficient, effective and equitable funding mechanisms.

Two issues arise out of competitive (merit-based) enrolment systems. The first is how merit is assessed, whether by previous educational background, academic achievement, entrance examination, interview, or some other method of selection. All these methods have pitfalls.

For more details, refer to Section 6.1.2: Methods of attracting, selecting and enrolling students below.

The second issue raised by competitive enrolment systems is the implications for equity. Students may fail to meet entry standards or perform badly in entrance examinations simply because they came from disadvantaged backgrounds. They may not have benefited as much as more affluent students from previous education. For these reasons, educational disadvantage can be transferred between generations of students and their parents. In this context "disadvantaged" applies to financial aspects (for example an inability to afford or participate in quality compulsory education) as well as to attitudes of mind. A student from a more affluent family may be more likely to appreciate the strong linkages between educational and vocational attainment, and accordingly place a higher value on education.

Nevertheless, competitive (merit-based) enrolment systems can be equitable, provided that alternative arrangements are put in place to ensure access to restricted-entry education and training for target groups (for instance, the socially disadvantaged). Targeting may be on the basis of:

☐ student (or family) income (addresses the student's ability – or lack thereof – to meet tuition fees and other training costs);

☐ gender (addresses the over- or under-representation of a particular gender in a particular occupation, for example men in nursing, women in construction trades);

☐ ethnicity (addresses under-representation in VET of a particular ethnic group).

The "affirmative action" policy instruments available to ensure equitable access to training through competitive (restricted-entry) enrolments systems include:

☐ pre-entry or bridging courses that allow students from disadvantaged backgrounds to meet the entry standards of competitive enrolment systems;

☐ scholarships or grants, which meet tuition fees and other costs of training and are allocated on the basis of the student's (or family's) income, that is, they are means-tested;

☐ non-discriminatory loans that are not subject to normal commercial lending criteria and that may include a public subsidy (reduced interest rates) and arrangements for income-contingent loan repayments;

☐ entry quota systems, which guarantee that a minimum number of places are reserved for students from priority target groups.

In quota systems, it is vital that all enrolled students (whether they are quota students or not) meet the course's minimum entry requirements. This is to ensure that all enrolled students have the ability to cope with the requirements of the course. Although students from non-target groups may need to achieve a higher standard for selection, the standard for successful graduation from the course must be the same for all students, otherwise quota students may be stigmatized as being sub-standard.

For more details on enrolment policies that apply in different countries, consult **Unit 6.1: The student enrolment process** on your CD-ROM.

6.1.2 METHODS OF ATTRACTING, SELECTING AND ENROLLING STUDENTS

Attracting students

Public VET institutions can attract potential students in a number of ways. A common approach is to use the media, that is, by advertising in community and national newspapers, on local radio and (for particularly well-resourced institutions) through television commercials. Public institutions may also organize special events or attend community venues such as shopping centres and career forums. They can also liaise with secondary schools and industry bodies.

Institutions commonly publish course promotional materials that describe offerings, training content and objectives, and entry requirements. Promotional material organized by vocational area, course level, entry level, content and venue should be readily available both in print and in electronic form. Such material may include brochures for distribution at targeted venues, a course information web site and a course information telephone line. It is becoming increasingly common for VET institutions to attract students via their own web sites. These give multimedia information about the training providers, the courses on offer and their enrolment procedures. They can include film, speech, photographs and be interactive in design.

A more selective approach to attracting students is through careers counsellors, who are well placed to advise students in their final year(s) of schooling on their future options for education, training and/or employment. Teachers in the upper years of schooling can also be influential. In some jurisdictions, a government agency maintains a comprehensive web site that offers generic information for school leavers on their employment options and the required levels of skills and competencies. Web sites take into account labour market data and also provide information on (or web links to) other web sites that outline relevant courses and identify appropriate VET providers.

For more details on these information services, refer to **Unit 6.4: Vocational guidance and job placement assistance**.

Through their linkages with local industries and the professions, VET institutions should also be able to recruit students who are already in employment, particularly when their employers are looking for higher levels of skills in their employees and may be willing to sponsor further training.

A public provider should also ensure that information is regularly updated and that telephone or email enquiries are responded to. The aim is to convert enquiries from potential students into enrolments. Local contacts are also important. The local reputation of an institution, developed through word-of-mouth recommendations from former students, or their families and friends, is often the most powerful influence on student choice. All potential students need to be given clear information about selection, enrolment and induction procedures, applicable fees and charges, study support mechanisms, delivery and assessment arrangements, and welfare and guidance services. Information on appeals, complaints and grievance procedures, disciplinary procedures, arrangements for the recognition of prior formal and informal learning as well as arrangements covering access, equity and anti-discrimination and harassment provisions is also vital.

A successful public VET institution with a consistent and active approach to customer service will ensure that enrolling students are matched with the course they need and want and are able to complete. Pre-enrolment counselling should cover the outcomes of the course, learning and assessment requirements and course delivery arrangements. The expectations and requirements of the course should be carefully communicated, so that the enrolling student makes an informed choice that leads to a successful engagement with the institution. It is important that any specific learning difficulties or physical disabilities are registered before the course begins, so that there is enough time to make special arrangements to support the student.

Enrolment procedures

The enrolment procedure of an open-entry system generally involves a student providing information required by the VET institution. This is customarily achieved by the student completing a standard enrolment form. Prospective students may be required to provide documentary evidence of their previous educational experience and attainment levels, and demonstrate that they meet the minimum entry standards for the training course.

In competitive (merit-based) enrolment systems, prospective students may be required to participate in a pre-enrolment process. Some jurisdictions operate quite elaborate pre-enrolment systems that are designed to optimize the match between student preferences and available places in training courses by drawing on some form of standardized score or other measure of their educational attainment. In others, it is left to the training providers to select their students, which they do by relying on end-of-schooling educational qualifications. Groups of institutions may operate a clearing system, where preferences can be stated, but public VET institutions pass on applicants to other institutions in order to make the best use of vacant places. In this way prospective students can avoid having to make several applications.

Applying the course requirements

The enrolment process should be agreed on and be consistent across all teaching areas of a public VET institution, with a common level of advice and support for learners in making enrolment decisions. The selection of students is usually based on system-wide entrance assessment and examination requirements, particularly for young people who are leaving school. Students will express preferences for courses and institutions, with admission based on results.

The selection of students may also be linked to specific course requirements. These will be developed by the VET institutions' departments with reference to individual courses or levels of study. Some courses may require the presentation of a portfolio of work to demonstrate competence and potential, while others may require previous experience in industry, the completion of subjects at a specified level, or the demonstration of a defined level of literacy and numeracy. Enrolments in an apprenticeship course will depend on the sponsorship of an employer.

Some training providers may elect to interview all their prospective students, while others will interview only those students who are neither well qualified nor unqualified for a particular course, and who may need more careful selection. Interviews can also help to disclose certain desirable personal attributes for a particular course that traditional end-of-schooling qualifications may not be able to assess (such as the maturity required for some paramedical professions).

Other training providers may conduct entry tests in order to rank prospective students, and allow selection to be undertaken on the basis of ranking indicated by such tests. These tests at least have the benefit of consistency, that is, all students are ranked according to the same criteria. However, it is not always apparent whether such rankings are related to a student's ability to benefit from the course. An obvious example is the pre-entry testing of mathematical ability when selecting candidates for an actuarial course. Tests which duplicate the information obtainable from school-leaving marks should be avoided, as they put unnecessary pressure on applicants and create tensions with local schools.

As noted above, selection processes may be modified:

☐ by pre-entry or bridging courses;

☐ by financial assistance through scholarships, grants and non-discriminatory loans;

☐ through the imposition of quota systems to encourage certain types of student.

Quotas encouraging participation by target (priority) groups may be introduced as a condition of public funding or they may be introduced by the training provider to meet its social obligations. The selection of quota students from the target group(s) and the selection of non-quota students generally take place separately. It is important that all enrolled students meet the minimum entry standard and that all must reach (or exceed) the same standard for graduation, although non-quota students may also need to reach a higher standard than quota students to be selected. In some countries, quota enrolment systems have become discredited, and are thought by many to be patronizing and/or unworkable.

Where students are selected competitively, the organization modifies its minimum entry standard according to the number of applicants per available place. The number of places may be limited by:

- the number of places that the government is prepared to finance (determined by government priorities and the government's fiscal position);
- the capacity of the training provider to deliver training (determined by its staffing levels and accommodation, equipment and other physical resources, and so on);
- the institution's autonomy regarding enrolments. In some jurisdictions, institutions can enrol significantly more students than they are funded for.

Although the decision to enrol additional students may improve access to training, it also may have adverse implications for:

- equitable access, since students may be charged higher tuition fees in order to cover the government funding shortfall; this may further increase the barrier to participation for students from disadvantaged backgrounds;
- training quality, since underfinanced courses may result in staff who are overextended, excessive staff/student ratios, insufficient facilities, and so on;
- students' learning progress, since students compete for the attention of overextended staff.

For more details on the methods of attracting, selecting and enrolling students in different countries, consult **Unit 6.1: The student enrolment process** on your CD-ROM.

Unit 6.2

GUIDING AND MONITORING STUDENT PROGRESS

6.2.1 STUDENT GUIDANCE AND MONITORING PROCESSES

The guidance and monitoring processes for students may involve induction, the recognition of prior learning, progress assessment, course evaluation, record keeping and managing students who might fail to complete a course. These processes should be managed according to policies which ensure consistency of approach across public VET institutions. The processes for measuring student performance are outlined in **Section 6.2.2: Measuring student performance** below.

The expectations of a student's involvement with his or her learning environment are established with the student's first formal contact with the VET institution before enrolment. They are then clarified through a formal induction process conducted during the first few weeks of the course.

Once a student begins a course, a teaching team ensures monitoring of that student's progress against the course's expected outcomes. Regular interaction with a teacher is an important element of learner success.

Guidance before the course

Student guidance generally begins with information that allows students to choose an appropriate training course that meets their expectations and learning needs and that they have the ability to complete successfully. Pre-entry information should cover the following aspects:

☐ course prerequisites (if any);

☐ course objectives and content (syllabus outline);

☐ mode(s) of course delivery (lectures, workshops, practical instruction, field trips, self-directed study, assignments, projects, and so on);

- learning support options and available institutional resources (teaching and support staff, classrooms, workshops, libraries, computer networks, other resources);

- cost of the course for students (tuition fees, other course-related costs including textbooks, stationery, course materials purchased by students, and so on);

- course assessment requirements and industry standards;

- course certification (what a student will receive as evidence of successful course completion);

- personal counselling, literacy support, disability support, equal opportunity and anti-discrimination provisions, grievance and complaints procedures, appeals processes.

Any advice given on the employment prospects for a graduate of a particular course may assist a prospective student but cannot be specific because the relationship between a qualification and employment prospects is determined by the labour market and so cannot be predicted with certainty. Some employers, for example, may seek specific skills, while others may look for more generic skills that they can build on through in-service training.

Information of this kind that covers all the courses offered by a VET institution may be collated into an institutional prospectus or calendar, which may be displayed on the institution's web site.

Course prerequisites can be expressed subjectively as the interests or aptitudes of potential students, and more objectively in terms of requisite previous educational achievement, for example the achieved school qualifications. The prerequisites may be advisory or made mandatory (that is, students who lack a mandatory prerequisite will be denied enrolment on the grounds that they are likely to fail the course).

Information on course objectives and content (syllabus outline) should leave a potential student in no doubt about the content of a course and what it intends to achieve, and should be up to date and accurate. Students have reason to be dissatisfied with a training course that does not match its stated objectives and content, and they should be able to seek redress for their wasted investment. Objectives are most informative if expressed as competencies (outcomes), for example a series of statements with the format: "On successful completion of this course, the student will be able to ..." and so on.

Modes of delivery should accurately express how the course will be taught by the VET provider, and institutional resources should indicate, without exaggeration, the human resources and teaching facilities that are available to support training delivery. Some indication of teaching staff qualifications and competencies, as well as staff's experience in industry and current industry links, may be helpful for potential students.

The information on the course costs to be met by students should be comprehensive and not only include quantifiable costs such as tuition fees and other fixed course-related charges but also any additional costs that students are likely to incur (for example travel and accommodation costs incurred during field trips or practical experience, and the purchase of course-related materials). A list of titles of textbooks and information on indicative costs (new or second-hand) or their availability through the institution's library will assist students. The list should clearly distinguish between required (mandatory) and recommended reading.

For some students, the major cost of undertaking training will be the opportunity cost of income forgone during the period of the course. Nevertheless, the actual fees and other course costs borne by students will be a significant factor in their decision on whether or not to participate.

Potential students are entitled to know prior to enrolment how their performance on a course will be measured, that is, the form of assessment that will be used to determine whether or not they have successfully graduated.

Before embarking on training courses intended to improve their employment or earning prospects, potential students are entitled to information about course certification. A potential student should be fully aware of the qualification awarded for successful completion of the course and its standing, for example:

☐ its acceptability to employers and other parties;

☐ its portability;

☐ its ability to offer progression to more advanced qualifications offered by the public VET institution or another training provider.

A VET institution may not be particularly well placed to inform students about risks associated with acquiring a certain qualification in terms of future employability, wages and so on, because a qualification's reputation is not determined by the institution but rather by the workplace and future employers.

Guidance while undertaking a course of study

Once enrolled and participating, students will generally continue to need guidance. Following enrolment, the information should cover the following aspects:

☐ timetables and training schedules of the course;

☐ procedures used by VET institutions to monitor progress throughout the course (for example class tests and assignments, individual competency-based assessment, and so on);

☐ procedures used to determine course outcomes (for example examinations, projects, competency-based assessment, and so on);

☐ the standard of behaviour expected of the staff and students, and any sanctions that may be imposed for unacceptable behaviour;

☐ advice or counselling on effective study methods;

☐ tutorial contacts and other forms of study support to enable students to overcome difficulties;

☐ student welfare services that may be provided by the VET institution;

☐ other extra-curricular activities and services for students that may be provided.

An autonomous VET institution at any particular time is likely to be delivering, simultaneously, a number of training courses that involve different groups of students (classes), teaching staff and teaching resources (classrooms, equipment, and so on). A timetable is required to eliminate (or at least minimize) situations in which students are required to undertake (or a staff member to teach) two components of a course simultaneously, or where there is double occupancy or use of a teaching space or equipment.

Students (and staff) will require access to, or printed copies of, the timetable in order for them to be at the right place at the right time to undertake (or deliver) training. In large complex VET institutions, computer software packages may be necessary to optimize timetabling, that is, to determine optimal times/locations/staffing of course delivery and to make the best use of the institutional assets and specialist resources available.

For more details on student guiding and monitoring processes that apply in different countries, consult **Unit 6.2: Guiding and monitoring student progress** on your CD-ROM.

Monitoring extra-curricular activities

Students enrolled at a VET institution should have a clear understanding of the institution's expectations concerning standards of behaviour. In particular, students should be made aware of what is considered (and is not considered) acceptable. They should also be made aware of what sanctions might be imposed by the institution in the event of unacceptable behaviour (for example cheating, plagiarism, bullying, and so forth), including formal disciplinary proceedings.

A VET institution may employ specialist staff to offer advice or counselling to students on effective study methods. Student services may extend beyond effective study methods to cover broader areas of counselling and welfare, including advice on mental and physical health, fitness and recreation, and how students may derive maximum benefit from their time spent in training.

Students should know about the institution's student welfare services and other extra-curricular activities and services, and how to access them. Ideally, this information should be contained within a student handbook that is freely available to all students and reinforced during induction.

For more details on institutional provisions for student welfare and other extra-curricular activities and services that may be offered (including the content of a student handbook), refer to **Unit 6.3: Student welfare**.

6.2.2 MEASURING STUDENT PERFORMANCE

A public VET institution will have procedures in place for monitoring the progress of its students through its training courses. These will help staff to identify early on any students who are not coping and who might fail or drop out. Student performance will be measured against the course of study and the planned sequence of learning and achievement. The learning achievement should be communicated to all and understood by everyone. In this way, the student and the teacher enjoy a common understanding of what is to be learned, how and in what time frame.

Assessment requirements and arrangements need to be explicit. The criteria against which assessment tasks will be measured are particularly important and will guide students to a clear understanding of what is required of them. In all cases, progress and assessment attainment should be based on objective observations against observable and measurable factors that take account of linguistic and cultural differences.

Student performance is based on the requirements of the training programme, which should be described in planned performance objectives matched against the course of study over its time frame. Student monitoring records will show the pattern of achievement by individual students over time, and ensure that they keep to the objectives and standards expected at different stages of the course.

Students are more likely to reach acceptable standards when they are in regular contact with their teachers; receive regular feedback on their learning and its assessment; have access to an appropriate range of learning resources; and are well supported in learning by their teachers, their fellow students and experts in generic skills.

Unsatisfactory attendance, non-participation or non-completion of set tasks put students at risk of failing to complete their course. The teaching department and the responsible teacher need to be aware of these risk factors, and be active in following up such problems. Any follow-up will begin at an informal level and then progress to formal processes where necessary.

The processes of measuring student performance should be conducted:

☐ throughout the duration of a course to monitor students' progress, to provide students with information on how they perform in a course, and perhaps to enable intervention by the staff if students are not coping with the demands of the course;

☐ at the conclusion of a course to determine whether students have met the course's requirements for successful graduation and, if so, are entitled to recognition of their achievement by appropriate certification.

Types of assessment

The evaluation of student performance can be carried out through various processes that, in general, fall into two broad categories:

(1) Norm-referenced assessment, which allows students to be ranked according to their performance in class tests and assignments. Ranking offers an indirect measure of the desired skills and competencies, but determining the overall course outcome (that is, whether a student is assessed as having passed or failed) is problematic. The pass mark may be set by the pre-determined number of graduates required.

(2) Standards-based assessment, which provides direct confirmation that students have acquired (that is, passed the course) or have not acquired (that is, failed the course) the desired skills and competencies. Ranking of student performance is problematic but should not be necessary.

Norm-referenced assessment involves testing the knowledge and understanding of a group of students (a class) through their individual (usually written) responses to a common assignment, (short) test paper, or (longer) examination paper, and so on. Norm-referenced means that pass marks and grades are set according to what should be expected of students achieving the normal standard for the course. Where norm-referenced assessment has been adopted for a course, a VET institution will generally require a comprehensive end-of-course examination or major assignment to be completed to determine course outcomes. The progressive results from class tests and assignments conducted throughout the course may also be included in this end-of-course assessment.

The written responses may be marked according to a marking schedule that identifies correct, incorrect and partially correct answers. Marks may be made for various parts of the assessment, then aggregated and expressed as a percentage. In practice, it is not always possible to distinguish objectively between correct and incorrect answers, and an element of subjectivity will arise in the marking schedule (particularly for essay-type responses to questions). Those marking the work are expected to exercise their professional judgement in assessing the standards achieved.

An apparent benefit of norm-referenced assessment is that students can be ranked according to their aggregated marks (percentages). The distribution of percentage marks of all students within a particular group should be "normal" (the so-called bell curve). The results of many students should be concentrated around an average mark (the mean or norm), with smaller numbers of students achieving either significantly higher or lower marks. This shows that the assessment methods are appropriate to a normal range of ability. If marks are clustered at the higher or lower ends of the range, the assessment is faulty.

Although its ability to rank students may seem to have benefits, there are problems with norm-referenced assessment. It is not always evident that there is a close correlation between aggregated marks awarded for responses to common assignments, tests or examinations, and the skills and competencies that the training course is intended to provide and that the assessment is intended to measure. More fundamentally, it is problematic to use norm-referenced assessment to decide:

☐ whether a student has clearly met (or has not met) the course requirements for successful graduation and certification;

☐ what constitutes the pass/fail percentage mark (for example if placed at the peak of the bell curve, then, for a normal distribution, one half of the class will be classified as having failed, irrespective of their skills and competencies).

In short, norm-referenced assessment judges whether students pass or fail arbitrarily on their ranking against a norm, rather than measuring their actual skill or competency.

Standards-based assessment (sometimes called criterion-referenced assessment) involves testing an individual student's ability to demonstrate mastery of a particular skill or competency. Assessment is carried out against a specified standard or criterion. Standards-based assessment requires that each training course be broken down into discrete modules or units, where each module describes a particular task that requires an identifiable skill or competency. Mastery of each module (that is, task) is assessed against a prescribed standard (or criterion) linked to it.

Where standards-based assessment has been adopted, the final course outcomes should be apparent by the end of the course. If standards-based assessment confirms that a student has met the required standards of skills and competencies for all components of the course, then clearly the student has also met the course requirements for successful graduation and certification. Although standards-based assessment is problematic for ranking students, its use to determine overall course outcomes (that is, a pass or fail assessment) is comparatively straightforward.

An advantage of standards-based (over norm-referenced) assessment is its ability to confirm that students meet the required standards of skill or competency for all modules (tasks) that constitute a training course.

A perceived disadvantage of standards-based assessment is that it does not readily allow students to be ranked in any meaningful way. Students are assessed as being able (or unable) to carry out a number of particular tasks according to prescribed standards (defined in course modules). These separate abilities are combined to give general evidence of a comprehensive set of skills and competencies that the training course is intended to provide. However, performance in the individual tasks cannot be meaningfully combined, unlike an assessment of overall skill or competence that allows ranking (such as norm referencing).

For more details on evaluating student performance in different countries, consult Unit 6.2: Guiding and monitoring student progress on your CD-ROM.

STUDENT WELFARE

6.3.1 THE PROVISION OF EXTRA-CURRICULAR ACTIVITIES AND WELFARE SERVICES

In addition to its delivery of education and training, a public VET institution may also provide a range of extra-curricular activities and welfare services for its students that are intended to enhance the benefit the students derive from training and to ensure their well-being. Where funding is available, this may include a range of recreational, social and welfare related components.

It is more likely, however, that VET institutions will be unable to offer all the services that might be deemed useful for students. The institution will prioritize a range of services that meet the most pressing needs of students. In particular, this will include mechanisms for addressing issues that may interfere with the completion of a course of study. A range of core services may be provided by VET institutions, while students can access other non-core services that may be offered by government and community agencies.

An institution may either provide services from its own resources; contract outside organizations to provide them on a fee-for-service or concessionary basis; or develop partnership arrangements with external agencies for delivering the service by referral.

Welfare services

The welfare services that are provided for students in training may include:

☐ financial support for students, including hardship funds and financial advice;

☐ health and accident insurance services;

☐ student accommodation services (on- and off-campus hostels, accommodation placement services);

☐ social, recreational and cultural centres;

☐   health and fitness centres.

To access these additional extra-curricular activities and welfare services, students will require information about them. This information may be contained in a generic handbook that is made available to all students at the time of their enrolment.

For more details on student handbooks, see **Section 6.3.2** below.

The information contained in a generic student handbook is often published separately from the information on training courses included in a VET institution's prospectus or calendar as described in **Unit 6.2: Guiding and monitoring student progress**.

The students who are required to pay significant tuition fees, particularly if from disadvantaged backgrounds, may need *financial support*. In some jurisdictions, financial support is provided by the state in recognition of the public benefit that derives from their training. This support may be offered through repayable loans or through non-repayable grants or scholarships. It may also be targeted, for example:

☐   on need – to the most disadvantaged students or to ethnic groups who are under-represented in training (grants);

☐   on merit – to the most able students (scholarships).

Autonomous public VET institutions may also decide to give their students financial support, either funded through operational income or privately through philanthropic trusts, endowments and the like. Such financial support may also be targeted on the basis of need and/or on merit.

Welfare services will also be able to advise students on sources of financial support, such as educational charitable trusts or preferential bank loans.

For more details on the financial support given to students, consult **Unit 5.3: Financing through cost recovery.**

Health and accident insurance schemes may be provided by a public VET institution to extend insurance cover to students while they are in training. Alternatively, students or their parents may be required to finance a compulsory accident insurance to cover accidents which may happen on the site of the VET institution. This insurance cover may be offered by private-sector insurers or, in some jurisdictions, by the State.

Student accommodation can potentially be an important constraint on participation, particularly for students enrolled in longer courses and for students who are required to travel considerable distances to undertake their training. A VET provider may own (or lease) and operate one or more hostels that provide accommodation for its students on a full- or partial-cost recovery basis. The hostels may be on campus, which would minimize transport costs for its students, or at another more distant location. Alternatively, a VET institution may limit its direct involvement in the operation of an accommodation service and will provide it by referral.

Many public VET institutions endeavour to meet the extra-curricular needs of their students by providing *social, recreational and cultural centres.* These centres may be operated in partnership with any organization that the students themselves may have set up to look after their broader interests. Social centres provide opportunities for students to meet in pleasant (and safe) environments, and cultural centres may help students from different and diverse ethnic backgrounds to overcome cultural barriers that may exist among them.

Health and fitness centres may promote a balance between (often sedentary) VET and healthy exercise, while providing the necessary access to health services for students who may become unwell. Health services may be delivered on campus by medical or nursing staff employed at the health centre or through referrals to off-campus health practitioners. A fitness centre will generally have access to gymnasium facilities and may be associated with sports fields, a swimming pool, and so on.

For more details on the provision of student welfare services (financial support, health and accident insurance, student accommodation, social, recreational and cultural centres, health and fitness centres) in different countries, consult **Unit 6.3: Student welfare** on your CD-ROM.

Employment-related services

A public VET institution may also provide employment-related services for its students, which might include:

☐ career and vocational guidance (prior to enrolment, during training and following graduation);

☐ job placement assistance (during training and following graduation);

For more details on vocational guidance and job placement services, consult **Unit 6.4: Vocational guidance and job placement assistance.**

6.3.2 THE PROVISION OF INFORMATION FOR STUDENTS

All students should have ready access to reliable and consistent course administrative information and general student information. This should cover the relevant policies and procedures of the public VET institutions and the services that are available.

Students enrolled at a public VET institution will generally be interested in:

☐ information on training courses, usually included in an institutional prospectus or calendar as described in Section 6.2.1; and

☐ information on student extra-curricular activities and welfare services (financial support, health and accident insurance, student accommodation, social, recreational and cultural centres, health and fitness centres, and so on) that may be described in a generic handbook, as outlined above in Section 6.3.1, and how to access these.

A general student handbook will cover information of interest and relevance to all students. It should be distributed to all students at or before enrolment so that they may refer to it as needed. Students will also require information about the teaching department they will be joining and the course they will be following for the duration of their study. This will be more specific and of relevance to students in a particular course. For this reason, the VET provider should ensure that all students receive this second level of information.

The student handbook may also include information on merit awards and scholarships that students may be eligible to apply for, and on the VET institution's expectations regarding their behaviour – as well as the sanctions that may be imposed in the event that these expectations are not met.

A student handbook may also outline what a student may reasonably expect of a VET institution, and what redress may be available to a student if those expectations are not met. Such provisions may be particularly important for an international student (for example on such matters as tuition fee refunds if a course is not delivered satisfactorily or an institution becomes bankrupt). In some jurisdictions, the rights of international students are protected by an agreed institutional code of practice, to which providers are required to adhere as a condition of their registration.

In jurisdictions where Internet access is readily available, the VET institution's web site has largely replaced the prospectus/calendar and student handbook as the principal sources of information on available courses and student services. Such web sites can be more easily accessed by prospective or current students than most published material. However, where there is limited access to the Internet, it is important that published material be available that provides prospective students with the information they require, at the very least in outline form as pamphlets and so on.

For more details on the provision of information on student extra-curricular activities and welfare services in different countries, go to **Unit 6.3: Student welfare** on your CD-ROM.

Unit 6.4

VOCATIONAL GUIDANCE
AND JOB PLACEMENT ASSISTANCE

6.4.1 THE PROVISION OF VOCATIONAL GUIDANCE

Students may derive benefit from vocational guidance while they are:

☐ considering various education and training options;

☐ undertaking their chosen courses;

☐ searching for a job after graduation.

For more details on vocational guidance provided after graduation, consult **Section 6.4.2: The provision of job placement assistance** below.

Vocational guidance for prospective students

Vocational guidance provided to potential students while they are still at secondary school should help them to consider their future vocational options, taking into account their interests, strengths and weaknesses, and their expectations for future employment. Such guidance should be given early enough to allow students to choose such options that may: (a) enable them to continue in courses of tertiary (post-school) education of their interest; and (b) provide knowledge and skills which fulfil their expectations for future employment.

An initial source of information for potential tertiary students is likely to be the careers counsellors employed by most senior secondary schools, often teaching staff members with the particular experience required for imparting vocational guidance. Information sources available to careers advisors via publications and web sites as well as to more enterprising students may include the following:

☐ education and training opportunities offered by VET institutions and other providers;

☐ labour market information on job opportunities, vacancies, skills shortages, wage levels, and so on, provided by government agencies, industry and the media (newspapers, web sites, and so forth).

In some jurisdictions, quite elaborate web site-based career assistance is provided for all the stakeholders (students, training providers, employers, careers counsellors) by the government as part of its strategy to enhance economic performance.

Linking learning to industry

A VET institution should be closely linked to the industries and professions represented in its training profile, since its task is to prepare students for employment in those industries. For this reason, a VET provider needs to use a variety of means to ensure that students have current and relevant information about their chosen vocational area. VET institutions should provide potential students with information that allows them to choose an appropriate course that meets their expectations and learning needs and that they have the ability to complete successfully. They should provide this information in close cooperation with representatives of the relevant industry.

Many VET institutions will, like secondary schools, employ dedicated staff with the particular knowledge and experience required for imparting vocational guidance. The advice they give is likely to specify how particular courses may lead to future employment and, for instance, may link competencies acquired during training with particular fields of employment and more detailed job descriptions.

VET institutions may also work cooperatively with employers' associations or even particular employers by facilitating open days, interviews and similar events that allow prospective employers to inform students of employment opportunities, and vice versa. Such arrangements may be a component of the job placement assistance provided by an institution. See also **Section 6.4.2: The provision of job placement assistance**.

Any advice given on the post-training employment prospects that a particular course may offer in general cannot be specific because the relationships between employment prospects and qualifications are determined by employers and so cannot be predicted with certainty. Some employers, for example, are interested in specific job-related skills, while others may look for more generic proficiencies in education and skills that they can build on through in-service training.

There is also an issue of objectivity: the interests of students in undertaking courses and of VET institutions enrolling them are not always congruent. It is the student, not the institution, who will bear the consequences of poor course selection.

The value of a vocational course is the insight it gives into the nature of work in a particular industry or job role, and the development of the skills needed for that job. The course of study becomes more closely linked to the industry requirements, when:

☐ industry practitioners have been involved in the course design ensuring that its content is relevant and up to date;

☐ training equipment matches that used in the industry;

☐ students have opportunities to have full-time periods of experience in a company while they are still studying to encounter the work environment;

☐ skills are demonstrated and assessed against industry standards, thereby ensuring a smooth transition from studying to employment.

For more details on the provision of vocational guidance in different countries, go to **Unit 6.4: Vocational guidance and job placement assistance** on your CD-ROM.

6.4.2 THE PROVISION OF JOB PLACEMENT ASSISTANCE

In addition to vocational guidance for potential and current students, a VET institution may from time to time provide job placement assistance. A student can benefit from this service by acquiring a job after graduation, and the VET institution's reputation may be enhanced. The provision of a dedicated job placement service for students may be desirable but it can also be beyond the discretional spending of the institution.

As noted in **Section 6.4.1: The provision of vocational guidance**, VET institutions may work cooperatively with employers' associations or even particular employers to inform students of job opportunities.

These arrangements may extend to industrial attachments or temporary placements in which students undertake a (usually unpaid) practical component of their course off campus using the facilities of local industry. Such placements allow students to benefit from hands-on experience and from the enhanced employment prospects that may result. Industry benefits to the extent that (usually unpaid) students contribute to production, even though "slowdown" time is required for their instruction. Employers can also check out prospective employees and recruit the most promising candidates.

Some countries practise workplace training, where the role of practical instruction and industry guidance is much greater. Workplace training offers trainees the chance to undertake most of their training on the job or at least on the premises of an enterprise. The teachers from the VET institution may deliver both the on-job and off-job component, or the company may have its own trainers. The off-job component is generally more generic than the on-job training, while the latter tends to be more job-specific to the particular enterprises. Costs may be shared between industry (offset by the students' contribution to production at reduced remuneration rates) and the government through public funding of the off-job component delivered by the provider.

Larger VET institutions may be able to support dedicated staff responsible for vocational and employment guidance, perhaps based in a service unit that provides support for other teaching units.

The task of liaising with local companies on employment opportunities and job requirements may be part of the expected workload of teachers or training instructors under the supervision of departmental directors, particularly in smaller institutions. As workplace learning expands, so too may the role of teaching staff in guidance and placement.

The alternative option for providing a job placement service is to secure support (usually from government funds) to develop partnerships with private, government and community agencies that specialize in job placement. This may be a more efficient use of public VET institutions' limited resources and it may offer a better outcome for students.

For more details on the provision of job placement assistance in different countries, go to **Unit 6.4: Vocational guidance and job placement assistance** on your CD-ROM.

MODULE 7

Staff management

Unit 7.1

STAFF SELECTION, RECRUITMENT AND APPOINTMENT

7.1.1 STAFF COMPOSITION IN AUTONOMOUS VET INSTITUTIONS

Depending on its size and complexity, an autonomous VET institution will have several categories of employees. Larger institutions are likely to have a wider range of staff, reflecting their greater degree of diversity. The categories will generally include most or all of the following:

☐ teaching staff;

☐ managerial staff – chief executive, senior managers, departmental managers, line managers within teaching or service departments;

☐ non-teaching specialist staff – including IT, library, public relations, technical support, and so on;

☐ student support staff – in vocational guidance, counselling, recreation and health, and so on;

☐ administrative staff – in finance, human resources, student records, clerical, and so on;

☐ maintenance staff – in charge of site, buildings and equipment, and so on.

Teaching staff

Teachers are customarily recruited from a particular trade or profession and should possess a National Vocational Certificate or Diploma or a higher level professional award associated with the relevant trade (usually of a higher level than the level at which they are required to teach).

Relevant prior workplace experience is commonly required as a condition for working as a vocational (trade) teacher, as evidence that the teacher possesses and can practise the specialist knowledge and skills.

In addition to a prerequisite level of specialist knowledge and skills, teaching staff will also need to have adequate teaching skills (a teacher certificate) if they are to be effective as teachers. These teaching skills may include the ability to:

☐ contribute to curriculum development and course design;

☐ plan for training sessions;

☐ develop knowledge, skills and work-related attitudes with their students through effective communication and the use of training aids;

☐ monitor and assess student progress.

Prior teaching and workplace experience and trade/professional and teaching qualifications may be recognized through a hierarchy of graded teaching positions, for example associate teacher, teacher, senior teacher and principal teacher.

Some jurisdictions determine national policies that set out the minimum qualifications required by teachers in VET institutions or by those delivering courses leading to nationally recognized vocational awards. The setting of entry standards for teachers may also be delegated to the governing councils of autonomous public VET institutions.

Managerial staff

The managerial staff of public VET institutions will need to have prior management experience and sometimes management qualifications. A qualification in Education Management, which has recently been launched in some universities and polytechnics, could be of particular value. Management experience and qualifications are recognized through a hierarchy of graded positions, for example: the VET institution's chief executive; senior manager; teaching department (training school) manager (director/head); campus manager; line managers in the course development department or other service departments, and so on.

Managerial skills may assume greater importance in senior management positions, whereas trade-related work experience and teaching experience are arguably more important at the level of teaching department (training school) managers.

Other staff

In general, non-teaching specialist staff (IT, library, public relations, technical support, and so forth) will be appointed for particular specialist skills that are not necessarily specific to VET. For example, the public relations staff of a VET institution are more likely to be skilled in the field of public relations than in aspects of VET, although an understanding of the latter could be a useful attribute.

Student support staff (vocational guidance, counselling, recreation and health, and so forth) are likely to have work experience and skills in communicating with and providing useful services for prospective, current and graduate students.

Administrative (finance, human resources, student records, clerical, and so on) and maintenance staff (in charge of site, buildings, equipment) are likely to have the generic skills required for the administration and maintenance of any organization that is characterized by the size and complexity of a VET institution. However, their skills may not necessarily relate to VET.

For more details on the composition of staff in autonomous public VET institutions in different countries, go to **Unit 7.1: Staff selection, recruitment and appointment** on your CD-ROM.

7.1.2 JOB DESCRIPTIONS FOR SENIOR MANAGEMENT, TEACHING AND NON-TEACHING STAFF

In many jurisdictions, the selection and recruitment of staff for positions in public VET institutions are based on matching the attributes of aspiring appointees with a job (or position) description for the vacancy. Usually the job description indicates:

☐ the job/position title;

☐ a list of superior staff position(s) – that is, to whom the appointee reports;

☐ a list of subordinate staff position(s) – that is, who reports to the appointee;

☐ the purpose of the position;

☐ key accountabilities – an outline of what is expected from the appointee, sometimes called key deliverables or defined in terms of performance indicators;

☐ a personal knowledge and experience specification – an outline of expected prior experience, desired level of formal qualifications and expected personal attributes and competencies.

In some jurisdictions, job descriptions are developed across the entire VET sector and are determined by a central agency. This arrangement may facilitate the negotiation of national award systems for the remuneration of managerial, teaching and non-teaching staff across the sector and may also facilitate staff transfers between public institutions. This practice does, however, diminish institutional autonomy. In other jurisdictions, staff job descriptions are for the governing councils of the public VET institutions themselves to determine.

A hierarchy of grades within positions, whether managerial or teaching, can be established through stating the appropriate differences in the job descriptions, for example through different key accountabilities, and so on.

For more details on job descriptions for senior management, teaching and non-teaching staff at autonomous public VET institutions in different countries, go to **Unit 7.1: Staff selection, recruitment and appointment** on your CD-ROM.

7.1.3 RECRUITMENT POLICIES, SELECTION AND APPOINTMENT PROCESSES

A key measure of institutional autonomy for a public institution is the extent to which it can determine its own recruitment policies and processes and select its own staff. In some jurisdictions, recruitment policies and processes remain the responsibility of a central agency, whereas in others the institutions themselves have the autonomy to recruit and select their own staff.

In some jurisdictions, managerial staff are commonly recruited for their demonstrated level of managerial skills, not necessarily associated with VET. In others, teachers are more usually promoted from teaching positions to take on managerial responsibilities. There are arguments in support of both practices in the recruitment of managerial staff.

A number of methods can be used to fill staff vacancies in public VET institutions. They include:

□ advertising through the mass media (newspapers and so forth), trade and professional journals, or the Internet (for example posting information on the institution's web site);

□ direct appointment/selection through internal staff promotion;

□ on-campus recruitment of the best students (through campus publications, posters, and so on);

□ the use of recruitment agencies (particularly for more senior management positions).

Just as for recruitment, selecting the most suitable candidate from a field of applicants can be carried out by a central agency or by the institution itself. The latter is preferable to the extent that it is the institution itself, rather than the central agency, that bears the consequences of poor selection.

Where an autonomous public institution has the authority to select its own staff, this selection should be carried out through due process in accordance with an explicit selection policy that ensures transparency and facilitates the selection of the most suitable candidate. In any case, the recruitment processes must comply with the provisions of employment legislation or regulation. The VET sector-wide agreements on the qualifications and grades of staff, pay systems and other conditions of work should also be made known to the candidates.

For more details on recruitment policies, selection and appointment processes in different countries, go to **Unit 7.1: Staff selection, recruitment and appointment** on your CD-ROM.

Unit 7.2

STAFF TRAINING
AND CAREER GUIDANCE

7.2.1 THE STAFF TRAINING SYSTEM

To be effective, a VET institution will require some form of staff training system to ensure that its staff, particularly its teachers, have the skills and competencies necessary for them to carry out their functions. In general, a staff training system will have a number of components, including arrangements for:

- the induction of new staff to acquaint them with the institution's expectations, regulations, processes and procedures;

- the conducting of training needs analyses at various levels (for example across the entire institution and its departments); and at an individual level to identify skills and competencies that staff members might lack (collectively and individually);

- the delivery of requisite staff training to address any identified skills gaps, delivered either within the institution by designated staff or by an external training provider contracted for this task;

- the development of individual training plans that identify what kind of training is appropriate to upgrade the skills and competencies of individual staff members, either through additional formal training or through other processes;

- the certification of teaching and other staff, which provides portable, tangible evidence of their skills and competencies;

- the career guidance, which enables individual staff members to devise career development plans that will facilitate their progression by promotion within the institution to positions of increased responsibility or authority.

The induction of new staff

Recently appointed staff at a VET institution are likely to function more effectively if they have a good understanding of the institution's expectations, policies, regulations, processes and procedures. This understanding can be expedited if the institution has formal provisions for the induction of new staff, customarily achieved through a short induction programme that will provide:

- introductions to the key members of staff with whom they are likely to have functional relationships while carrying out their duties;

- briefings on the institutional policies, rules and regulations of which they need to be aware if they are to meet expectations regarding their performance and behaviour;

- an awareness of the institutional procedures relating to workplace health and safety;

- briefings on the institution's routine administrative procedures (for example arrangements for remuneration, applying for annual leave, taking sick leave, and so on);

- an informative tour of the institution's training facilities (classrooms and workshops, teaching aids, and so on) and staff amenities.

For more details on staff training systems in autonomous public VET institutions in different countries, go to **Unit 7.2: Staff training and career guidance** on your CD-ROM.

7.2.2 INDIVIDUAL TRAINING PLANS

Training needs analyses

The identification of skills and competencies that staff members may be lacking can be carried out through training needs analyses at various levels. These analyses may be undertaken by the VET institutions' own staff or by external consultants under contract, and may apply across the entire institution to identify generic skills gaps across functional components of the institution (for example in particular teaching or service departments) or at the level of individual staff members.

The output of the training needs analysis should be an assessment of:

- the skills that are necessary for the delivery of requisite training outputs by the institution, training/service department, or (most commonly) individual teachers;

- the level of skills of individual teachers to undertake training delivery.

The desired outcome of the training needs analysis should be the provision of appropriate training (or such other arrangements as deemed necessary) in order to remedy any identified shortages of skills.

If a skills gap is identified, the requisite formal training may be provided. In some jurisdictions, this training is provided by a state entity set up specifically for this purpose. In other jurisdictions, a dedicated staff-training department of another public provider or a private-sector training provider contracted for this task may deliver the requisite training.

Individual training plans

Individual staff members – teaching and non-teaching – can be helped to upgrade their skills and competencies if the VET provider encourages the development of individual training plans. In general, these plans pick up on the outputs of the training needs analyses of individual staff members and identify what kind of training would be most appropriate for them.

The training intended to upgrade staff competencies may be provided through formal training programmes as well as industrial attachments, sabbaticals, refresher leave, overseas study tours, attendance at seminars and conferences, and so forth.

The training for VET teachers, whether delivered through formal training courses or other processes, may be subject-specific or pedagogical in nature. In the case of VET managers, it is more likely to be management-oriented. Ideally, the development and review of individual training plans should be a mandatory component of the regular performance reviews of all members of staff.

7.2.3 CERTIFYING TEACHERS AND OTHER MEMBERS OF STAFF

Provisions for the certification of teachers and other staff members should provide tangible evidence (via credentials and awards) of their skills and competencies, and may be taken into account when selecting new staff and negotiating conditions of service.

Credentials may attest to the level of skill or competency in:

☐ a profession, discipline, trade, or field of study (that is, subject-specific skills and competencies that are generally recognized across other fields as well as teaching);

☐ teaching (that is, specific to the pedagogy of teaching).

The consistency and portability of credentials and awards for teaching staff may be facilitated when certification is undertaken external to the VET institution by a national certifying agency. However, some providers may choose to recognize the skills and competencies of their own staff's skills by issuing internal credentials.

Some teaching credentials may recognize both subject-specific and pedagogical skills (for example qualifications in the teaching of science such as BSc, Dip Tchg, or BEd (Science). The credentials of non-teaching staff are more likely to be generic (for example attesting to the general level of education of clerical staff) or subject-specific rather than pedagogical (for example an accounting degree for a staff member of a VET institution's finance department).

For more details on certifying teachers and other staff members of public VET institutions in different countries, go to **Unit 7.2: Staff training and career guidance** on your CD-ROM.

7.2.4 CAREER GUIDANCE FOR STAFF

The objectives of career guidance for staff should be to:

- □ enable individual staff members to identify how they can best advance their careers while remaining employed by the VET provider;
- □ facilitate the retention of current staff in whom the institution may already have made substantial investment;
- □ facilitate the recruitment of prospective staff by providing clear information on their potential for progression within the institution.

Ideally, the development and review of individual career development plans should be a mandatory component of the regular performance review of all staff, and should provide opportunities for:

- □ VET institution's employees to inform their managers of their own career aspirations within the institution;
- □ managers to give employees a reality check on their career aspirations, taking into account individual training plans, the imperatives (if any) for staff retention and the fiscal constraints (if any) on staff promotion and so forth.

For more details on career guidance for the staff of autonomous public VET institutions in different countries, go to **Unit 7.2: Staff training and career guidance** on your CD-ROM.

STAFF REMUNERATION
AND BENEFITS

7.3.1 STAFF REMUNERATION

The benefits of institutional autonomy

VET institutions will have a number of arrangements by which the remuneration of the teaching and support staff is determined. These arrangements may vary among countries, depending largely on the degree of the public VET institution's autonomy.

In some countries, the staff of public VET institutions are civil servants who are appointed by a central agency of the government, usually a civil services commission or equivalent. Their conditions of employment, including their remuneration and benefits, are determined centrally. VET institutions may only fill positions that are approved by the central agency, and new staff are generally appointed to a particular level on an approved salary scale for an approved class (for example those of teacher, support staff, and so forth).

In such jurisdictions, since salaries typically account for about 75 per cent of the costs of a public VET institution, the ability of institutions to match their input costs to their outputs is substantially constrained. Thus their autonomy (ability for self-management) is also substantially constrained, and the benefits of such autonomy – operational flexibility, responsiveness, cost-effectiveness and cost-efficiency – are largely lost. A common result is that staff adopt an attitude of a job for life within the public VET institution and the wider public service.

In the countries that allow public institutions high autonomy, the staff are appointed by institutional governing councils or by senior management acting under delegated authority. Levels of remuneration are negotiated by the VET institutions' management with the prospective staff appointee, without preventing the intervention of a staff union on behalf of its members that may have negotiated agreed levels of remuneration for particular positions. The levels of remuneration for senior managerial staff are more commonly arranged on an individual basis. In some countries, levels of remuneration and other conditions of employment may be negotiated collectively by unions representing all (or most) of the staff and an agent representing an association of two or more VET institutions.

The essential difference in these other countries is that the levels of staff remuneration are more closely aligned to the staff member's perceived value to the VET institution, and also provide the institution with an essential component of self-management – the ability to select and appoint the most appropriate person to carry out a job.

A VET teacher employed to teach a particular trade or profession will also have alternative employment opportunities in that profession. A qualified plumbing tutor ought to be able to find alternative employment in the labour market as a first-rate plumber. The negotiated salary should reflect this, perhaps with a margin for teaching competencies.

Although employees of autonomous public VET institutions may no longer have the certainty of a job for life, they are also more likely to be compensated at the true labour market value of their competencies. This freedom can encourage positive attitudes, including ambition and entrepreneurship, among the staff. Monetary and other rewards can more than compensate for the degree of job uncertainty.

Autonomous public VET institutions also benefit in that they have greater freedom to match their input costs (mainly salaries) to what they deliver (outputs). Indeed, this freedom is a prerequisite for the introduction of output-based funding systems. It allows a public VET provider to address staffing mismatches (the over- or undersupply of teachers in particular fields) by recruiting additional teachers when there is an undersupply, or by redeploying or carrying out redundancies when there is an oversupply. Teachers deemed surplus to the institution's staffing requirements should be fully compensated by way of fair redundancy provisions.

Government interventions

Even in those countries in which public VET institutions have the autonomy to recruit, select, appoint and dismiss their own staff, governments will inevitably intervene in the labour markets through employment policies and enabling legislation and/or regulation. For example, many governments legislate to ensure that their expectations are met in respect of the behaviour of employers, unions and employees in the industrial relations arena, for instance in wage setting, resolving disputes, and rights and responsibilities in respect of industrial action.

In many jurisdictions, salary levels are prescribed by:

☐ occupational class (for example teaching staff);

☐ ranking (for example head of department, supervising teacher, senior teacher, teacher, associate teacher or equivalent); or

☐ step (for example from step 1 through to step 10 on a ten-step teacher salary scale).

Negotiated salary agreements customarily include provisions for regular reviews and adjustments. Salary reviews are usually undertaken on an annual basis through performance review processes and in some circumstances may lead to promotions – or in rare instances to demotions. Details of these processes are outlined in Unit 7.4: Staff performance appraisal and promotion.

In addition to negotiated salary scales, monetary compensation offered by a public VET institution may include various allowances that are intended to compensate staff for any work-related costs incurred by them, including:

☐ travel, meal and accommodation costs incurred while on business;

☐ overtime to compensate for additional hours worked;

☐ costs for special clothing;

☐ telephone costs if on call;

☐ costs for safety equipment;

☐ costs for work-related tools.

There may also be a performance-based component represented by ad hoc one-off bonus payments or their equivalent through which exceptional performance may be recognized.

On social equity grounds, governments also customarily legislate to enforce:

☐ a minimum working age;

☐ a minimum hourly wage rate;

☐ statutory holidays;

☐ minimum provisions for annual leave;

☐ provisions for other forms of leave (sick and parental leave, and so on).

For more details on arrangements for staff remuneration in autonomous public VET institutions in different countries, go to Unit 7.3: Staff remuneration and benefits on your CD-ROM.

7.3.2 STAFF BENEFITS

In addition to salaries, allowances and bonuses, the teaching and support staff employed by VET institutions may be entitled to a range of other benefits, which may include:

- □ training and retraining;
- □ retirement pensions or superannuation;
- □ medical insurance;
- □ health-care provisions;
- □ childcare provisions.

These benefits may be offered centrally and cover all teaching and support staff employed across an entire public VET sector or they may be offered by individual institutions to all their staff as part of their recruitment and retention policies. Portability may be an important issue, particularly for long-term arrangements that offer retirement pensions or superannuation.

Training may be offered to public VET institutions' staff as part of staff development, and *retraining* may be offered as an alternative to redundancy, when there are changes in the demand for teachers. For details on staff training arrangements in public VET institutions, refer to **Unit 7.2: Staff training and career guidance**.

A key issue in arrangements that provide *retirement pensions* or *superannuation* is that they be portable, that is, the arrangements should ensure continuity and not terminate every time an employee moves to another job. Thus provisions for retirement pensions and superannuation are often offered by third parties, which may include the government or private-sector retirement pension/superannuation funds.

Retirement pensions and superannuation schemes are generally funded by employee contributions (often a designated percentage of salary) and may be co-funded by employer (autonomous VET institution) contributions as a component of the institution's staff recruitment and retention policy.

The issue of portability is partially addressed in centralized systems where employees of autonomous public VET institutions have identical status to all other public servants and can move freely between institutions or between a public VET institution and other public-sector employment. However, such arrangements can preclude career movements from the public service into private-sector employment, particularly for long-term public servants, who may effectively be locked into public-sector retirement pensions or superannuation schemes. Such rigidity can reinforce an unhealthy dependence on the public sector as principle employer and can stifle positive attitudes, including ambition and entrepreneurship.

Medical insurance can be offered as a component of a VET institution's recruitment and retention policy. Medical insurance services are generally

197

offered by specialist medical insurers under contract to the autonomous VET provider.

In principle, a public VET institution is well placed to offer on-campus *facilities for health care* if these facilities are also provided for students. However, in some jurisdictions, staff requiring health care use the same services that they would access during non-working hours, and the VET institution's contribution extends only to the provision of medical or sick leave.

The crèche or equivalent *childcare facilities* offered by a VET provider for its students who have dependants may reasonably be made available to staff members with dependants as a component of its recruitment and retention policy. In some jurisdictions, childcare provisions are mandated and funded by the government as part of their social policy objectives.

For more details on staff benefits in autonomous public VET institutions in different countries, go to **Unit 7.3: Staff remuneration and benefits** on your CD-ROM.

Unit 7.4

STAFF PERFORMANCE APPRAISAL AND PROMOTION

7.4.1 STAFF PERFORMANCE APPRAISAL

The purpose of appraisals

Managers in VET institutions will commonly undertake periodic staff performance appraisals, usually on an annual basis, as an important component of staff management. These appraisals can serve two functions:

(1) They assess the performance of staff regarding their expected outputs (service delivery).

(2) They provide staff with feedback on their performance and outputs, including identification of their strengths and weaknesses, and can help further career development.

In principle, the aggregation of staff performance appraisals may provide insight into the accountability of the institution. Poorly performing teaching and service departments can be identified and remedial action undertaken to ensure that adequate accountability is restored.

Identifying potential units of excellence within the VET provider may improve awareness of particular strengths and allow experiences to be shared. An improved awareness by staff of their particular strengths and weaknesses may facilitate career development planning as well as the development of individual training plans. These plans will aim to conduct appropriate training for individual staff members as well as help managers to upgrade their skills and competencies.

For details on individual staff training plans, refer to **Unit 7.2: Staff training and career guidance**.

The process

The staff performance appraisal process generally involves a supervising manager interviewing a particular staff member. If the interview is likely to be contentious (that is, lead to a dispute between the staff member and supervising manager over the assessment of performance), the presence of a third party (independent observer/recorder) may be beneficial. This third party should preferably have skills in human resource development (HRD).

The aim of the initial staff performance appraisal is, in general, to assess the staff member's performance against the job description under which the appointment was made. Customarily, the job description will specify key functional relationships, the key tasks that the staff member is expected to undertake, and the staff member's expected personal and professional development. It will also specify the expected knowledge, experience, skills and aptitudes required for the job.

Accordingly, the staff performance appraisal should assess for the review period under consideration:

☐ how successfully the staff member has accomplished the listed key tasks (produced planned outputs);

☐ whether the staff member has demonstrated the expected knowledge, expertise, required skills, aptitudes and personal attributes set out in the person specification;

☐ whether the staff member has related appropriately to all the other staff members where a key functional relationship exists;

☐ whether the staff member's personal and professional development during the review period has met the requirements set out in the plan.

The assessment will be subjective to the extent that the job description and person specification are subjective. It may be possible – and indeed desirable – for the staff member and supervising manager to agree where possible on more objective performance targets for subsequent appraisals. This also reduces the potential for dispute.

The outcome of the performance review should be a written appraisal that sets out:

☐ how the staff member measured up to the job description and person specification;

☐ the strengths and weaknesses of the staff member and implications (if any);

☐ revised (objectives) performance targets (if any);

☐ agreed intentions of the need for a salary increase, promotion (if any);

☐ agreed changes to the staff member's individual training plans (if any).

The written appraisal should be agreed to, dated and countersigned by both parties and held in the staff member's personal file.

A formal arbitration process involving other independent managers may need to be invoked to resolve any disputed assessments to the satisfaction of both parties. As noted above, the presence of a third party as an independent observer/recorder may reduce the likelihood of disputed assessments.

For more details on arrangements for staff performance appraisal in autonomous public VET institutions in different countries, go to **Unit 7.4: Staff performance appraisal and promotion** on your CD-ROM.

7.4.2 THE USE OF PERFORMANCE APPRAISAL FOR STAFF PROMOTION

Staff performance appraisals allow the management of VET providers to rank their staff according to their performance. They also enable the institutional management to:

- recognize well-performing staff through salary increases, bonuses, and/or promotions;
- provide directions and/or incentives for poor-performing staff to improve their performance;
- provide incentives for all staff to improve their performance through training and personal development;
- impose sanctions on non-performing staff, including dismissal.

In many jurisdictions, salary levels are prescribed by:

- occupational class (for example teaching staff);
- ranking (for example head of department, supervising teacher, senior teacher, teacher, associate teacher or equivalent); or
- step (for example from step 1 through to step 10 on a ten-step teacher salary scale).

New staff are customarily appointed to a particular step within a particular ranking, depending on their previous experience and qualifications. The progression to higher steps within a particular ranking may be automatic subject to satisfactory performance in each year. However, automatic progression is often blocked between certain prescribed steps by a so-called "performance bar". Progression between these steps may be strictly on merit. Generally without exception, progression between ranking scale is on merit, that is, through promotion.

Often for reasons of cost containment, stringent restrictions are applied to the number of staff who may be approved for progression to higher steps across performance bars or who are promoted to higher rankings. Since bonuses do not have costs that carry forward to subsequent years, they could be allocated as tangible recognition to well-performing staff in situations when cost-containment precludes promotions.

Not unexpectedly, staff members will have a keen interest in bonuses and promotions allocated on the basis of staff performance appraisals. The appraisal process must be robust and transparent, since staff will scrutinize it closely and must have confidence in it to eliminate concerns. Particular attention must be paid to ensuring that there is strict comparability between the staff performance appraisal processes across different teaching and support departments.

For more details on the use of performance appraisals for staff promotion in autonomous public VET institutions in different countries, go to **Unit 7.4: Staff performance appraisal and promotion** on your CD-ROM.

MODULE 8

Course development
and evaluation

Unit 8.1

DEVELOPING A COURSE
FOR A NATIONAL VET QUALIFICATION

8.1.1 NATIONAL VOCATIONAL QUALIFICATIONS FRAMEWORKS

Vocational qualifications

A national VET qualification is an award which recognizes that learning has taken place and that certain outputs have been achieved by the learners. These outputs will be expressed as achievements in meeting certain skill or competency standards that are based on job requirements.

"Competence" or "competency" is the ability or state of being competent, that is, adequately qualified, capable, or effective. "Skill" is defined as the ability to do something well, as expertise, or as a particular ability. Although competence and skill are often assumed to be synonyms, skill can have the connotation of being manual, while competence has the connotation of knowledge (for example skill in carpentry, competence in accounting). In this handbook, though, skill and competency standards are considered synonymous with occupational standards (for example skill or competence in carpentry or accounting).

A national VET qualification is a body of knowledge defined by three basic elements:

(1) the title of the qualification (which may include the qualification level);

(2) the learning outputs expressed through meeting certain skill (competency) standards;

(3) the assessment (testing) requirements as standard criteria and procedures for the person to demonstrate the acquired knowledge and skills (competencies).

Some VET qualifications involve the assessment of mostly practical skills and are described as competence-based qualifications: the assessment criteria and procedures set out the competences that the learner is required to demonstrate. Other VET qualifications also test and accredit theoretical knowledge, without which the practitioner cannot understand the technology, carry out work, and explain to others why the work should be done in a certain way. And it is a requirement of some qualifications that candidates have a certain amount of job experience.

Competencies are most certainly learned and can be expressed as a set of standards that together determine a course curriculum. The curriculum describes the content of what is delivered by a VET course; practical mastery of the content should enable learners to demonstrate that they have acquired the competences that satisfy the required standards. As competence-based qualifications are standards-based, the student's assessment is also standards-based. Standards-based assessment involves deciding whether a student meets (passes) or does not meet (fails) a prescribed standard.

For example, the qualifications offered by industry bodies frequently expect that graduation can only be achieved after a specified period of practice. In this case, the qualification is also a licence to practise. Therefore, most vocational qualifications involve the development of practical skills, some background knowledge and practical experience. Accreditation of all three leads to the award of a qualification, and the proportions of each tend to determine the level ascribed to it in the qualifications framework.

National qualifications frameworks

A national qualifications framework is the agreed system of qualifications that operates in a particular country. A qualification is awarded by an approved body and is recognition that a person has achieved certain levels of learning outcomes, standards or competencies. A certificate is evidence of achievement in one or all aspects of the qualification.

Qualifications frameworks are devices to support the coherent integration of qualifications and they aim to provide national consistency in recognition of educational and training outcomes. A qualifications framework will provide directions on:

☐ the principles that explain the design and philosophy of the framework. This will include how and where the qualifications can be achieved as well as the operating principles of the framework: transparency, simplicity, quality, comprehensiveness, flexibility and relevance;

☐ the structure of qualifications involving their coverage, scope and the sectors in which the framework operates. Some frameworks are comprehensive and cover the entire education system, from school to vocational colleges and universities, whereas others are for vocational qualifications only. Qualification descriptors will also explain each qualification level and the required skills, knowledge and competences that need to be attained. Qualifications may be whole qualifications or consist of units or modules;

□ the legal status of the framework – voluntary, regulatory or statutory;

□ the basis of qualifications – the attainment of learning outcomes, competency (occupational) standards, or the completion of a curriculum; the formulation of learning outcomes determines the emphasis on practical competencies or knowledge-related components;

□ the recognition and credit mechanisms for learning and credit transfer arrangements for all modules of all qualifications. A framework may also incorporate mechanisms for the recognition of parts of qualifications, groups of learning outcomes or competencies. These are called credit systems. Recognition of prior learning is also a credit system that recognizes the skills and knowledge acquired through education or work and life experiences;

□ the types of awards or credentials – certificates, diplomas or degrees;

□ the protocols for issuing a qualification that will ensure national consistency and standard information on the certification and avoid confusion over titles.

The advantages of the qualifications frameworks are that they provide opportunities for:

□ the national and international recognition of qualifications;

□ flexible learning and career mobility without age limit;

□ the recognition of prior learning;

□ linkages between work-based qualifications and academic qualifications;

□ modular course offerings;

□ the provision of credit for part of a qualification; and

□ certification.

National vocational qualifications should ensure that different VET providers are working to the same standards. Their graduates should have an agreed minimum level of skills and knowledge so that employers know what they can expect of students.

In most countries, there are variations between the standards achieved by different VET providers, with some maybe having an established reputation for excellence in particular fields. Nevertheless, a national system of skills assessment and awards should provide some assurance that a threshold of quality can be relied on.

As so many trades and professions need qualifications, a national organizing framework, which can group occupations into occupational families of related skills or economic activity, can be helpful. Occupations within that family can then be grouped according to level. So, for instance, an occupational family such as "construction", may encompass: trades such as carpentry, plumbing, scaffolding; professional occupations such as architecture and quantity surveying; and services skills such as heating, air conditioning and ventilation design. The levels of training can be defined according to the educational level required for entry; the degree of supervision needed to do the job; or agreement about the degree of practical skill or intellectual ability required.

A qualifications framework will have operating procedures that outline the processes to be followed. A national advisory board or qualifications authority may be responsible for monitoring the implementation of the framework and for supporting national and cross-sector consistency. This advisory board will include representatives from stakeholder groups, such as the community, employers, the VET sector and higher education, as well as experts that can advise on implementation and monitoring.

The role, function and responsibilities of the stakeholders are often established in the legislation or charter covering the framework. For a framework to function effectively, quality processes need to inform the activities of the advisory board and the implementation of the framework.

The development of qualifications frameworks

In developing a national qualifications framework, a high-level forum involving government, employers, training providers and possibly trades unions needs to agree on the occupational categories to be used and the levels of qualifications to be contained within each category.

National VET qualifications may be developed, maintained and approved by a designated department of state or central agency charged with these roles. Such a government-led structure may operate through appointed committees of experts and industry, involving VET professionals, which are assigned the task of setting skill standards, and developing and maintaining each of the qualifications or families of qualifications.

Once qualifications have been agreed to and registered on the framework, they should be subject to review by stakeholders and experts on a regular basis, to enable refinements and updates to be made over the years.

In some other countries, national vocational qualifications may be developed by public/private or entirely private organizations, such as industry bodies. In this case, the practitioners of a certain profession or trade will agree on which skill standards and training content are required for a particular occupation and its related qualifications. VET professionals and employee representatives also need to participate in this work. Such industry organizations may be based locally, in chambers of commerce, or they may belong to professional associations. They are commonly employer-led, from a desire to see standards within their professions controlled. To receive national status, the VET qualifications will nevertheless require approval from government-appointed competent bodies.

Qualifications-awarding bodies

Once it has been decided which skill standards are required for a qualification, the standard-setting body may organize skills assessment tests itself or it might permit other bodies to do so. The assessment of the required skills and knowledge should involve people who are themselves competent in carrying out assessments. The criteria for the approval of an awarding body should include that such a body:

- ☐ is competent to design and offer the required tests;

- ☐ has a robust system for appointing and training assessors and examiners;

- ☐ has the required level of quality assurance to offer consistency in assessments and to avoid fraud;

- ☐ has good links with skills standard-setting bodies so that the qualifications are kept up to date and meet employers' requirements.

The external assessment of skills

Qualifications-awarding bodies also control the work of those who carry out assessments leading to the qualifications. Indeed, there may be national qualifications for assessors. Depending on the mix of theoretical and practical assessment, assessors who observe and assess the work of students in a practical setting as well as those who mark examination papers and theoretical tests, will need to meet certain requirements. The first type of assessment requires that the assessor be face to face with the students; the second type of assessment can be done at a distance, by sending scripts to be assessed or by computer. Although teachers are still responsible for continuously assessing the learning of their students, assessment leading to the award of qualifications may be done by others.

Professional assessors are generally experienced teachers. VET institutions may, therefore, have to make their staff available to work for an awarding body and perform assessments on students from other institutions. This may be a private arrangement, and be separately paid, but it is generally thought to be beneficial for teachers to be approved as examiners or assessors. The advantage of external assessments for national qualifications is that they are more likely to protect the institution against fraudulent standards or fraudulent testing practice.

In their course delivery practices, VET providers have to meet the requirements of standard-setting and awarding bodies, which may mean that they have to fulfil certain requirements regarding staff qualifications, training resources and the conduct of tests and other assessments.

209

Courses leading to national VET qualifications

VET courses are structured learning experiences with specified outcomes. A VET course usually involves a number of features, of which the most important are the curriculum reflecting the detailed learning content of a course and the way a course is delivered. Learning content may be structured into modules and research activities. Several courses of study may lead to the same VET qualification. VET providers are the individuals and organizations that supply education, training and assessment services, and they include public and private institutions and workplaces.

National qualifications frameworks may also provide information on the courses that can deliver certain qualifications as well as give a list of institutions that are accredited to deliver these courses. The information can include some or all of the following:

☐ the name/title of the course;

☐ the name/title of the qualification (for example, Welder General, Level 3);

☐ a summary of course objectives (provision of knowledge and skills recognized by an award);

☐ anticipated outcomes (for example how the course is related to employment opportunities);

☐ a list of prerequisite courses, that is, other courses that must have been completed prior to entering the listed course;

☐ a list of co-requisite courses, that is, other courses that should be undertaken concurrently with the listed course;

☐ the course duration, for example in hours/days/weeks/years;

☐ the course level, normally expressed as a descriptor (such as pre-entry, entry, graduate, post-graduate, and so on) or expressed numerically according to a defined scale of levels;[1]

☐ the course credit value, for example a numerical value that allows a comparison of course load (for example 20 credits) with a full-time, full year of study (for example 120 credits) or, alternatively, that allows a comparison of the listed course (for example 20 credits) with a more substantive course of which it may be a subcomponent or module (for example a two-year course of 240 credits);

---

[1] For example in a multi-level framework, which in some jurisdictions spans both VET and higher education, the first level may be the least complex and the last level the most complex. Levels depend on the complexity of learning: lower levels may equate to approximately the same standard as senior secondary education and basic trades training, middle levels may equate to advanced trades, technical and business qualifications, and the highest levels to advanced graduate and postgraduate degree qualifications.

☐ a list of course modules (if a modular course), where each module has a credit value;

☐ a list of providers accredited to offer the course and their contact details.

The information contained within a national vocational qualifications framework can be of significant benefit to the stakeholders:

☐ students can access the framework to determine how the various courses registered on it are interrelated and, accordingly, may be assisted with career planning;

☐ students may be able to benefit through provisions specified in the framework for the recognition of prior learning;

☐ employers may be able to contribute to the qualifications, course and curriculum development processes by being permitted to articulate their skills needs; their involvement may result in courses that are more relevant to their requirements; they are also able to link qualifications with the expected competencies of potential employees;

☐ students and employers can readily identify courses that are quality assured;

☐ the government can be assured – if registration on the national framework is a precondition for public funding – that it is funding only quality-assured education and training;

☐ VET providers have access to up-to-date information on the national qualifications, with changes communicated promptly to them.

For more details on national vocational qualifications frameworks in different countries, go to **Unit 8.1: Developing a course for a national VET qualification** on your CD-ROM.

8.1.2 DEVELOPING A NATIONAL VOCATIONAL TRAINING COURSE

There are two approaches that can be taken in developing a national vocational training course: either it can be based on endorsed competencies, agreed assessment standards and qualification pathways or it can be based on a curriculum document related to learning outcomes and required knowledge.

A national vocational training course is accredited by a national training authority and as a consequence is recognized nationally. On the successful completion of a course, a recognized credential or statement is issued. This may be referred to as a qualification.

Although the design of a VET qualification is best left to experts in this field, VET courses are usually developed by education and training specialists. Commonly, a course involves a large number of features, some of which are listed in **Section 8.1.1** and which may be registered on the national qualifications framework.

The centralized approach

When a set of competency standards (a subset of which may be packaged as a course) is being developed, the main recognition authority within the training system oversees the consultative process, which involves the participation of employer groups or industry training boards, and trade unions. National vocational training courses may be developed by a variety of organizations and institutions, and will be available via a national register to other VET providers for delivery.

National VET course or curriculum committees may be established to develop a training course. The input from relevant industries and professions is crucial, but this information should also be tempered with advice from experts in training delivery and pedagogy. A template for setting out the course is provided by the accreditation authority.

The following four stages are essential in course development. First, a group of experts must agree on the education and training objectives and the content of the training course. The content may be expressed as topics to be studied or skills and knowledge to be acquired. The group must also agree on the level of competence for each skill, and whether it is to be exercised under supervision or not. The agreed content must be expressed in such a way that those who use the specification will interpret it as consistently as possible. Arrangements must be made for the group of experts to review the course content from time to time to ensure that it continues to meet employers' requirements.

Second, teaching and learning support materials need to be produced. These materials may include anything that is required to support the teaching of a new programme, such as textbooks, teacher guides and online materials. Some countries may apply a national curriculum which determines what is to be taught; input from experts in curriculum development, who can advise on the balance and integration of generic, theoretical and practical training, the application of a modular approach, the mode of delivery, and so on, would facilitate this process.

In some other countries, however, the development of a total learning support package for a complete qualification is unlikely, as teachers are expected to adapt their support materials to suit their own approach.

Third, the assessment panel from the qualifications-awarding body assesses the course and recommends whether it should be accredited. The panel also determines the length of the period of accreditation. Accreditation is the formal recognition that a vocational course conforms to the national principles and guidelines for accreditation and to a national qualifications framework. This means that:

☐ its contents and standards are appropriate to the qualification;

☐ it fulfils the purpose for which it was developed; and

☐ it is based on national competency standards, where they exist.

The qualifications-awarding body must also agree on the form of assessment to be used. The qualification needs to be assigned to a level within the framework, and the title of the qualification agreed and registered with the national authority responsible for the framework. Assessors are appointed and then visits to training centres arranged.

Fourth, a subsequent task is to determine how the curriculum is to be delivered: decisions on the administrative arrangements within assessment centres for registering candidates, organizing assessments and dealing with results and certificates all need to be reached.

For more details, see **Unit 8.3: Curriculum development**.

The VET institution-based approach

Sometimes individual VET providers, particularly those that specialize in subject areas, propose and develop their own national vocational training courses. Indeed, some designated VET providers may be commissioned to develop a national vocational training course and its curriculum. Such an institution will have specialist staff to carry out this function, for example curriculum managers.

In some countries, any autonomous VET provider may be allowed to develop and seek registration of a national VET course, which, once registered, becomes accessible to all other providers.

The development of a national VET course/curriculum by a training provider, whether a mandatory or discretionary function, requires similar consultation processes to those followed by the national course/curriculum committees outlined above. In particular, input will be required from the central agency responsible for qualifications frameworks, from relevant industries and/or professions and from experts in course and curriculum development.

The stages of course development are similar to those listed above, although the regulatory process may differ.

The VET provider's academic board or other body with responsibility for the courses offered by an institution has to approve a proposal to develop a new course with an associated qualification. Such a proposal should be accompanied by data to justify the course.

The specialist staff then decide on the course objectives and the means of achieving them. Some VET providers have specialist advisory groups drawn from relevant employers. The course designers need to agree on the mix of theoretical content and practical experience, decide what it is that graduates need to know and be able to do, and then decide how this knowledge and skill should be assessed. A senior manager with curriculum management responsibilities should supervise the development group. See also **Unit 8.3: Curriculum development**.

The course outline, together with details of resource requirements (teaching time, equipment, materials, and so forth), and the assessment requirements are validated by the academic board or other group responsible for accepting the proposed course. The course details may be scrutinized by colleagues from other disciplines in order to ensure consistency of standards across the institution. For planning purposes, agreement needs to be reached on the course length and maximum teaching time at this stage. A vocational course and qualification proposal may also need to be examined by a relevant professional body.

The new course is then submitted to a national awarding body for approval so that it can be fitted into the national qualifications framework and assessed independently according to the national arrangements. If a national VET system allows individual providers to make their own awards, the provider will then make arrangements for the conduct of examinations and other course assessments.

Quality assurance

The quality of national VET delivery may be assured through the following arrangements:

☐ All qualifications registered on the national qualifications framework are quality assured.

☐ VET courses that lead to national qualifications are delivered by accredited VET providers that are quality assured.

☐ The skills assessment process for the awarding of such qualifications is quality assured.

☐ A moderation system is in place to ensure national consistency in the awarding of national qualifications.

A VET qualification is registered on the national qualifications framework only if:

☐ the information on the qualification listed in Section 8.1.1 above is provided in the prescribed format and detail;

☐ due process had been followed in its development, for example the qualification has been designed by a competent group; consultation with all the stakeholders has been adequate; arrangements are in place for the qualification to be refined and updated over the years.

For a detailed format on registering a VET qualification on a national qualifications framework, consult **Module 10: Quality assurance in education and training.**

The registration and accreditation of VET institutions to deliver certain courses is usually the responsibility of the central agency. Registration is a generic assessment of the institution's ability to deliver quality training. Accreditation is a more specific assessment of a VET institution's ability to deliver a national qualification. A registered provider may have accreditation for only some of its vocational training courses.

Accreditation means that a VET institution has the necessary teachers, resources and equipment to deliver a course and assess students' achievements. These conditions and resources can be set out in a report of the accreditation panel following an inspection and/or perhaps by referring to the institution's asset register or whatever documentation the panel may request.

VET institutions and national awarding bodies need to be registered and accredited if they are to assess knowledge and skills and to award national qualifications. Skills assessment may also be the task of the central agency responsible for the national qualifications framework or for issuing vocational awards.

In a devolved VET system, skills assessment may be carried out by the accredited VET institution or by a registered assessor. Moderation processes may be required to ensure that accredited VET providers and assessors make consistent and reliable judgements on the work of students seeking qualifications.

For more details on quality assurance processes, including registration, accreditation and moderation, refer to **Module 10: Quality assurance in education and training.**

For more details on developing a national vocational training course in different countries, go to **Unit 8.1: Developing a course for a national VET qualification** on your CD-ROM.

Unit 8.2

DEVELOPING
A PROVIDER COURSE

8.2.1 THE MAIN DEVELOPMENT STAGES
OF A PROVIDER COURSE

The provider course

VET courses fall into two broad categories:

(1) Courses that lead to national qualifications. These national courses are normally developed or determined by national VET curriculum/course committees (of the agencies charged with this function) or by specialist staff at a VET provider, with appropriate external input; these courses have automatic credit transfer arrangements and can be delivered by any accredited provider.

(2) Courses that meet local needs. These provider (or tailor-made) courses are normally developed by a particular VET provider on its own initiative, often are whole qualifications with no or limited provisions for credit transfer of their components, are quality assured but are not necessarily registered on a national qualifications framework, and remain the intellectual property of the initiating provider. Some provider courses offered by large VET institutions may, in fact, be delivered across a whole country.

From time to time, an individual VET provider may identify a local training need and be required to develop a specific course. This usually occurs when there is a gap in the provision of current programmes or there is a trend in industry or the community to train a particular client group.

Provider courses that aim to suit the needs of particular customers are likely to be short courses designed for a specific purpose, for instance, to update employees on new regulations for electricians. The most likely evidence of attainment is a course attendance certificate, which is not accepted as a nationally recognized qualification.

There are three main types of provider courses:

(1) customized competencies/accredited courses within the national qualifications framework, and students undertake formal assessment. For instance, standard course units are adapted to suit an unusual work context;

(2) copyright and/or licensed courses, which consist of modules/competencies developed to meet specific industry needs, or courses licensed by industry organizations. They may also include nationally accredited modules/competencies if appropriate;

(3) non-assessed courses for which there is no assessment or credit transfer with a nationally accredited course.

For details on national courses, refer to **Unit 8.1: Developing a course for a national VET qualification**.

Course development stages

The development stages of a provider course can be broken down into three steps:

Step 1: Identifying the need for the course
This includes: conducting a feasibility study in order to justify the course; identifying the proposed VET outcomes that will be covered by the course; listing the units of competency on which the course is based.
A feasibility study should provide assessments of:

☐ the demand for particular skills and competencies that is not currently being met;

☐ course training objectives – which skills and competencies should the course deliver?

☐ employer demand for particular skills and competencies – will employers recognize a proposed course?

☐ student demand for the proposed course – will students enrol in sufficient numbers in the proposed course to warrant its development, delivery and return to investment?

☐ the capacity of the VET provider to deliver the course – does the provider have the requisite resources to deliver the course? If not, how could any deficiencies be remedied?

☐ the costs of course development and implementation and how these costs are to be met.

Step 2: Course development

This involves devising, with the advice of employers: the course content and specifications for assessment requirements, including continuous in-house assessment and end-tests; the resources required for the course, costing and resource procurement details; the specifications for course entry and exit; and assuring quality of the course delivery.

The course development process is carried out by the provider's course development committees (teams), which may include representation from the provider's senior management and from enterprises, industries and professions.

Experience in course and curriculum development is a competence that some or many teachers will need to acquire. Training in course and curriculum development is often part of tertiary teacher training programmes offered by specialist teacher training institutions.

The academic board of a VET provider may exercise oversight of the course development process and approve recommendations from course development teams. The academic board may have (internal) responsibility for institutional accreditation to deliver a provider course under the delegated authority of a central quality assurance agency.

Step 3: Course endorsement

This may be overseen by the academic board at a local level. A VET provider's course development committee ensures that the project design, products and processes meet customer and regulatory requirements.

Provider shorter courses are, however, rarely taken to the academic board for approval. There is more likely to be blanket approval for the work of the course development department or a VET provider's training department (school), allowing it free rein to develop short courses within an agreed earnings target.

For details on the organization and functioning of the academic board, refer to **Unit 3.3: Alternative organizational structures of autonomous VET institutions**.

For details of the main development stages of a provider course in different countries, go to **Unit 8.2: Developing a provider course** on your CD-ROM.

8.2.2 COURSE REQUIREMENTS

Course outcomes

The educational and employment outcomes of a provider course need to be identified along with the competency standards and general competencies.

Course content

The course content may be expressed as topics to be studied or skills to be acquired. The team must also set a standard, that is, agree on the level of competence for each skill, and whether it is to be supervised or not. The agreed content must be expressed in such a way that those who use the specification will interpret it as consistently as possible. Arrangements must be made for the group of experts to review the course content from time to time to ensure that it continues to meet employers' requirements.

Whole versus modular structure

Decisions are to be made on whether and, if so, how the course is to be broken down into learning units or modules. A modular structure offers significant advantages (for example enhanced opportunities for the transfer of credits between courses that include the same or similar modules), but it also requires additional work on its structure. In particular, the course development team will need to decide whether all the modules of the course are to be compulsory or whether students will be able to select some optional modules in addition to compulsory modules (if any). The course designers will also need to consider in detail how each module will contribute to the course's training objectives.

The course outline, whether modular or otherwise, will need to be developed into a curriculum that specifies in sufficient detail *what* is to be taught. To carry out this process, the course development project team will need members with experience in curriculum design. The curriculum should specify the topics to be covered and the level of detail. It may also determine *how* the proposed course is to be taught. Curriculum should include sufficient information to enable teaching staff to develop individual teaching plans for each session or period of course delivery – typically of one hour's duration or shorter.

For details on the curriculum development process, refer to **Unit 8.3: Curriculum development**.

Designing the assessment of student progress

Course design should also include planning on how student progress is to be evaluated. Student progress will need to be evaluated:

☐ throughout the course to provide students with information on their performance, and to enable intervention to be taken by teaching staff if students are not coping with the demands of the course;

☐ at the end of the course to determine whether students have met the course's requirements for successful graduation and, if so, are entitled to recognition by appropriate certification.

The evaluation of student progress can be carried out through a number of processes, which, in general, fall into two broad categories: norm-referenced assessment and standards-based assessment.

For more details on evaluating student performance, consult **Unit 6.2: Guiding and monitoring student progress**.

Course entry and exit levels and course duration

An initial task of a course development project is to produce a course outline or structure to ensure that the course meets the training objectives identified by the feasibility study. To inform course design, early decisions are required on important course specification parameters, including:

☐ course entry level(s) – determines the level(s) of VET students entering the course, without precluding two or more entry points and a requirement that students must have successfully completed course prerequisites (that is, have previously graduated from prescribed pre-entry education and training courses);

☐ course exit level(s) – descriptor(s) or numerical value(s) usually related to those used for the national qualifications framework, without precluding two or more exit points at different levels of the course. For details on course levels, refer to Unit 8.1: Developing a course for a national VET qualification;

☐ the duration of the course – determines the workload required for students to complete the course successfully, without precluding different durations for different modes of delivery (for example full-time, part-time, distance learning and so forth), and is often stated as an EFTS unit (1.00 EFTS is the workload of a student enrolled in a full-time, fullyear course).

Evaluation of the course design

Procedures should exist for the evaluation of the course design to ensure that the course is meeting its training objectives.

For more details, refer to **Unit 8.4: Course evaluation**.

Identifying resource requirements

The final stage of course development – once decisions have been taken on course outline and specifications, course modules and their contributions to training objectives, the methodology of evaluating student performance, and procedures for course evaluation – is to identify the resources required by the VET provider to deliver the course. These will generally include:

☐ human resources – teaching and support staff, taking into account the skills and competencies of instructors, how these match those of current staff and how identified deficiencies can be remedied by employing specialist contract instructors, and so forth;

☐ accommodation – classrooms, workshops, laboratories, and so forth;

☐ equipment – tools, instruments, and so forth;

☐ teaching resources – teachers' notes, student handouts, and so on.

Quality assurance issues

A newly developed provider course should comply with quality assurance requirements as it is often a prerequisite for public funding. Public providers that deliver their own courses are expected to be registered and accredited for delivering publicly funded courses.

The registration of VET providers is commonly a function of the central agency responsible for the national qualifications framework or it may be delegated to a quality assurance body in the VET sector. The registration of a VET provider amounts to a generic assessment of its ability to deliver quality training, and takes into account:

☐ the VET institution's governance and management capacities;

☐ the quality of its teaching and support staff;

☐ the general adequacy of the institution's resources, including accommodation, equipment and student facilities.

Course approval for a provider course usually applies to a particular course and, like registration, may be a function of the central agency or of a quality assurance body established for the VET sector. Course approval is based on an assessment that due process has been followed in course development, that is:

☐ the course has been designed by competent staff;

☐ consultation with the stakeholders has been adequate and training objectives are realistic;

☐ the proposed course should meet the specified training objectives;

☐ arrangements are in place for the course to be refined and updated over the years.

Where VET institutions have developed rigorous internal processes for quality assurance, the course approval process may be delegated to the providers themselves. Internal course approval committees may be set up as part of the VET institution's quality assurance system. This delegation should be subject to periodic review and to an audit by a national quality assurance body established for the VET sector or, alternatively, by some other central body.

Provider accreditation is an assessment of a VET institution's ability to deliver and conduct assessments of a particular provider's course/qualification or broader vocational fields. It should take into account the resources available to the provider for delivering the proposed course(s).

Registration, course approval and accreditation may be specified as a condition of receiving public funding for provider qualifications. By imposing this condition, the government can be assured that it is funding only quality-assured qualifications. A VET institution may have accreditation for only some of its provider VET courses.

In jurisdictions where registration, course approval and accreditation processes are delegated to public VET providers, moderation processes are necessary to ensure that consistent and reliable judgements are being made. The implementation and maintenance of moderation processes are generally the responsibility of the central agency or, in more devolved systems, of the quality assurance body established for the VET sector.

For more details on quality assurance processes, including registration, accreditation and moderation, refer to **Module 10: Quality assurance in education and training.**

For details on course requirements in different countries, go to **Unit 8.2: Developing a provider course** on your CD-ROM.

Unit 8.3

CURRICULUM DEVELOPMENT

8.3.1 THE CURRICULUM DEVELOPMENT FRAMEWORK

The degree of involvement of providers in the curriculum development of VET courses varies from country to country. Within a national qualifications framework, the curricula of courses may be strongly determined by national VET qualifications requirements, since they consist of endorsed units of competency standards and skills assessment procedures. This may leave individual VET providers with little freedom to develop curricula for the national qualifications that they wish to be accredited for delivering.

The curricula of provider courses are developed by a particular VET provider on its own initiative. In this case, a VET provider may establish course/ curriculum development committees to cover the various vocational fields of relevance. They may include representation from:

☐ the VET institution's senior management;

☐ employers, enterprises, industries and professions served by the institution;

☐ curriculum and course development specialists as well as teaching staff.

The first step usually taken by a VET institution that has identified a training need for a new course is to conduct a feasibility study. Subject to a satisfactory outcome of the study, the next step is to develop a course content and outline. This includes details on its modular structure, if any, the broad course content covering the constituent modules, specified entry and exit levels and the credit value for the course as well as a methodology for student assessment.

For details on developing a course outline, including feasibility study, course content and course requirements, and student assessment, refer to **Unit 8.1: Developing a course for a national VET qualification** and **Unit 8.2: Developing a provider course**.

The course outline describes *how* the proposed course is to be taught and then needs to be developed into a course curriculum, which clearly specifies *what* is to be taught, including the topics to be covered by the teaching staff and to what level of detail. The curriculum should include sufficient information to enable the teaching staff to develop their own individual teaching plans.

The VET institution's teaching staff should be closely involved in course and curriculum development. The academic board generally exercises academic oversight and may also be responsible for approving the proposed curricula prior to course delivery. In some jurisdictions, approval of the course and curriculum by the VET provider's academic board is a necessary condition for registration of the course on the national qualifications framework.

For details on the role of the autonomous VET provider's academic board, refer to **Unit 3.3: Alternative organizational structures of autonomous VET institutions**.

For details on curriculum development frameworks in different countries, go to **Unit 8.3: Curriculum development** on your CD-ROM.

The effects of national and institutional policies on curriculum

Curriculum development should encompass everything that the institution expects the student should learn or experience. It may even go beyond the demands of achieving a particular qualification. A framework for curriculum development can be influenced by national policy or by the overall purposes of the institution. For instance, the government may decide to use VET institutions to support national campaigns to improve computer literacy or to address particular health issues. Funding would, therefore, follow to help establish a basic course curriculum in support of such campaigns.

Certain groups of learners might be expected to continue their general education. Young apprentices often work to a national framework that adds continued general education to their work experience and job-related training. In this case they will be required to complete all aspects of the curriculum before they can fully graduate.

The mission statement of an individual VET provider may include certain aspects of curriculum relevant to the personal development of all learners. There may be considerable pressure for learners to perform highly in national qualifications in order to maintain the reputation and prestige of the institution, which might lead to particular tutorial and support arrangements and consistent demands to meet or exceed expectations. There may be competitions and awards for activity not directly related to qualifications. These aspects are sometimes referred to as the "ethos" or the "hidden curriculum" of a VET institution.

Other VET institutions may be more relaxed, helping learners to achieve but leaving it up to them as to how hard they work. The ethos of such a practice is that the learning experience should be enjoyable and fun. The curriculum may include residential trips, outdoor pursuits and recreational activities, with students being expected to participate in these events in order to develop aspects of their personalities outside working life. Such activities are sometimes referred to as extra-curricular, that is, they are outside the main curriculum or course requirements.

Discussion of how the VET institution's mission translates into a curriculum framework for the institution as a whole is a matter for the academic board, which should offer advice on how curriculum frameworks should apply to courses across the institution. For example, the academic board may recommend that all full-time students should have tutorial meetings with both academic and personal tutors; and that a college-based record system should be maintained of students' academic assessments as well as of their extra-curricular activities.

The academic board may also decide that, before leaving, all students must demonstrate a particular level of attainment in general education standards, such as in written work, verbal communication and mathematics. Few VET providers include compulsory sports in their programmes but quite a few expect students to join in sports or other chosen recreational activities. The resources for such extra work have to be found from the unit of resource made available to each student, but if these extra-curricular activities accord with values that the VET provider feels strongly about, then such adjustments will be made.

8.3.2 THE MAIN STAGES OF CURRICULUM DEVELOPMENT

There are certain standard stages in the development of curricula as well as factors that need to be taken into account when determining the curriculum requirements for a course leading to a national VET qualification:

- □ determining the course objectives: what is to be learned should be expressed as learning outputs that can be observed or assessed. Course outputs need to be based on nationally endorsed units of competencies developed with appropriate industry bodies;

- □ determining the course content, in conjunction with experts from the relevant industry sectors. This will include identifying the mix of practical and theoretical studies, the need for continued general education (for example, mathematics) to support specialist learning and contextual study to increase understanding of the industry. There may be a need for generic studies, such as drawing, or health and safety;

- □ determining work standards: at what level are the skills or knowledge to be exercised and under what conditions (for example under supervision or in particular work conditions)?

- □ determining training methods: this will include location (workshop, on-the-job, classroom-based) and style (explanation, demonstration, project-based,

225

research, individual or team work). A VET provider may further develop detailed teaching and training strategies. These are often disseminated as teacher guidelines, which are intended to assist teachers in developing their own teaching plans and offering suggestions for delivering the curriculum;

☐ time requirement factor: some skills-based qualifications are not time-bound. Tests are administered when students are ready, and they can proceed at their own pace. Nevertheless, in any training setting there must be some consideration of the time likely to be needed for the average learner to achieve the course objectives;

☐ arranging the course content: depending on the circumstances, the content can be arranged in number of ways (see below);

☐ determining skills assessment methods: the assessment should follow the design of the curriculum and match the learning objectives. Assessment should suit the purpose of the learning. For instance, there is no point in giving a multiple-choice paper test for aspects of IT; these tests should be computer-based. Written essay examinations have limited relevance in practical subjects. National awarding bodies will determine the form of final, national assessments. In-course assessments should assess learning, rather than be rehearsals for the national tests;

☐ curriculum pilots: where there is to be a major national change in curricula, there should be a pilot phase to test the planned changes. This phase can be problematic, since there is often pressure to effect the desired changes quickly. The "pilot" students may also suffer if the experimental curriculum does not offer them what they need during their course. Nevertheless, there needs to be some kind of trial to determine whether the quantity of content, the proposed pace of learning and the outcomes of the proposed changes in the curriculum are appropriate. Such a pilot phase must be accompanied by independent evaluation;

☐ resource management: this should include preparing staff for any changes or the recruitment of new staff; the development of teaching and resource materials; new equipment and accommodation requirements;

☐ course curriculum evaluation: how is the curriculum to be introduced, delivered and evaluated? Evaluation is normally based on feedback received from major stakeholders, in particular course graduates and their employers. This feedback may be obtained through various survey techniques, including surveys of graduate destinations (tracer studies) and surveys of employers' opinions.

Structuring the course content

The design of the course content should allow for flexibility in learning and delivery through, for instance, the use of learning modules. When there are mixed-ability learners or people with varied entry points, the content may be arranged in small chunks (modules or units), usually accompanied by resource materials that allow independent study. These may be paper- or computer-based. Students generally need close guidance to adhere to the objectives, but such a design may also be suitable for distance learning. An alternative use for a modular course structure is the roll-on roll-off programme, where enrolment is continuous throughout the year, and learners enter and leave as their circumstances demand. This design of curriculum may permit students some choice of content or the order in which it is learned. It also allows assessment to be organized at the end of each module or unit, so that qualification credits are accumulated gradually.

The linear course design demands that content be organized in a logical sequence, and that most students follow the course at the same time and at the same pace. Course plans follow the sequence, and assessments are fitted in where the design demands. Tests may need to be taken at certain stages or all assessments may take place at the end of the course. This pattern is suitable for short courses.

The project-based curriculum allows students to learn in small groups, so that practical skills are exercised while achieving a larger-scale objective. Such a method is thought to combine experience and problem-solving in such a way that learning is reinforced, making it both more effective and enjoyable than the other design structures.

The curriculum should also allow for equitable access by taking into account the learning needs of groups at risk. This could be reflected in differently structured learning and assessment methods.

The knowledge, skills and competencies embodied in a curriculum may be generic (that is, relate to a broad range of vocational fields), specialist (that is, relate to a narrow vocational field or even to a particular job), or include both generic and specific components. Alternatively, they may be theoretical (that is, abstract or conceptual knowledge) or practical (that is, manual skills or knowledge that are related to a particular utilitarian task).

The integration of generic (theoretical) and practical (specific) skills training is considered in **Section 8.3.3** below.

For details on developing and implementing VET curriculum in different countries including examples of curricula, go to **Unit 8.3: Curriculum development** on your CD-ROM.

8.3.3 INTEGRATING GENERIC AND PRACTICAL KNOWLEDGE AND SKILLS

Generic knowledge and skills (often called employability skills) are those that are useful in many occupations and in employment and adult life in general. The generic knowledge and skills components that are often included in, or assumed for, a VET curriculum involve:

☐ basic literacy – the ability to read, write and comprehend;

☐ basic numeracy – the ability to count, measure and make arithmetic calculations;

☐ interpersonal skills – the ability to get on with other people, function as a team, and so forth;

☐ communication skills – the ability to express ideas, opinions, requests, conclusions and recommendations;

☐ capabilities to collect and analyse information;

☐ time management skills – the ability to plan and organize activities, and use time efficiently;

☐ another language proficiency;

☐ computer skills – the ability to use a keyboard and common computer packages;

☐ workplace skills – having an understanding of the respective rights and responsibilities of employees and employers, including relevant labour laws, job safety rules, working time schedules, and so on;

☐ skills that are required to gain employment or establish an enterprise, to progress within an enterprise or expand personal employment capability.

Some of these skills can be more easily taught than others, but employers frequently demand that a personal assessment of graduates includes a report on such attributes and the potential of graduates to develop them further.

A substantial proportion of these generic skills should be acquired during their general education, and the benefit of them cannot be entirely captured by a particular employer (that is, these skills offer the same benefits to all employers). Their acquisition may be reflected in an entry level that is prescribed for the course.

The needs of prospective students who have not previously acquired these generic skills during their general education could be met by a VET provider through delivering:

☐ generic skill components as stand-alone modules or units of competency, in-house, as part of the VET curriculum; skills assessors can gather evidence on both generic and specific industry competencies;

☐ generic pre-entry training or bridging courses;

◻ general adult (second chance) education and training courses offered by an adult education provider.

Course design will need to consider the extent to which generic and specialist learning are integrated. Ideally, generic skills should be developed through the design of the specialist content, although this may be difficult for those learners who need remedial support.

Economies can sometimes be made by teaching students from different courses together in some common aspects of the curriculum. Where most learning is on the job, some generic skills teaching may have to be outsourced to another provider. Without very close linkages between the on-the-job and off-the-job training elements, this type of integration is extremely difficult to manage.

The generic skills curriculum usually requires close links between different staff groups in the VET provider: technical and trade specialists need to collaborate with teams of generic skills specialists in the design and delivery of programmes. For instance, literacy skills may need to be developed in the context of technical content because teaching materials have been specially designed to match the technical course. While such collaboration is informative for all concerned, it sometimes creates organizational hurdles that need to be overcome.

Generic skills need to be incorporated into all vocational courses to complement specific industry competencies and to develop richer learning experiences. Because of the growing importance of generic skills, national guidelines are sometimes introduced for course developers to ensure that the skills are explicitly incorporated into new competency standards and curricula.

Delivering practical instruction

The delivery of practical training requires a VET institution to provide students with access to the materials, tools and equipment that they will encounter in a workplace setting where these practical skills are utilized. The access to practical training can be achieved in several different ways:

◻ A VET provider might set up workshops with the required materials, tools and equipment to simulate a workplace setting, and deliver the entire course on campus.

◻ A VET provider might deliver theoretical components on campus and might contract industry to provide off-campus access to a workplace setting.

◻ An ITO might deliver practical components as on-the-job training and contract a VET institution to deliver theoretical components off the job (that is, on campus).

For details on integrating generic and practical knowledge and skills in different countries, go to Unit 8.3: Curriculum development on your CD-ROM.

COURSE EVALUATION

The need for course review

VET qualifications, the courses and curricula leading to them as well as the way they are delivered need to be reviewed, over time, as they may become less relevant to student learning interests and to industry's need for skilled workers. Curriculum is particularly sensitive to changing job requirements. Course delivery processes may need to be reviewed in order to maintain the quality of the course.

VET courses fall into two broad categories. First, there are VET courses that lead to national qualifications. These courses are normally developed by designated national agencies or by specialist staff in VET institutions with appropriate external input. Such courses may have automatic credit transfer arrangements and can be delivered by any accredited provider.

Second, there are VET provider courses that meet identified local demand. These courses are normally developed by individual providers on their own initiative. They may be whole qualifications with no or limited provisions for credit transfer of their components. They need to be quality assured but are not necessarily registered on a national qualifications framework; they then remain the intellectual property of the initiating provider.

For details on national courses, refer to **Unit 8.1: Developing a course for a national VET qualification**. For details on provider courses, refer to **Unit 8.2: Developing a provider course**.

The purpose of an evaluation is to assess the quality and suitability of a course. The evaluation can focus on a whole course or particular aspects of it, such as course design, teaching and learning, skills assessment, delivery and outcomes. Each accredited course must outline the processes in place for its ongoing monitoring and evaluation throughout the period for which it is accredited. It is also necessary to demonstrate ongoing monitoring and review when a course is being re-accredited. This procedure should be followed for the accreditation of every course.

The licensing bodies or course development committees that deal with national VET qualifications and course registration within the quality assurance frameworks need to establish the criteria and procedures for undertaking course evaluation. VET providers should have course evaluation policies that reflect national and institutional requirements.

Accredited courses should have nationally agreed quality arrangements that stipulate the evaluation processes to be followed. Individual providers need to adopt similar guidelines for tailor-made courses. From time to time there will be other reasons for the individual VET provider to evaluate courses or aspects of a course, such as the learning resources, teaching methods, skills assessment approaches, the delivery modes such as work-based or online delivery. Courses are often evaluated by focusing on graduate outcomes or employer views of the course to ensure that the course is maintaining its relevance in the market-place.

The scope for course evaluation

When planning an evaluation, the VET provider needs to ask the following questions:

☐ What is the purpose of the evaluation?

☐ When is it best to carry out the evaluation?

☐ Which data will be collected?

☐ Who are the main stakeholders?

☐ How will the findings be presented?

The scope of a course evaluation can vary according to its purpose but the following general issues may be explored:

☐ Course relevance – Does the course continue to meet the needs of industry, enterprises and community groups? Are the course objectives appropriate and achievable? Is the content appropriate, both in subject and level? Have unforeseen gaps emerged in knowledge and skills? Have there been any changes in national competency standards? Have there been any changes in regulatory requirements?

☐ Course design – How well is the course structured? Did the content fit the time allocated to it? Do additional course modules need to be developed? Should there be specialist options for some students?

☐ Course delivery – Has delivery been successful? Were delivery methods appropriate? Have students encountered any unexpected difficulties?

☐ Skills assessment – Was student assessment appropriate and was it fit for purpose? Did the course deliver what was intended in terms of student success?

☐ Cost-efficiency – Did costs match the proposed budget? Was the delivery efficient in terms of the resources used and the outcomes achieved? Was the content taught the most cost-efficient way of imparting the knowledge, skills and competencies? Could the same knowledge, skills and competencies be acquired using a different curriculum content?

☐ Feedback from stakeholders – What do students and employers think about the course and its curriculum in the light of experience? Are staff comfortable with the course design and delivery methods as well as clear about their role? Do the stakeholders think that any changes are necessary?

Evaluating the relevance of the course

Certain procedures will be required to ensure that VET courses and their curricula remain relevant. If a course is relevant, then the skills and competencies offered by it are appropriate to the current needs of learners, enterprises and professions.

The knowledge that provides a theoretical basis for skills and competencies, like all other knowledge, will continue to increase incrementally but is unlikely to change substantially over a short time interval. The foundation subjects that underpin much of VET, such as mathematics and elementary physics and chemistry, have changed very little over the past century.

However, because of technological innovations and structural change, the requirements for new skills and competencies can change significantly over a short time interval. In other words, skills and competencies change more rapidly than the knowledge that is required to acquire and practise them.

The issue of course relevance may not always be answered by the feasibility study. A course may be feasible, that is, the VET institution may be capable of developing and delivering it and students may decide to enrol in it, but this does not necessarily mean that it is relevant for their needs and for the skills needs of industry.

Because course relevance is one of the parameters that define training quality in general, course evaluations are also legitimate components of the quality audits carried out by a VET quality assurance body.

For more details on quality assurance, refer to **Module 10: Quality assurance in education and training**.

Any changes carried out to a national VET curriculum need to be accompanied by a formal independent evaluation conducted by a team working under contract to the relevant national body or funding agency. Any risks of course irrelevance will be mitigated if the evaluation is carried out by an independent agency rather than by the agencies that developed the course.

A VET provider might set up an internal evaluation team, consisting of teachers, managers and employers, to review the course content and delivery and assess its effectiveness.

Other stakeholders with an interest in the relevance of a VET course may also wish to undertake curriculum evaluations. This can be done by a national or local employers' association or by an ITO. The government funding agent also has an interest in course evaluations as they provide information that will help the agent to make VET funding decisions. Generally, though, the government funding agent relies on the assessments of other agencies, including quality assurance bodies.

The frequency with which evaluations are carried out is a matter for the evaluating bodies to decide, and may, for example, be determined by the overall cycle of VET providers' audits undertaken by a quality assurance body. Course committees need to be responsive to expressions of concern from any stakeholder that curricula are becoming obsolete.

Assessing curriculum compliance

An important aspect of course evaluation is the extent to which the teaching conforms to the curriculum. Compliance with the curriculum is an internal matter for a VET provider, and should be assessed as part of its internal QMS. Compliance is also relevant for a quality audit undertaken periodically by the VET quality assurance body. For details, refer to **Module 10: Quality assurance in education and training**.

Assessment techniques

The data-gathering methods used in course evaluations may include: questionnaires, interviews, case studies, action research and participant observation. An evaluation protocol, which sets out the conclusions and recommendations of the evaluation, needs to be produced.

The responses and assessments of the stakeholders (students, graduates, and employers) are essential for a robust course evaluation. They can be obtained through:

☐ an employer satisfaction survey – determines the extent to which employers are satisfied that course graduates have acquired the necessary skills and competencies;

☐ a graduate satisfaction survey – determines the level of graduate satisfaction with a course, influenced by their employment outcomes/prospects;

- a graduate destination survey (tracer study) – determines whether graduates find employment (or continued learning) and determines the relevance of their previous training to employment and further learning;

- a student satisfaction survey (as well as data on student enrolments and performance on the course) – determines the level of student satisfaction with a course;

- a teaching staff survey will assess teachers' satisfaction level with the course design and delivery.

For details on these assessment methodologies, refer to **Unit 4.2: Assessing industry demand for VET courses.**

A course evaluation has no purpose unless it aims to improve a course. A satisfactory evaluation provides evidence that a course is meeting its objectives and that the teaching and support staff involved in its delivery are meeting their performance targets.

Where the course outcomes are not as intended or where many students have dropped out, further investigations are needed. Those involved in course development and delivery (course/curriculum committees, a VET institution's academic board, and management and teaching staff) need to respond appropriately in the case of an unsatisfactory evaluation. Appropriate responses may include:

- making changes to the course curriculum and delivery patterns to improve its relevance;

- making improvements in course delivery, for example providing enhanced teaching resources, replacing non-performing staff, and so on;

- closing or replacing a course.

Decisions about course changes or closure will generally be taken by the VET institution's academic board or senior staff group.

For details on course evaluation carried out in different countries, go to **Unit 8.4: Course evaluation** on your CD-ROM.

Unit 8.5

FRANCHISING VET COURSES

What can be franchised in education and training?

A VET provider may wish to deliver programmes of learning that have been developed by some other agency and are not publicly available on the national register of accredited programmes. These programmes could be from another VET institution, a higher education institution or an industry organization. A commercial arrangement will need to be negotiated to deliver these programmes and, in most circumstances, fees will be charged to the participants, so that all the costs will be fully recovered.

Two broad categories of VET courses were identified in **Unit 8.1: Developing a course for a national VET qualification** and **Unit 8.2: Developing a provider course**:

(1) national courses that lead to national qualifications; and

(2) provider courses developed by a particular VET institution on its own initiative and leading to a new provider qualification.

A usual condition for the registration of a new provider qualification on a national qualifications framework is that it becomes accessible to all VET providers. The decision by a VET institution on whether to register a new provider qualification that it has developed needs to take into account the benefits of registration – enhanced portability and uptake of the qualification by other VET providers – as well as possible disadvantages:

☐ the intellectual property rights of the initiating VET provider are extinguished;

☐ a new qualification may have to be adjusted to the registration format applied by the national qualifications framework (for instance, a whole qualification may need to be broken down into modules as a condition of registration, and so on).

A provider qualification that is not registered on a national qualifications framework remains the intellectual property of the VET institution that developed it. The qualification may be used in a number of ways, including:

☐ selling the course to another provider;

☐ contracting another provider to deliver the course on behalf of the initiating VET institution;

☐ franchising the course for delivery by another provider.

Selling the course saves the purchasing institution the costs of course development, but the onus on obtaining approval to deliver the course transfers to the purchaser. Once accreditation to deliver the approved course has been obtained, the VET provider that has bought an education and training course developed by another institution is then able to award its own qualification. However, the purchasing VET provider will still need to have its own QMS.

In the case of *contracting* a separate provider to deliver the course, the contracted VET institution will have the same status as a satellite campus, and will be subject to the initiating VET provider's QMS.

Franchising is an arrangement that allows other providers (franchisees) to deliver the course/qualification developed by another VET institution (franchiser). A franchise agreement – a legal package that sets out the terms and conditions of the relationship between franchiser and franchisee – will need to be reached.

The agreement should prescribe the conditions that the franchisee must meet in delivering the course, including the major characteristics of the course, its curriculum, course teaching resources, marketing plan, geographical area of training delivery, quality assurance arrangements and payment of fees (if any) to the franchiser for (intellectual property) rights. Under the franchise agreement, the course approval and accreditation functions remain with the franchiser.

The VET provider that has developed a course can franchise the whole course or parts of it, such as, for instance, a skills assessment system or a set of the course's teaching resources.

In jurisdictions where individual VET providers are expected to develop curricula for national qualifications, they can also franchise curricula to other providers that are willing to deliver the course leading to a national qualification.

The advantages of course franchising

Where a particular provider has developed a VET programme, it is sometimes to the advantage of both the provider and others if franchise arrangements can be made. This means that the developing VET provider can issue a licence to another provider to offer the course the developing provider designed.

The benefits of a franchise arrangement for the initiating VET provider (franchiser) are that:

☐ portability, access to and the uptake of the qualification are extended to other regions (often a more cost-effective strategy than establishing a satellite campus for this purpose);

☐ the development costs of the course and qualification (including course approval and accreditation) are shared with other organizations through fees charged for the right to deliver the course/qualification;

☐ it provides an opportunity to generate income.

The benefits of a franchise arrangement for the franchisee are that the full costs of course development, course approval and accreditation, and often of setting up a QMS, are borne by the initiating institution. However, this benefit is offset by the fee charged by the initiating provider for the right of the franchisee to deliver the course/qualification. For instance where the provider is not approved to offer higher-level courses, a franchise from a university can offer local students the opportunity of following higher-level courses without having to move to the university location.

There are risks to both parties. Financial agreements must be made clear from the outset, and limits established to growth. The responsibilities of each party for the quality of provision and the supervisory responsibility of the franchising VET provider must also be unambiguous. The terms on which the franchise will end should be set out, and any penalties calculated.

For details on franchising VET programmes in different countries, go to Unit 8.5: Franchising VET courses on your CD-ROM.

MODULE 9

The management
of training delivery

Unit 9.1

THE ORGANIZATION
OF TRAINING DELIVERY

9.1.1 ORGANIZATIONAL AND MANAGEMENT STRUCTURES

The organizational and management system

The autonomous public VET institution is responsible for its own organiza-tional and staffing structures. The design of these structures and the roles and responsibilities assigned to the staff determine how training delivery is managed. In practice, however, these structures often reflect government and industry advice and are organized along industry-wide lines or specializations. These decisions can determine the number and specialization of the VET insti-tution's schools, faculties or departments.

The organization and management of VET delivery are determined by the following major factors:

☐ the vision or philosophy of the institution;

☐ the size of the institution;

☐ the operating environment, which may be one site or multi-campus;

☐ the industry structures for which the VET institution offers services;

☐ the diversity and levels of educational and training programme offerings (ranging from basic education to diploma level) across several fields of occupations;

☐ preferred delivery options (school-based or industry-based or combined);

☐ the student and other client groups and the related support services;

☐ the available resources – physical, human and financial.

An autonomous VET provider needs to interpret the above factors and develop a structure capable of operating in the complex conditions of the education and training markets. Senior management will be concerned with the strategic planning framework and the performance indicators on which to measure the outcomes for the whole organization. Departmental heads will need to organize their staff, financial resources and VET delivery methods to respond to industry and community needs. Teaching and training staff will need to organize the delivery of the training programme for individuals and groups of students.

Senior management

This level will comprise:

- a governing council;
- a chief executive;
- a management team of the chief executive and senior managers (executive or senior management group).

In a small group of staff which includes the chief executive, there may be a person with general curriculum responsibility for the courses and programmes. There should also be a finance manager. In an autonomous VET institution, the finances are handled at a very senior level.

Depending on the size of the VET provider, other responsibilities may be combined or be held by separate senior managers, but they should include human resources (for appointments, professional development and discipline); estates (for capital developments, regular maintenance and some procurement); and student services (for marketing, advice and guidance, health, safety and welfare).

The above structure of the autonomous VET institution implies a minimum of three layers of management. Some responsibilities are however shared by each member of staff. For instance, VET quality assurance is the personal responsibility of each individual, as is good health and safety practice.

Departmental delivery structures

The structure of an autonomous VET institution will include some form of breakdown into departments and cost centres based on specific education and training fields, each managed by a designated head of department. In larger institutions, a number of training departments may be aggregated into larger units commonly called faculties or schools.

A head of department, programme leader, or faculty head are the academic managers (line managers). They manage teachers and tutors, grouped into delivery teams, and are responsible to the VET institution's senior management team for the efficient running of the courses and the welfare of students within their study area.

Where institution-wide coordination is required, management decisions may be taken at higher levels within the institution's administrative structure. Examples of such situations include:

☐ deciding on access to common teaching spaces or major pieces of equipment;

☐ the timetabling of classes for students undertaking courses delivered across several departments.

The department or school may also employ specialist staff who indirectly support the delivery of training. These members of staff – who in some instances may also have part-time teaching roles – may include:

☐ curriculum development specialists;

☐ industrial liaison staff (field-specific training), and so on.

Functional departments

Training delivery will necessitate the management of a range of support functions, which include:

☐ facilities management and related issues, such as room allocation, timetabling, parking;

☐ financial management – budgeting and costing, income generating, fees and charges;

☐ student services management – housing and income support, careers and employment, welfare and childcare, health;

☐ marketing and publicity;

☐ educational support services to students – language and study skills, resource centres and libraries and computer centres;

☐ educational support services to teachers – the development of curriculum and teaching and learning resources, professional development, liaising with industry and community.

The technical and administrative support services cited above may be organized at departmental level, particularly in larger institutions, but for reasons of efficiency these services can also be organized within a separate section.

Functional managers make sure that administrative and support systems run smoothly. For instance, the libraries and learning resource centres, MISs, and examination registration systems must be closely linked to the education and training programmes. Where a VET provider operates on several campuses,

243

there may need to be a campus manager. Teamwork is an essential skill for such an institution. In some way, each member of staff is dependent on other colleagues to ensure that everyone does their job properly. The quality of overall management and liaison and the level of cooperation between colleagues determine how smoothly the VET provider operates.

Support staff who provide general administrative services are usually employed by functional sections that span the institution rather than being located within particular training departments/schools. These services may include:

☐ human resource management (recruitment, appointment, leave, training, welfare, and so forth);

☐ information management support (ICTs);

☐ student management and welfare (enrolments, fees and grants, academic records, and so forth);

☐ liaison with general education schools and industry, vocational guidance and counselling;

☐ financial management (accounts, payroll, and so forth).

Some services – such as cleaning and maintenance services – are often outsourced to external suppliers.

The appointment, roles and responsibilities of VET institutions' governing councils are outlined in **Unit 3.1: The governing council and its procedures**. The appointment, roles and responsibilities of chief executives are outlined in **Unit 3.2: The role of the chief executive**.

For more details on the different organizational arrangements for teaching and support staff, refer to **Unit 3.3: Alternative organizational structures of autonomous VET institutions**.

For more details on staff with non-teaching functions, refer to **Unit 6.2: Guiding and monitoring student progress**, **Unit 6.3: Student welfare**, **Unit 6.4: Vocational guidance and job placement assistance** and **Unit 8.3: Curriculum development**.

Course management

The organization of VET delivery should be viewed through a single course delivery process. There are various ways of defining a "course", which then determines the way in which training delivery is managed. First, a course may be a complete programme of study provided for a group of learners who are enrolled together and study at more or less the same pace. Even within this pattern, arrangements may need to be made for students who need remedial help, for those who have relevant previous experience and can progress faster, or for those who want to follow different options.

Second, a course may be a single subject, planned by one or two teachers, which combines with other such subjects to make up a programme from which each student chooses. Modular programmes are usually offered in this way, with suggested pathways of study which provide routes to particular types of employment.

Third, training may be work-based, which means that some skills and experiences are acquired and assessed at work, and supplemented by additional practical work or theoretical study in the VET institution, perhaps on one day a week. This type of study requires close collaboration between the VET institution's teachers and work-place supervisors or training officers.

Each of these models requires particular organizational back-up. Each course needs a set of teachers or instructors who are experts in a subject discipline. These teachers may be grouped into a department or programme area for management purposes, with a team leader who is their line manager and organizes their day-to-day work. The second course pattern also requires careful oversight of the curriculum by someone who has management responsibility for the whole teaching programme, to ensure that choices are kept open, that modules are available in the right sequence and that students who are "picking and mixing" from a menu of courses are properly supervised.

In the first course model, the team leader may also be the course tutor, with responsibility for the students' progress. In the second model, the course tutor has to be selected from any one of the teaching team. In the third model, the direct supervisor of the student is likely to be the employer or training officer at work, so that the VET provider's course leader is mainly responsible for the smooth running of the programme and for maintaining close links with employers.

Therefore, delivery of VET courses needs at least three basic types of staff roles:

(1) groups of subject teachers and a planning specialist working together;

(2) a course leader, who oversees the day-to-day management of the course and liaises with employers where necessary;

(3) a personal tutor, who ensures that individual students make satisfactory progress.

Delivery teams may also include instructors who supervise workshop practices and do some skills assessments, as well as technicians, who provide technical support to specialist teachers. Individual staff may have a number of roles which are recognized in their pay and conditions.

The modes and organization of delivery may also be determined by the different client groups. Basic adult education classes are delivered in small groups or through the use of language laboratories or tutors. Vocational practical classes in trade subjects, such as welding or cooking, will be delivered in simulated work environments, so that the students are able to use the appropriate equipment. Vocational theory classes, such as classes in business studies or welfare studies, may be delivered in lecture as well as classroom mode.

For examples of organizational structures, sample job descriptions and more details on the organization and management of training delivery in different countries, go to **Unit 9.1: The organization of training delivery** on your CD-ROM.

9.1.2 MANAGING OFF-SITE LEARNING

Not all learning in VET courses delivered by training providers will occur within the confines of the institution's campus. There will be a range of procedures that determine off-site learning management and they will vary according to the client group. Some examples of off-site learning include:

☐ the practical components of institution-based courses delivered in workshops;

☐ workplace learning, which is training delivered entirely or predominantly in the workplace;

☐ distance learning and off-campus e-learning.

Learning workshops on campus

Practical components are often an important part of VET programmes. They can be delivered on campus in specialized teaching spaces that are not part of the main location of the institution, for example in science and language laboratories, technical workshops, nursing suites, computer science laboratories, and so on. The appropriately equipped specialist laboratories and workshops simulate settings that students are likely to encounter in their future industrial workplaces.

Learning in the workplace

It is also typical for certain occupations that practical instruction takes place away from a main building, for instance, marine studies at a dockyard or aeronautical studies at an airfield. The danger here is that both students and staff develop an "annexe" mentality, and have little contact with the management and facilities of the VET provider. They may also have inferior resources for study and recreation. Care needs to be taken to maintain links with such groups and to ensure that their course plans keep them linked to the library, student support services and professional development opportunities.

Some countries increasingly practise workplace training, where the role of practical instruction and industry guidance is much greater. Workplace training offers students an opportunity to undertake most of their training on the job or at least on the premises of an enterprise. Teachers from the VET institution may deliver both the on-the-job and off-the-job component or the company may have its own trainers.

For details on appropriately equipped laboratories and workshops, and so forth, refer to **Unit 9.3: Managing capital assets**.

An alternative approach to workplace training are full-time industrial attachments, where students are sent to work in companies with specialist equipment and appropriate working environments. These real (rather than simulated) workplaces can include scientific laboratories, construction sites, factories, health clinics, and so on.

Students who are primarily work-based need to be encouraged to feel part of their VET provider and to use its facilities well. Their course tutor has to maintain close links with employers to ensure that course content is relevant and that opportunities for the assessment of workplace skills are well planned. Careful records have to be kept to maintain good-quality linkages between off-the-job and on-the job training. VET institution's staff may need to be given time to visit students and employers at their place of work, and to assess their progress.

Learning in the workplace requires careful management, particularly if health and safety issues arise which may involve employees in the workplace and/or the general public (for example hospital patients) as well as the students themselves. A VET institution may manage the practical components of training delivered in the workplace by:

☐ contracting a suitable person already employed in the workplace to supervise the students;

☐ deploying designated institutional staff in the workplace (for example clinical training tutors).

The costs of contracted supervisors, dedicated teaching spaces within the actual workplace and the costs to the workplace (for example time lost to the enterprise/workplace as a result of providing practical experience to students) may be met by the VET institution. Alternatively, the company costs related to student workplace instruction may also be covered by the government.

Distance learning and off-campus e-learning

Off-site learning has rapidly expanded in recent years with the development of distance learning and off-campus e-learning. Distance learning and e-learning are becoming synonymous as the Internet and email are rapidly replacing printed course material sent by post. Often these modes are supported by a study centre on campus that is available to the students or by an online notes and email communications system. Communicating regularly with the tutor, combined with a clear statement on assessment requirements, can help to ensure that the programme is being effectively managed.

There is a common view that distance and e-learning can increase both the availability and accessibility of VET at lower cost levels. In some countries, however, this has not always been found to be the case. Distance learning and e-learning require the preparation of specific course materials designed for these forms of delivery, and developmental costs can be substantial (particularly for more specialist courses involving small student numbers).

Making available reading material on line does not take the place of lectures and tutorials, particularly for younger students experiencing their first contact with VET after leaving school. Post-school VET is generally more student-centred than school education, which is strongly teacher-centred. Experience is demonstrating that distance learning and off-campus e-learning are more suitable for mature students and students undertaking second or advanced qualifications.

However, younger students can benefit from on-campus e-learning, where, in addition to the benefits of a student-centred, problem-solving approach to learning, they also have access to institutional staff through lectures, seminars and tutorials.

For details on student-centred learning and on-campus e-learning, refer to **Unit 9.3: Managing capital assets**.

Even further away from the support offered by institutions are distance-learning students, who are studying either through correspondence or via Internet links, and have less frequent contact with their teachers because they are directing their own study pace. Their supervision is usually part of the workload of full-time lecturers, although it may be contracted out to part-time specialists. In any case, these students need to maintain regular tutor contact as their link with the institution. Distance-learning courses should be subject to the institution's normal quality-assurance procedures. The workload of staff who supervise such students is calculated differently from that of the staff who teach regular classes (see Unit 9.2: Managing staff resources).

The special needs of off-site students

A VET institution should make adequate provision for the needs of off-site students in the following areas:

☐ policies, implementation plans and actual provision of student service delivery;

☐ clearly defined contacts for service; easy access to up-to-date course and career information and essential learning equipment and materials;

☐ the staff and resources allocated to coordinate off-site delivery and learning and support service delivery;

☐ a comprehensive induction into courses and information to familiarize students with all aspects of the institution and all the services available;

☐ appropriate communication between the VET provider and student and between students, for example by newsletters and a student network support;

☐ feedback-providing opportunities to enable programmes and student service delivery to be evaluated;

☐ adequate training and technical support in the techniques used for on-line learning;

☐ clear guidelines on all course requirements and schedules, especially weekly commitments and assessment tasks;

☐ advice on the practical difficulties of learning off-site and what is needed to manage those challenges successfully.

The most important challenge facing off-site students is developing a good level of personal exchange between teacher and student. There should be protocols that encourage regular communications and opportunities to meet face to face, either on- or off-campus.

The special needs of staff

Instructional staff need to have appropriate professional development to acquire the skills necessary to deliver training in this way. For instance, using the workplace as a primary learning site suggests a significant change in the way teachers view learning and its relationship to work. Understanding the nuances of work relationships in industries and enterprises and reflecting that in the learning materials are important. Utilizing the workplace as a useful learning resource is also beneficial.

The design of courses delivered at a distance is a specialist skill. Although VET providers may be able to buy some of the commercially produced materials to use with their students, the materials may need to be produced or adapted in-house, which may be undertaken as part of a specially funded project. Such projects may be implemented collaboratively with other providers or with a VET professional association, with staff released from their regular teaching work to compile them. This is particularly true for courses delivered through what is now referred to as a virtual learning environment (VLE).

The virtual learning environment

A VLE uses certain features of information and learning technology (ILT) such as making content available electronically, using email and discussion groups, having online assessment, and so on, and combines them into one piece of software and one integrated environment, all the features of which may currently be used separately. Therefore, when setting up a VLE careful technical decisions need to be made about equipment location and networking, software purchases, systems management and trouble-shooting. Teaching staff can perform very different roles, whether in the design of materials or in student supervision by email and Internet discussion groups. It is important that technical staff work closely with teachers, so that the purposes of such learning are not forgotten. Some very different management skills will be required in the new learning environments.

As well as variations in the contracting arrangements for staff working with distance or self-directed students, these courses of study will have different budgetary requirements. They cannot work on standard calculations of average class size and course length, so fee structures and costing formulae need to be adjusted.

For more details on the arrangements for managing off-site learning in different countries, go to **Unit 9.1: The organization of training delivery** on your CD-ROM.

Unit 9.2

MANAGING STAFF RESOURCES

The management of staff offers a range of challenges in the VET institution. It is important for the manager to negotiate mutually agreed work directions by providing leadership through setting clear goals for the staff and by using a strategic planning process. Staff need support to ensure that their individual goals in the delivering of VET are in accordance with the institution's strategic plan. These goals are best established within a framework of consultation. The manager can strengthen morale by being available to discuss issues of concern, by encouraging team-building activities and by giving staff recognition for their work.

For information on HRD and employment issues in VET institutions, refer to **Module 7: Staff management**.

For the VET provider as a whole, an important financial indicator is the percentage of income spent on staffing, as this is always the highest budget item. The less is spent on staff, the more money is available for investing in resources and other development. In some situations, the teaching load of a staff member in a specialist area may not warrant a full-time or full-year appointment. Accordingly, a member of the teaching staff may be appointed to a part-time position or to a fixed-term contract position of less than one year to suit the requirements of the course delivery. The indicator of FTE staff total may, in fact, be a combination of full-time posts, part-time teachers or those paid by the hour, which allows for greater flexibility in the use of the staffing budget.

Teaching load

The allocation of the teaching staff resources of a VET institution to its opera-tions involves making decisions on an appropriate teaching load for staff. These decisions should make reasonable provisions for:

☐ "student contact hours" (SCHs) or "student guided hours" – the time spent in the actual teaching and supervision of student learning (for instance in supervising distance learning);

☐ non-teaching time required for other necessary non-teaching duties;

☐ teacher time required for appropriate modes of delivery and an appropriate class size(s);

☐ staff leave and sickness.

SCHs or "student guided hours" is a measure of teacher load. It is also a measure of planning of training delivery and funding. The calculation of SCHs for planning and funding purposes is based on the following. Each training package or curriculum nominates the number of hours that an average student under normal conditions might be expected to take to demonstrate a particular competency or set of learning outcomes in a module or course. The calcula-tion of SCHs takes the predicted hours of training for a course within a year and multiples it by the benchmark class size.

The total number of SCHs is also commonly used as a measure of planning training delivery by an education and training course or a VET institution as a whole. The total number of SCHs is used as a principal parameter in the service and funding contracts signed by a VET institution and a government agency. The number of SCHs and funding rates per 1.0 SCH directly determine the amount of institutional funding to be allocated by the government.

Teaching load is also influenced by the requirements for and expectations of non-teaching time, for example whether teachers are expected to under-take curriculum development or applied research or are supposed to visit industries where their graduates may be employed. If teachers are supposed to be involved in a large number of non-teaching activities, then their SCHs should be reduced commensurately. Staff employed in management spine posts can expect to have considerably reduced teaching hours. Instructors who supervise practical work may have different terms and conditions from lecturing staff. This generally means that they may have higher numbers of SCHs.

Norms for appropriate teacher load expressed in SCHs vary among the VET systems of different countries but in general they decrease as the level (or complexity) of VET programmes increases. The notion of caseload allows a limit to be set for the number of students who might be supervised by a teacher, where students are required to make extensive use of learning centres and self-directed study. Generalizations are difficult but, in a number of countries, 20 teaching hours per week or 800 teaching hours per academic year is regarded as a substantial teaching load.

The teacher load in SCHs is customarily expressed as hours per day, hours per week and weeks per year. It may be included as the prescribed maxima in employment contracts, taking into account entitlements for annual leave and other provisions of employment, including professional development. Refer to **Unit 7.1: Staff selection, recruitment and appointment**.

Another measure of teaching load is the "equivalent full-time student" (EFTS). It is the workload undertaken by a VET institution to train a student in a full-time course for a full year. Different courses of different durations will deliver different numbers of EFTS. Accordingly, delivery of EFTS can be assigned to teachers as their workload.

Allocation of teacher load will take account of the ratio of full-time equivalent (FTE) staff to the number of EFTSs, an average time taught per year as a basis for calculating EFTS, and an agreed average class size. The description of distance learning and self-directed study (refer to **Section 9.1.2**) showed that this calculation cannot be very exact in some cases.

EFTS is also used as a planning and funding indicator. An institution may commonly plan the number of enrolled students as well as the number of EFTSs to be delivered. Obviously a full-year course will require more resources than a one-week course. Accordingly, an output of 1.00 EFTS delivered for courses in particular education and training fields and at different qualification levels will require different resources and will attract different funding rates. Therefore, 1.00 EFTS is also a "funding category" on which basis the resource allocation for VET providers may be arranged. The planning indicators and definitions of full-time and full year training are determined by the national VET funding agencies.

A measure of the FTE teacher will vary according to the terms applied by each VET provider. In principle, it is the number of hours taught, divided by the teacher standard contracted hours per year.

On the planning of training, refer to **Unit 4.1: Supply and demand factors in planning for training delivery**.

Non-teaching time should make adequate provisions for the following activities:

- preparing for the delivery of lectures, demonstrations, practical experiences, and so forth;

- the marking and assessment of student work subsequent to training delivery;

- professional development, industrial refresher leave, and so on;

- meeting with students, graduates and the industries where they are/may be employed;

- course and curriculum development and maintenance responsibilities (if any);
- applied research responsibilities (if any), and so on.

The appropriate modes of delivery may include:

- lectures – generally applicable to the delivery of the more theoretical components of VET;
- tutorials – generally involving smaller groups (or one-to-one teaching) and allowing greater interaction between teacher and student(s);
- practical work undertaken in workshops and laboratories, and so forth;
- clinical training undertaken in health centres, and so forth;
- self-directed study – the teacher's involvement is limited to initiating study, providing guidance as required and assessing learning outcomes;
- supervisory work – applicable to undergraduate research.

Student-to-staff ratio

An appropriate class size(s) depends substantially on the mode of delivery and may range from: several hundred students accommodated in a large lecture theatre; a few tens of students in entry-level tutorials, workshops and laboratories; less than ten students in advanced-level tutorials, workshops and laboratories; to the supervision of one or two students doing research degrees.

The appropriate student-to-staff ratio for a course, department, or a whole VET institution will vary among the VET systems of different countries but in general – as for SCHs – they decrease as the level (or complexity) of VET programmes increases.

The desired quality of training delivery is also an important consideration in determining appropriate student-to-staff ratios. Individual students have enhanced access to teaching staff as student-to-staff ratios are reduced and, in principle, the quality of learning is also enhanced. However, the relationship is non-linear, that is, beyond a limit, committing additional teaching staff to a training course has no effect on its quality. Evidence suggests that the quality of the teacher is more important for learning outcomes than the student-to-staff ratio: for example a single quality teacher of 40 students may achieve better learning outcomes than two inferior teachers with classes of 20 students each.

However, trying to achieve efficiency gains (that is, achieving more teaching for the same cost or the same teaching for less cost) by increasing student-to-staff ratios becomes counter-productive when the concomitant reduction in quality becomes unacceptable. Some countries have attempted to achieve efficiency gains by increasing student-to-staff ratios to offset the increasing cost as a result of mass participation in post-school education (VET, higher education). This understandable response to the fiscal challenge of mass participation has undoubtedly reduced the quality of post-school education.

Generalizations are difficult but, in a number of countries, a student-to-staff ratio of around nine to 20, averaging around 15, is common. This figure is only a crude average and depends quite substantially on the ratio of practical-to-general/theoretical content of the training courses in question.

Arrangements for support staff are generally dictated by the provisions for teaching staff and generally include workshop technicians, laboratory assistants and other support. They may be allocated to a particular teaching space – a workshop or laboratory – rather than to a particular member of the teaching staff.

The level of provision of support staff can be generalized across departments and whole VET institutions as a support-to-teaching staff ratio. Norms for the level of provision vary from country to country but in general increase as the level (or complexity) of VET increases. Generalizations are difficult but, in a number of countries, one support staff for every two to four teaching staff is regarded as adequate provision.

Provisions for staff leave and sickness

The allocation of the teaching staff resources of a VET institution to its training operations should also make reasonable provisions for staff leave and sickness. The consequences of staff leave are predictable, since provisions are generally included in staff employment contracts (refer to **Unit 7.1: Staff selection, recruitment and appointment**). The consequences of staff sickness are less predictable but can be minimized by:

☐ ensuring that there is an appropriate level of redundancy in the number of teaching staff to cover expected absences through sickness;

☐ maintaining flexibility in timetabling arrangements (see below), which enables classes to be deferred if necessary to allow teachers to recover;

☐ using contracted part-time relief teachers (often retired teachers who are prepared to undertake teaching of short duration at short notice).

Timetabling

Timetabling is a critical factor in the effective allocation of teaching and support staff resources to training delivery, and is necessary to optimize the scheduling of training delivery to minimize possible clashes concerning:

☐ the double occupancy of a teaching space;

☐ the dual use of an essential piece of equipment;

- a teacher delivering different components of a course(s) simultaneously;
- a student attending different components of a course(s) simultaneously.

The standard components of management information systems (MISs) operating in autonomous VET institutions in many jurisdictions generally include:

- a student management package – enrolments, passes, credits, qualifications awarded, and so forth;
- an accounting package – financial management, budgeting and asset registers;
- a payroll package;
- facilities management – maintenance, stock control;
- a timetabling package – optimizes timing of course delivery to minimize clashes;
- communications – private automatic branch exchange (PABX) and voice mail;
- IT – email, Internet, and so on;
- a library package – an inventory of holdings, issues, returns, overdues.

With the exception of the student management package, most if not all of the packages listed above will have applications outside autonomous VET institutions and so are likely to be commercially available.

For details on the timetabling packages of a VET institution's MIS, refer to **Unit 3.5: The VET institution's management information system**.

Programme managers who are responsible for resource planning and monitoring will plan timetables and deploy staff according to a given unit of hours of equivalent contact time per year per full-time member of staff. It is generally expected that staff will exercise some flexibility over their deployment, to meet fluctuations in demand or to provide cover for absent colleagues. As professional staff, teachers are not generally expected to be too rigid in their interpretations of their contracts, but neither should managers demand too much.

Professional judgements have to be made by VET institution managers about the target average class size for particular courses. A lecture-based course that can be economically delivered to a large group of students offsets the high costs of courses where small class sizes are necessary, for instance where students have learning difficulties or where a high level of one-to-one supervision is needed, for instance in teacher training. Workshop classes using machines may be limited in size on safety grounds. Where technical staff are available to assist teachers with supervision, numbers can be higher, space permitting.

Where courses run continuously over the year or where there are large numbers of distance-learning students, overlapping schedules of staff have to be drawn up to ensure that students have continuity of contact. Resource management is highly dependent on computerized MISs, which provide links between student enrolment and attendance, staff timetables, course timetables and monitoring data in the form of reports to managers. Each programme area or department is a cost centre whose manager is responsible for achieving financial targets and balancing budgets for staff and other resources across a range of courses.

For details on MISs, refer to **Unit 3.5: The VET institution's management information system**.

These systems mean that FTE staff posts can be linked to target student numbers, and that comparisons can be made between the staff/student ratios of each department. Providers may use commercial software packages approved by the funding bodies to manage staff deployment and related information. A managed learning environment (MLE) system refers to the whole range of information and processes that support learning and the management of learning within an institution. The use of such systems has important implications for the updating and contracting of teaching and technical staff.

For more details on managing staff resources in autonomous VET institutions in different countries, go to **Unit 9.2: Managing staff resources** on your CD-ROM.

Unit 9.3

MANAGING CAPITAL ASSETS

9.3.1 THE LAYOUT OF INSTITUTIONAL BUILDINGS

The direction for capital development

VET institutions need to be flexible, adaptable and able to accommodate changes in the demand for skills. Although the layout and design of educational buildings is a job for an educational architect, professional teaching staff also need to be involved at a very early stage. Buildings support the work of teachers, and the needs of the education and training process are paramount. For a new building, projections of the total size of the institution, together with the spread of its curriculum and requirements for specialist teaching space, are necessary. In view of the speed of educational change and the likely impact of new learning technologies, the maximum flexibility over the use of space is needed.

The provision of new VET facilities should be linked to the government's VET strategies. Some countries have planning frameworks, sometimes called strategic asset management (SAM) plans, which cover all aspects of the acquisition, maintenance, operation and disposal of their VET assets.

When a VET system is being developed, the management of the physical resources of the public training providers is normally undertaken by an agent acting on behalf of the government, such as a department of state or a funding body. Central intervention and direction by the agent is necessary until adequate capacities and systems are in place at the institutional level. These management capacities and systems are necessary prerequisites for institutional autonomy.

The government agent may determine the direction for the capital development programme as well as the requirements for the operation and maintenance of individual VET institutions. In implementing capital development, the central agency is often guided by a set of norms or standards that take into account training fields/levels, staffing and delivery objectives, and include norms for the allocation of teaching and non-teaching areas in VET providers (refer to **Section 9.3.2: Managing teaching spaces** below).

In some developed VET systems, capital funding may form part of an undifferentiated bulk funding allocated to each autonomous VET provider, generally based on measures of outputs (for example the number of EFTS enrolments, course completions, or graduations). This capital funding is provided, along with recurrent operational funding, to meet the input costs of training delivery by the VET institution. In some other VET systems, the central funding agency retains control over capital works programmes across the VET sector, while the providers have complete autonomy in the use of their operational funding.

The transition from a centrally managed system to a system of self-governing VET institutions resourced through an output-based funding system requires carefully phased implementation and should be managed centrally in accordance with a well-developed policy and a robust accountability framework.

For details on output-based funding, refer to **Unit 5.1: Efficient, effective and equitable funding mechanisms**.

The development of VET assets should also take account of the VET institution's size and training delivery profiles. The experience of a number of countries shows that efficiency is best achieved in a VET system in which there are fewer but larger institutions. Economies of scale are difficult to achieve with large numbers of small VET providers.

A number of countries are also finding it beneficial to merge small monotechnic institutions into larger VET institutions that offer more comprehensive education and training provision. A flexible response to changing labour market needs and the effective use of buildings and equipment is difficult to achieve in an institution that serves only a single labour market or a limited group of trades. VET institutions that have a wide subject base also have pedagogical benefits.

In the short term, closing down all existing VET facilities and regrouping them onto single independent sites is not a feasible option. However, small VET institutions can be brought together administratively as larger multi-campus institutions, pending the possibility of consolidation on fewer sites as opportunities arise.

Space areas

The facilities for institutions that deliver tertiary education – including higher education and VET – usually provide for most or all of the following:

☐ a common teaching space – for example lecture theatres, classrooms, seminar or tutorial rooms, common-use computer learning rooms and some parts of modern learning centres;

☐ specialized teaching space – for example science and language laboratories, technical workshops, nursing suites, computer science laboratories;

- information services – for example libraries, resources centres, computer centres, project rooms and communications hub;

- staff accommodation – for example offices for teaching and support staff and department/faculty/institutional administration;

- staff and student services – for example common rooms, food services, health and career services, sports and recreation facilities, cultural and community facilities;

- residential accommodation – accommodation for students and/or staff as well as management.

The following types of teaching areas all have different space requirements, which may mean that different courses need different-sized classrooms, or that class sizes will vary with the discipline:

General teaching
- Lecture theatre (or close seating arrangements)

- Teaching of informal groups

- Teaching with demonstration facilities

Specialized teaching
- Commerce and business (computer terminal rooms)

- Science and technology (laboratories)

- Art and design studios (other than for large-scale work) and drawing offices

- Crafts, large-scale art and design, home economics, dressmaking, carpentry, plumbing (workshops with benches)

- Catering and hairdressing

- Welding, motor vehicle work, metal trades, installation trades (with large machines).

Design and construction projects

As the demand for tertiary education at all levels has been rising, so too has the demand for adequate and functional facilities. Adapting existing facilities to allow them to meet strategic demands more effectively may be more practicable than embarking on the construction of new specialist facilities. Where new VET facilities are necessary, their design should allow maximum flexibility.

In order to develop existing space, VET institutions must justify to their funding body why new developments are necessary. The funding body may be the government or a non-governmental agency, or it may be a bank that is providing most of the capital. To assess how much space development is required, VET institutions must derive their requirements for classrooms and facilities from their projected enrolments and curriculum needs and compare them with those currently available so that they can identify areas of over-supply or shortage.

A strategic view of accommodation requirements should be planned well ahead, and kept up to date in parallel with the strategic plan. The VET pro-vider's property strategy should be based on a fundamental review of the institution's estate and provide a plan for its management and development. The strategy should offer clear direction for a period of at least three to five years in advance.

For publicly funded VET institutions, there are usually some national guide-lines and norms for the space requirements for general teaching, practical workshops and library/private study space. If not, they need to be developed in order to provide consistent guidelines to planners. Space norms for prac-tical workshops may vary according to the subjects taught. Business studies offices, engineering workshops, and art and design studios, for example, all have different needs for space per student.

The calculations are based either on gross floor space, divided by the number of EFTSs or the required number of workspaces at any one time. In addition, there is a fixed percentage for administration (about 9 per cent), as adminis-tration requirements do not markedly increase as student numbers rise. Space for circulation, storage, recreation and canteen/restaurant facilities are also needed, in broad proportion to the daily student population.

The use of space should be as efficient as possible, both in terms of utili-zation over the course of a day, week and year, and in terms of designs that do not waste space on unnecessary circulation. Unused space still has to be maintained, heated or cooled, and cleaned.

Agreed criteria can be used to judge the effectiveness of a VET building project proposal and the likelihood of the project being successfully completed. General criteria are that:

☐ the building meets clearly documented objectives related to the delivery of VET programmes;

☐ the building is effective in its planned use of space and will be flexible and adaptable throughout its projected life;

☐ the project represents good value for money in terms of the necessary capital investment, and the building is worth at least what it costs;

☐ new facilities are designed so that they have a lower cost in use over their whole lifetime than the existing ones;

☐ sustainability and environmental matters have been considered (there is no unnecessary consumption of materials, and energy costs are low);

- the project can be brought forward reasonably quickly, the construction is economic, with few financial or other risks;

- the new building should make an appropriate architectural contribution to the VET provider's main assets, the locality and the community within which it operates;

- the new buildings should inspire people to participate in education and training, and should be appealing to all their users;

- VET environments must conform to industry standards in occupational health and safety and building codes.

For details on the layout and norms of VET institutional buildings in different countries, go to **Unit 9.3: Managing capital assets** on your CD-ROM.

9.3.2 MANAGING TEACHING SPACES

Central oversight of capital assets

In a developing VET system, the government agent responsible for the management of the physical resources of institutions should have systems and processes in place that allow all the physical resources to be overseen. Establishing a dedicated capital works directorate (or equivalent) would facilitate this in the medium term.

As the VET institutions develop their own management systems and capacities required for enhanced autonomy, the role of the capital works directorate should progressively change from planning and implementing capital works programmes to monitoring the performance of institutions in managing and developing their own facilities. Monitoring is necessary to protect the government's ownership interests.

For details on the government's funding and ownership interests, refer to **Unit 5.1: Efficient, effective and equitable funding mechanisms**.

The governing councils and the management of autonomous VET institutions will eventually take over the responsibility for the planning and implementation of capital works programmes. In VET systems where this responsibility is devolved, each autonomous training provider will need to have its own capital works directorate (or equivalent) within its management structure.

The functions of a capital works directorate – whether centralized or devolved – include the compilation of a comprehensive database of all the facilities used by the system or institution. The following information should be available for all physical assets and infrastructure:

- a unique building identifier;

- □ the gross floor area (in m^2);
- □ the net or usable area (in m^2);
- □ the date of completion/age of building;
- □ current replacement value (updated annually);
- □ annual operating costs per m^2 gross floor area (updated annually);
- □ information on the condition of the asset, for example "a facility condition index";
- □ a schedule and current value of deferred maintenance;
- □ a schedule of functional deficiencies and the current value of required refurbishment/upgrade costs.

This information should be gathered through a structured facilities audit. To obtain a copy of guidelines for a facility audit developed by the Tertiary Education Facilities Management Association (TEFMA) of Australasia, refer to "**Guidelines for strategic asset management. How to undertake a facilities audit. AAPPA. 2000. 24pp.**" on your CD-ROM (see "Resource Documents").

A space inventory generated by a facilities audit enables a capital works department to develop a space planning system, which provides estimates for the space requirements of any institutional function or teaching programme. It is based on a system of accepted space norms, which depend on the field/level of training and on the actual use of the facility; these norms form the essential basis of a space planning and management system.

Examples of space norms applicable to VET institutions are available from Australia, Canada, New Zealand, the United Kingdom and the United States. For a copy of the guidelines for space planning developed by the TEFMA of Australasia, refer to "**Space planning guidelines. AAPPA. 2nd Edition. 29pp.**" on your CD-ROM (see "Resource Documents").

The facilities department of a VET provider will oversee the management of accommodation and equipment but it will also receive a great deal of input from the teaching departments, who will identify training-related needs. The facilities department is responsible for the general management of centrally managed teaching spaces, including repairs and maintenance, space management, audio visual services and refurbishment projects. At times, it may be necessary to hire additional teaching space, which may be undertaken through a leasing or purchasing arrangement.

The senior management group is responsible for identifying the needs of teaching facilities, seeking input from staff and students and making recommendations on such matters as priorities for upgrading centrally managed spaces and developing policy and guidelines for the management of facilities. These senior managers will also monitor the usage of accommodation and equipment in order to maximize their resources and identify training areas that are growing or in decline. Space utilization and efficiency benchmarks will be used.

The efficient use of facilities

The building and running of VET institutional facilities account for a substantial part of public training expenditure. The planning and design of institutional facilities have an impact on the training outcomes, which is significant but hard to quantify.

The efficient use of physical facilities is essential if VET institutions are to cater for rising student intakes. An important step in this process is to rationalize the number of institutions and review the VET delivery profile as outlined in Section 9.3.1 above. Bringing more students together on a single campus increases the scope for the more efficient use of capital assets.

First, an important prerequisite is to encourage the concept of institutional rather than school or faculty ownership in the culture of the VET institution. Accordingly, general-purpose lecture theatres, classrooms and laboratories should not be owned by or dedicated to the use of a single section or department.

This requires that all lecture theatres, classrooms, seminar rooms and other common teaching areas are pooled as a common resource. A central computerized timetabling system should apply across the VET campus. The system may include procedures, exclusions, preferences and similar caveats. All bids by sections, departments and faculties/schools for teaching space can be allocated space and time according to the timetabling system's rules.

The same principles apply to specialist teaching areas, such as workshops, laboratories, computer teaching rooms and clinical training suites. Nevertheless, some specialist facilities/workshops may need to be managed by the specialist staff who use and maintain them. The challenge, however, is to design multipurpose teaching spaces, so that they are not left empty when not being used by specialist groups of students.

Second, those designing timetables need to match teaching group size to room capacity, and the timing of teaching, so that all available spaces are efficiently used. Agreed space norms should provide some guidance on the relationship between teaching space, numbers of students and timetabled hours of study. These should take into account daytime and evening study; the range of timetabled hours used on different courses in the VET institution, their distribution over the year and the type of curriculum offered as well as the type of students. For instance, postgraduate and high-fee employed students may well expect better-quality accommodation than 16-year-olds. Part of the space calculation may be to consider which courses might be offered outside the main building.

The following issues are important when planning and timetabling courses:

☐ the position of breaks in the day – simultaneous or staggered. Some VET institutions like to plan lunch breaks so that all students are free to join in leisure activities, but this results in many empty classrooms.

☐ day starting and finishing times – an early afternoon finish is a waste of classroom space;

☐ the programming of "twilight" (late afternoon) and evening classes;

☐ the timetabling of examinations, which require large spaces to be vacated for long periods in the summer term, disrupting other teaching programmes.

The non-availability of space is a constraint on the efficient use of specialist teachers, and vice versa, so space requirements need to be carefully considered alongside staffing and curriculum requirements.

A central computerized timetabling system can increase the efficient use of accommodation. Such systems are commercially available and can be operated in conjunction with other components of a VET institution's MIS. For details on other components, refer to **Unit 3.5: The VET institution's management information system** and **Unit 9.2: Managing staff resources**.

For instance, experience in Australia and New Zealand indicates that common teaching areas provided at the rate of 1 m^2 per 1.0 EFTS can achieve occupancy rates of 65 per cent over a 40-hour week if allocated by a central computerized timetabling system.

Computerized space management systems can be helpful in a large institution as they are reputed to deal effectively with about 95 per cent of the task, leaving only about 5 per cent that needs to be managed to take account of staff and student personal requirements.

Third, apart from common and specialist teaching areas, a considerable amount of space may be used for student-managed learning. In some countries, VET providers are recommended to have at least 9 per cent of the total floor space devoted to learning resource centres, and up to a maximum of 17 per cent of space. This has shifted the space requirements for most VET providers. Such space may be flexibly used for both teaching and self-directed learning.

Library requirements are also governed by space standards, depending on the amount of private-space study time or research requirements.

For day-release groups of employed students, private study requirements may be less or they may need to study at home. Workspace or an agreed square metre size should be provided for each student estimated to need the library at any one time. There is never likely to be enough of this space. Moreover, the change in study patterns created by the rapid development of learning technology is such that the space requirements for personal study have also changed.

"Supporting space", that is, the space not used directly for teaching, is likely to be around 40 per cent of the total area. This typically comprises 15 per cent for administration, catering and communal areas, and so on, and 25 per cent for balance (corridors, foyers, WCs, central storage, and so on).

The provision of adjacent equipment bays – and mobile cabinets used to store specialized equipment that can be brought out when needed – can facilitate the creation of multifunctional spaces. A central computerized timetabling system can also be applied to such spaces, ensuring that adequate time for reconfiguring, setting-up and cleaning is programmed into the timetable. Savings can be accrued through a more effective use of what are usually the most expensive spaces in a VET institution.

Room utilization surveys should be conducted from time to time to assess the overall efficiency with which the VET provider is using its space and the degree to which managers are maximizing their resources. Such a survey usually takes place over a typical teaching week, and each room is visited every hour for that week, and the number of students present in each space recorded. Based on this sample, demands for increased space can be assessed and the present level of space wastage calculated. Efficiency of space usage can be dramatically increased by regular room utilization surveys, and managers held accountable for their use of this expensive resource.

For more details on managing teaching spaces in autonomous VET institutions in different countries, go to **Unit 9.3: Managing capital assets** on your CD-ROM.

9.3.3 MANAGING EQUIPMENT AND LEARNING TECHNOLOGIES

Teaching aids

The effective delivery of VET requires that providers not only have adequate teaching space but also adequate teaching aids and a proper range of equipment. Various traditional and newer teaching aids that enhance teacher-centred learning include:

☐ simple photocopied handouts;

☐ wall-charts, blackboards, whiteboards, laser pointers, and so forth;

☐ overhead projectors (for the projection of slides and transparencies);

☐ video projectors linked to video recorders (to allow videotape presentations, and so forth);

☐ video projectors linked to personal computers (PCs) (to allow the presentation of computer-based learning materials, and so forth);

☐ databases and computer-based self-learning materials.

The most common new piece of equipment in VET institutions in recent years has undoubtedly been the desktop computer. Computer resource rooms that contain sets of stand-alone or networked desktop computers that allow individual – or at least small group – access to a single keyboard and screen have become the norm.

Teaching equipment and desktop computers in particular have a short life, whether this is because of heavy use or rapid obsolescence. Their rapid depreciation – particularly in comparison with the depreciation of fixed assets such as buildings – needs to be taken into account in financial planning to allow for new purchases. Carrying out routine maintenance as a practical component of a training course on equipment maintenance could help to reduce the costs of maintaining and repairing teaching equipment.

For details on making provisions for depreciation, see **Unit 5.4: Managing assets and revenue**.

Specialist equipment

The equipment in specialist science laboratories and technical workshops is intended to simulate vocational settings and introduce students to the practical skills and competencies that they might need when employed in the workplace.

In order to improve the efficiency of specialist teaching areas, it is important to address the mix of training equipment and numbers of units of equipment. Some VET providers have large numbers of the same kind of equipment in their workshops, such as, for instance, many turning and milling lathes. These are large machines that occupy most of the workshop space and can only be used for training students in one single metal trade. The implications of such an approach are that the VET provider limits its capabilities to diversify training programmes and respond flexibly to the demand for courses.

An alternative approach is that workshops accommodate different types of equipment or multifunctional equipment that permits students to be trained in a larger variety of trades, depending on the demand for them; the same item of equipment may become available for different VET courses. Savings can, therefore, be made, because it is no longer necessary to build and maintain what is usually the most expensive space in a VET institution; savings can also be made in the purchase, maintenance and replacement of specialist VET equipment. Computer workshops and laboratories applying the same hardware but different types of software can be used to deliver almost a dozen different VET courses, such as CAD/CAM, design and architecture, software writing, Internet-related courses, and so on.

As noted in **Section 9.3.2**, the provision of adjacent equipment bays and mobile cabinets in workshops can facilitate the creation of multifunctional spaces. This is a strategy that enhances the efficient use of workshops and laboratories by enabling different combinations of VET courses and/or different types of equipment to be used in the same teaching space.

A trend away from teacher-centred learning towards student-centred learning has resulted in the emergence of new forms of learning environment. A learning centre approach builds on traditional teaching environments such as classrooms, seminar rooms and computer resource rooms and combines them with the provision of information services. The juxtaposition of traditional teaching environments with resource facilities such as libraries, Internet access and facilities that encourage group work (project rooms, general-access computer facilities) has shifted the emphasis from assimilation or rote learning to learning through doing and problem-solving.

The provision of information services in a VET institution is akin to providing a gateway for both staff and students to be able to search for and obtain information. A learning centre should be more than just the holding of books in a library or the provision of sets of desktop computers for individual student use. The information services centre, as many libraries are now known, serves as a communications and data hub for the campus.

Often, the information services centre is responsible for the VET institution's MIS and is also the physical location of hardware that provides the network and computing capabilities of the institution. In smaller VET providers, all these services should be located in a single unit to achieve desired economies. Although a degree of disaggregation is feasible in larger VET institutions, the collocation of hardware is still desirable in order to minimize back-up, support facilities and give technical support.

A particular challenge is presented by the speed of change in new ICTs. Many VET institutions have made changes to their approaches to teaching and learning as they have increased the availability of ICTs and other electronic resources (e-learning). As a consequence, staff need to acquire new skills (and so need support), courses and classrooms need to be redesigned, and students' expectations also change. Some staff become very enthusiastic about particular developments in learning technology and their potential application. Such enthusiasms need to be managed to find the right balance between encouragement, visionary management and the avoidance of wasted time and other resources.

For instance, at the time of writing, a number of teachers were exploring the potential of "m-learning", through the use of mobile and hand-held IT devices, such as palmtop computers, mobile phones, laptops and tablet PCs, in teaching and learning. This could either be a short-lived fashion or it could herald the start of some powerful changes in teaching and learning methods.

For more details on MISs, go to **Unit 3.5: The VET institution's management information system**.

Modern learning technologies

There are a number of new terms that are applied to technology in education. Since they are often used in definitions of e-learning, it is helpful to take a closer look at them as well as at current definitions of e-learning.

IT

IT is used most commonly to refer to the key components of computing technology: the software, hardware and the skills required to use a stand-alone computer or laptop effectively, for instance to produce handouts or worksheets.

ICT

In further education ICT commonly refers to the extra dimension afforded by networking computers to allow the communication of information via email, shared access to databases and software and MISs, which link together the business aspects of the education and training provider. In this sense, ICT covers the use of technology to communicate both within and between organizations.

However, in schools and higher education sectors, ICT is used in a broader sense to cover a full range of activities associated with both learning and running the core business of providers of education and training, in the same way that ILT (see below) is used in the further education sector.

ILT

The term ILT is also used in further education to refer to the application of IT and ICT in the running of the core business of the institution – learning and teaching, the management of information and business systems and resources to enable successful learning.

E-learning

This term is defined as:

☐ a spectrum ranging from Internet-supported distance learning in which the learner has limited physical contact with a tutor or other learners, to teacher-led, classroom-based activity involving occasional computer-delivered or facilitated assignments; or

☐ learning with the help of ICT tools; or

☐ any form of learning that uses ICTs. The learner could be a pre-school child playing an interactive game; a group of students collaborating on a learning project via the Internet; a student watching an animated learning material on the maintenance of air conditioners – they all qualify as a form of e-learning.

Management arrangements

Learning technologies require capital investment, technical support, curriculum planning and clear overall management. Learning technologies are typically the responsibility of the senior manager for curriculum, together with the institution's staff development team, learning support staff and technical staff. These responsibilities may include purchasing new equipment and training in its use, or a particular approach to an aspect of study, such as common or generic skills, which requires a team approach to teaching. Some developments are the result of individual enthusiasms, but these need to be harnessed into strategically relevant changes which benefit the maximum number of students and staff colleagues.

Capital investment can only be made from planned resources in the VET institution. Equipment purchases are generally made from the income earned by autonomous VET providers, although there may be specialist grants from government or industry to support particular programmes. Institutions must manage equipment purchases and updating through their regular management processes. Items above a certain cost are generally approved for purchase by senior staff, and should be part of a planned programme of investment in, and replacement of, equipment.

Technical support is multifaceted. It involves the management of purchases and support services; problem management; staff training; software development and support; access and availability; and network management. Often, technical support staff have very good specialist knowledge about the procurement, management and maintenance of specialist equipment. Their skills need updating as much as teachers' skills do.

As with the planning of buildings, learning technology should efficiently support the planned curriculum. There is no point in acquiring interesting pieces of equipment if the curriculum does not require it. Equally, it may be more cost-effective to lease an infrequently used piece of equipment from an employer or to arrange for students to have a demonstration from a manufacturer. In general, though, students should not be training on outdated equipment, and the training environment should compare well with the students' present or future workplace.

For more details on managing equipment and learning technologies in autonomous VET institutions in different countries, go to **Unit 9.3: Managing capital assets** on your CD-ROM.

Unit 9.4

MONITORING COURSE PROGRESS AND OUTPUTS

9.4.1 MONITORING TEACHING

Teaching cannot be separated from learning. Teachers are being effective if their students are learning. However, although teaching can be observed, generally it is only the outcomes of learning that can be observed. It can be useful for VET managers to carry out teacher observation in order to gain a snapshot of the teaching skills and effectiveness of their staff, but this needs to be combined with an examination of student work. The aims of such observations should be made very clear to the staff, and negotiated with the teachers' trade union or professional association. Such aims might include:

☐ gathering evidence for teachers' annual appraisals;

☐ assessing the effectiveness of a new course;

☐ gathering evidence for newly appointed teachers in their probationary period;

☐ offering support to a newly qualified teacher;

☐ obtaining judgements on the quality of teaching in the VET institution as a whole, to provide evidence for managers or for an external organization;

☐ carrying out routine quality assurance on courses or departments.

Some of these aims may conflict with each other, that is why it is important that the objectives of the observations be clarified at the outset. Observations may be conducted by:

☐ senior staff only;

☐ line managers;

☐ a trained team of observers, working across VET institutions;

☐ groups of professional peers;

☐ specially contracted independent consultants.

Observations should take into account course and lesson plans as well as some student work. The observer may wish to talk to students about the lesson. The fundamental questions to be asked during an observation are: "Was the lesson consistent with course requirements and the planned outcomes? Were the students learning?" Following the observation, the teacher should be given feedback, and a written record may be made of the conclusions.

Some VET institutions use student questionnaires to obtain students' views about their courses, about the teaching and sometimes about the teachers. This is a sensitive area, and needs to be managed with care, but students are the customers, and their views are relevant to judgements about teaching staff competence.

Course managers should keep a course file with all the relevant data about the course and its requirements. The file should also contain copies of course plans and staff work records. Such a record should enable managers to judge the progress of courses against plans, and to make any necessary changes quite rapidly. Careful record keeping also means that if there need to be changes in staffing, for instance as a result of illness, the course can progress smoothly, without interruption or repetition.

The internal monitoring of teaching may be more appropriate for a devolved VET system, because autonomy for a training institution generally includes the authority for self-assessment of its teaching staff – usually subject to periodic external audits of its monitoring processes.

For details on staff performance appraisal, refer to **Unit 7.4: Staff performance appraisal and promotion**.

In some VET systems, publicly funded training providers are supposed to follow the quality guidelines monitored by a national training authority. In this case, the delivery of training and the competence of teachers will be audited as part of the compliance process. The teaching audit process will involve the availability of mentoring for new teaching staff and the provision of advice and direction on instructional approaches. It will also examine the role of course coordinators in monitoring teaching and compliance with curriculum as well as the assurance that all staff utilize the best teaching resources. The audit process may also canvass views from students on teaching and teachers. They might be asked questions on their teachers':

☐ technical competence of the training subject matter;

☐ use of appropriate learning and teaching methods and materials;

☐ organizational skills; and

☐ presentation and communication skills.

Monitoring the course delivery for compliance with the curriculum is intended to ensure that what teachers actually teach is consistent with what they are expected to teach: the prescribed curriculum. Although compliance monitoring can be viewed as a commendable objective, there are arguments against the practice. For example:

☐ the interpretation of a curriculum has a degree of subjectivity;

☐ overzealous insistence on adherence to a curriculum may suppress innovative approaches to teaching delivery;

☐ monitoring reinforces a teacher-centred approach to learning (for example teachers who encourage student-centred learning could be perceived to be not teaching to the curriculum).

Accordingly, greater attention could be given to monitoring student progress and learning outputs/outcomes. Refer to **Section 9.4.2** below for details on monitoring student progress.

For more details on arrangements for monitoring teaching in different countries, go to **Unit 9.4: Monitoring course progress and outputs** on your CD-ROM.

9.4.2 MONITORING STUDENT PROGRESS AND OUTPUTS

Progress monitoring

A VET institution will have procedures in place for monitoring the progress of its students. This will allow the early identification of students who are not coping and who are at risk of failing or dropping out.

Students should be supported by a number of formal and informal structures and processes that assist in their progress, involving:

☐ teachers and peers and their effective relationships with students;

☐ VET institution's units: study support, welfare, library staff; disability support, and so on;

☐ the moderation of assessment items by teachers and the validation of assessment processes and tools with industry representatives;

☐ equal opportunity and anti-discrimination regulations; appeals and grievances procedures.

Teachers can monitor the progress of students by ensuring that they have adequate opportunity to provide feedback to the staff on any issue of concern. This can be achieved through group discussions at the end of each course element, through the application of structured midcourse questionnaires, or through other mechanisms such as a pinboard, where participants can write up and display their comments about the progress of a course.

Students should have a clear understanding of how their progress through the course as well as the overall outcome for the course will be assessed. Monitoring of the learning progress may be carried out through regular assessments, which in general fall into two categories:

(1) norm-referenced assessment through class tests and assignments. Ranking offers an indirect measure of the desired skills and competencies that the training course is intended to provide, but determining the overall course outcome (that is, whether a student is assessed as having passed or failed) is problematic;

(2) standards-based assessment, which provides direct confirmation that students have acquired (that is, passed the course) or have not acquired (that is, failed the course) the desired skills and competencies, but meaningful ranking of student performance is problematic.

Records kept of this monitoring will show the pattern of achievement by individual students over time, and ensure that they keep to the objectives and standards expected at different stages of the course. Personal or course tutors can intervene by providing guidance to individual students about how they can keep up with any problematic aspects of their studies.

The assessment of students undertaking practical components of VET courses off-campus may be accomplished by:

☐ contracting a suitable person already employed in the workplace to assess the VET institution's students;

☐ deploying designated institutional staff in the workplace;

☐ registered training assessors.

Employers' assessments of students may also be used to monitor progress. It is useful for learners to know that their employers and teachers are working together to ensure the development of skills and knowledge, and that each contributes to judgements of the students' competence. Some VET institutions also use employers to assist with assessments in the training institution, while other assessments may be conducted in the workplace. Agreement is needed on the standards to be applied in the recording and reporting requirements for such assessments; workplace supervisors also need training in assessment.

For details of monitoring learning progress in on-the-job training, refer to **Unit 9.1: The organization of training delivery**.

For details on monitoring the learning progress of students, refer to **Unit 6.2: Guiding and monitoring student progress**.

Measuring course outputs

Arguably, the monitoring of course outputs and outcomes provides the most informative data on the progress of a course. These data help to ensure that courses are relevant to future employment and training needs.

VET course outputs are the knowledge, skills and competencies and levels thereof acquired by its graduates. These outputs are somewhat intangible, variable and therefore difficult to measure. For reasons of simplicity, various proxies for knowledge, skills and competencies are used as measures of the outputs of VET providers. All these proxy measures have some limitations and often include:

☐ a measure of "equivalent full-time students" (EFTSs) or "student contact hours" (SCHs)/"student guided hours" of curriculum delivered;

☐ the student retention rate (the number of students staying on the course to the end as a measure of student motivation and satisfaction);

☐ the student graduation rate (the percentage of those retained who have been awarded the qualification) as well as the levels of qualifications acquired;

☐ measures of students' satisfaction.

EFTS is a better measure of student volume than course enrolments as it takes into account course length. However, it does not take into account students who fail to complete their courses or measure the number of students participating in short VET courses.

Course completions do not take into account those students who fail course assessments. Counting graduations as an output measure may also provide a perverse incentive for institutions to pass all their students, with a potentially adverse effect on quality. A better measure might be the percentage of those enrolled in the course who are awarded the qualification.

Student retention and graduation rates as well as the measures of EFTSs or SCHs are commonly utilized by VET providers keen on monitoring their course outputs.

Drop-out rates, determined from the differences between course enrolments and subsequent completions of the course, do not provide any information on why students have not completed the course. These can range from: inadequate pre-entry preparation; family circumstances (for example poverty); stringent assessment standards; or low course quality (for example inferior teaching, irrelevant curriculum). Further assessment is required, particularly of course quality, to interpret drop-out rates.

Measures of student satisfaction with a particular course can be derived from questionnaire surveys conducted by VET institutions, or independent market research organizations. Such surveys should be a regular part of course evaluation. VET course outputs are also measured in order to benchmark (that is, compare the rates of retention and success) a course against other groups in the same VET institution or elsewhere (through using data from qualification-awarding bodies or the funding agency).

For details on course quality monitoring and assessment, refer to **Module 10: Quality assurance in education and training**.

Measuring course outcomes

The principal measures of the learning outcomes of a VET course are:

☐ the employability of graduates, that is, their ability to find and retain jobs in the occupations in which they have been trained; and

☐ their capability to undertake further learning in the occupational knowledge areas in which they have been trained.

The data on learning outcomes are commonly provided by:

☐ graduate satisfaction surveys;

☐ graduate destination surveys; and

☐ surveys of employer satisfaction.

Graduate satisfaction surveys produce reliable data when questionnaires are completed by graduates in 6-12 months after graduation. Some VET providers also survey graduates' satisfaction at the conclusion of their courses. Their subjective feelings of satisfaction – or otherwise – with the courses that they have just completed are not necessarily translated into successful employment or other desirable outcomes.

Graduate destination surveys or tracer studies determine outcomes for graduates from particular VET courses (or institutions), for example to employment, to unemployment, or to further education and training. These surveys provide measures of the effectiveness of the courses (or VET institutions).

A variant of tracer studies are reverse tracer studies, which examine the training and career paths of employees in different occupations and help to understand the role of VET courses as a path to employment in these occupations. These surveys provide measures of the relevance of courses to local occupational structures and job opportunities.

Surveys of employer satisfaction with graduates from courses (or VET institutions) provide measures of their relevance for the employers' particular skills needs.

These surveys are generally undertaken by the institutions themselves or by service organizations. Most VET providers will employ part-time students to conduct surveys of employer satisfaction, taking a sample of employers each year. The more closely institutions work with their local and national employer bodies, the easier it is to ensure employer satisfaction with training outcomes.

For details on service organizations, refer to **Unit 2.1: Service-providing agencies** and **Unit 2.2: Associations of public VET institutions**.

For details on employer satisfaction surveying techniques, refer to **Unit 4.2: Assessing industry demand for VET courses**.

For more details on the arrangements for monitoring the progress of student learning in different countries, go to **Unit 9.4: Monitoring course progress and outputs** on your CD-ROM.

MODULE 10

Quality assurance
in education and training

Unit 10.1

QUALITY MANAGEMENT SYSTEMS

10.1.1 QUALITY CONCEPTS AND MANAGEMENT ARRANGEMENTS

Why quality assurance?

A major impetus in the adoption of quality management systems (QMSs) in VET has been the rise in the need for accountability, especially with regard to publicly funded operations. As the consumption of education and training services grows, QMSs are now regarded as a useful way of reassuring clients and government about the beneficial outcomes of a VET provider.

The QMSs use various indicators and focus on improving different aspects of educational and training institutions. Some aim to improve customer satisfaction with education and training, whereas others concentrate on improving service productivity and reducing costs by, for example, focusing on strategic planning, leadership, control, customer focus, risk management and results or future plans.

QMSs were developed in the commercial sector where they focus on customers, products and financial success for shareholders. Although these concepts have been adapted to the nature and needs of public VET institutions, there are limitations to measuring education and training outputs and outcomes and their quality.

It is useful to distinguish between qualifications, courses and VET providers, since quality often refers to all of these aspects:

☐ qualifications are awards which recognize that learning has taken place and that certain knowledge and skills standards have been achieved and can be practised by the learners;

☐ courses are structured learning experiences with specified objectives, curricula and outcomes;

☐ providers are public and private VET institutions and companies that supply VET and related services.

The quality assurance of VET providers is commonly achieved through their institutional registration, certification and accreditation. For details on institutional certification and accreditation, go to **Section 10.1.2: Certification, approval, accreditation and audit processes** below.

The concepts of quality

Quality can be defined in three different ways:

(1) quality as excellence;

(2) quality as fitness for purpose;

(3) quality as a value for investment.

Quality as excellence

Quality as *excellence* is a comparative attribute determined in relation to similar qualifications, courses and providers. Those qualifications, courses and providers that fare better or best (score highly on a determined scale) are judged by constituents and consumers as excellent and are, therefore, considered to be of high quality. A QMS based on this definition may involve benchmarks against which the performance of qualifications, courses and providers can be assessed and ranked.

The underpinning factor are standards, which can be applied to successful practices in VET. There are various ways of measuring activities, which have resulted in the development of benchmarking and best-practice concepts in education and training: evidence of student satisfaction, course assessment questionnaires, graduate destinations surveys and audits of quality management systems and processes are commonly used.

Quality is a relative concept. Standards are set relative to perceived best practice in an area of work. There may also be legally accepted minimum standards. A VET provider can, for instance, set its own quality and performance standards on what is an acceptable level of success by its students.

Benchmarks or standards may be developed:

☐ for individual VET institutions to be applied to their own internal quality assurance processes;

☐ for the VET system of a particular country;

☐ by international standard-setting agencies (for example ISO 9000 provisions).

ISO 9000 is a generic management standard developed by the ISO that contains eight quality management principles. These principles can be used by the senior management of any organization – including a VET institution – as a framework to guide their staff towards improving performance. The eight principles are:

(1) Customer focus

(2) Leadership

(3) Involvement of people

(4) Process approach

(5) System approach to management

(6) Continual improvement

(7) Factual approach to decision-making

(8) Mutually beneficial supplier relationships.

For details on each of the above quality management principles underlying ISO 9000, go to "**Quality management principles underpinning ISO 9000. 4pp.**" on your CD-ROM.

A key advantage of the application of this approach to VET systems and institutions is that it provides clear and comparable information about the performance of qualifications, courses and providers. A key disadvantage, however, is the considerable expense of maintaining an up-to-date assessment system and its benchmarks as well as organizing external assessment. This approach can also fail to take into account the specific context and goals of particular VET institutions.

Quality as fitness for purpose

Quality as *fitness for purpose* assesses the performance of qualifications, courses and providers against certain standards, the institutions' stated outcomes or intentions. The fitness-for-purpose approach ranks courses, providers and qualifications as equally excellent if they reach the established performance standards. On balance, quality defined as fitness for purpose is generally considered by most jurisdictions as the most workable approach.

The diversity of VET provision makes it difficult for comparisons to be made between similar qualifications, courses and providers, so it is important that common benchmarks or standards underpin quality assurance processes (refer also to **Section 10.1.2: Certification, approval, accreditation and audit processes** below).

Two further major dichotomies may arise in quality assurance:

☐ whether the quality assurance of qualifications, courses and institutions focuses on the inputs to VET, on its outputs and outcomes, or on all of these;

283

- whether the quality assurance of qualifications, courses and institutions is internal (that is, undertaken by a VET institution's own staff through internal processes) or external (undertaken by an external agent and through external processes).

In practice, the quality assurance of qualifications, courses and institutions usually involves considering both inputs and outputs, irrespective of how quality is defined. For example, by assessing performance against stated VET standards, outcomes or intentions, quality defined as fitness for purpose is clearly focused on (stated) outputs and outcomes but may also take into account the inputs in assessing performance. A QMS that is based on excellence assesses and ranks the performance of qualifications, courses and providers against certain benchmarks, and is of necessity focused on VET outputs.

Quality as value for investment

Quality as *value for investment* is based on stakeholders' perceptions of the cost and time required to achieve certain quality standards in delivering VET qualifications and courses and its implications to the VET institution's performance. This approach treats the quality of education and training as a form of investment in which returns have yet to be assessed. Generally, stakeholders may not be able to judge returns, and hence quality, reliably. Nevertheless, the inclusion of stakeholders' views should be an important element in all forms of quality assessment.

VET providers may achieve excellence by concentrating resources into particular programmes to attract the best staff and equipment, and so on. System-wide excellence may, however, be unaffordable and not value for investment.

Therefore, assuring the quality of learning may include making assessments of the quality of inputs to learning, such as:

- course quality (for example design, curriculum, qualifications);

- the quality of students (for example selection, monitoring, guidance);

- the quality of the staff (for example competence, leadership, management skills);

- the quality of teaching delivery (for example teacher behaviour, teaching spaces, equipment and teaching aids).

Assuring the quality of learning may also include making assessments of the quality of major outputs and outcomes from learning, such as:

- the levels of qualifications (knowledge and skills) acquired;

- the employability of graduates;

- graduates' capacity for further learning.

For more details on assuring the quality of learning through assessing the quality of inputs to and outputs from learning, go to **Unit 10.2: Assuring the quality of learning**.

Implementation arrangements

The key elements of implementing a QMS include:

- ☐ management commitment;
- ☐ a communications strategy across the organization;
- ☐ the development of objectives;
- ☐ the development of operational principles;
- ☐ process mapping;
- ☐ measuring outcomes through key performance indicators (KPIs);
- ☐ documentation of the processes; and
- ☐ staff training.

Different QMSs recognize similar sets of operational principles that are introduced by the generic management standard (ISO 9000) – a focus on the customer, well-designed processes and procedures, a systematic approach to management, and so on.

In a VET institution, the aforementioned quality operational principles can embrace issues such as:

- ☐ student-centred learning;
- ☐ measuring all processes by the impact they have on student learning;
- ☐ setting clear goals and offering leadership within the institution to meet these goals;
- ☐ good relationships between managers and other staff, so that ideas for maintaining quality can be shared;
- ☐ good management and administration, leading to effective and efficient operational work;
- ☐ the constant review of institutional procedures and outcomes to ensure that the best possible performance is achieved;
- ☐ good quality and timely management information that is shared to underpin decisions;
- ☐ good partnerships and networking with other organizations in the supply chain.

Achieving quality is not something that can be delegated. Everyone in an organization is responsible for quality. Everyone is someone else's customer, and is dependent on the quality of work done by others. If a chain of responsibility ends anywhere, it is on the desk of the chief executive. In practice, large VET organizations often assign a senior manager to be responsible for quality, and there may be a team of quality managers working on audits, inspections and the maintenance of quality assurance systems. However, such teams cannot manage quality. They can audit and reveal problems, but line managers and all employees have to work on their own performance.

Once the parameters of quality assurance have been agreed on, there need to be regular checks on performance against these standards. These may be reviews of student and employer reactions to courses. They may be audits by the staff team of its own performance or of the performance of colleagues' teams. There may be external audits by government departments, funding agencies, or independent assessors employed by a VET institution, its awarding bodies, or professional associations. The purpose of such audits is to ensure consistency of performance over time and between different teaching departments.

For more details on internal and external quality monitoring and assessment processes, refer to **Unit 10.3: Quality monitoring and assessment**.

For more details on concepts and management arrangements for QMSs in different countries, go to **Unit 10.1: Quality management systems** on your CD-ROM.

10.1.2 CERTIFICATION, APPROVAL, ACCREDITATION AND AUDIT PROCESSES

Traditionally, the quality of VET providers is validated through provider certification/registration processes and the quality of courses is assured through course approval and provider accreditation processes.

Certification and registration

Certification and registration are quality assurance processes intended to ensure that providers are capable of delivering quality VET. Technically, they may have slightly different meanings. Under ISO 9000, for example, certification refers to the issuing of written assurance (the certificate) by an independent, external body that has audited a VET institution's management system and verified that it conforms to a required standard. Registration means that the auditing body then records the certification in its client register.

The VET institution's management system has, therefore, to be both certified and registered. For practical purposes in the ISO 9000 context, the difference between the two terms is not significant and both are acceptable for general use and are interchangeable. Certification, however, seems to be the term most commonly used worldwide.

In general, VET institutions must be registered and also accredited to be able to deliver courses that lead to certain national qualifications, that is, courses that are recognized on national qualifications frameworks. The accreditation process checks that VET institutions are capable of operating their own QMSs and of meeting their obligations to quality assurance agencies – usually the same agencies responsible for national qualification frameworks – and to relevant industry groups.

Registered VET institutions may also apply for accreditation and course approval to offer provider courses that do not lead to national qualifications and are not recognized on national qualifications frameworks. For course approvals, VET institutions are generally required to supply details of the design of their courses and any additional material necessary to show that the proposed courses fit within VET institutions' QMSs.

Course approvals provide stakeholders (for example students) with an assurance that approved courses have been checked for quality. Approved courses are coherent programmes that are based on clear and consistent aims, content, outcomes and skills assessment practices. Some VET institutions may offer a range of courses, some approved, others not approved.

The assessment of off-campus industry-based training may be carried out by assessors who are part of the QMSs of accredited organizations. Most workplace assessors are registered by accredited ITOs.

The quality of VET courses is closely related to the quality of the VET institutions that deliver them, and the processes for validating VET institutions and course delivery (accreditation) inevitably overlap. Reducing registration and accreditation to a single standard would better reflect the interrelated nature of quality in VET and would reduce compliance costs for VET providers currently facing both processes.

Working towards accreditation

VET providers may use internal or external specialist teams for advice on quality management and on ongoing checks for the audits of QMSs. The process of accreditation begins with these steps:

□ selecting the QMS for accreditation and identifying the necessary requirements and documentation;

□ gaining management commitment and involvement in the process;

□ coordinating the process with a clear communications strategy, a plan and a schedule of activities;

□ assigning resources;

☐ assessing the gap analysis in the institution;

☐ undertaking process mapping;

☐ documenting the planning, operation and control of the processes;

☐ devising effective internal audit and improvement strategies.

After this initial preparatory stage, a VET provider's team prepares to meet the criteria of the QMS by addressing the gaps identified while implementing any changes or improvements. Usually, when this work has been completed, an internal audit is undertaken before a certifier is selected and the audit is scheduled.

Certification involves an independent evaluation of the VET institution, including management, activities, policies and procedures. The audit will also cover the methods for measuring quality, such as staff and customer satisfaction surveys. Certification encourages continuous improvement as well as internal and external recognition and acknowledgement.

Maintaining quality

Assuring that quality once demonstrated by VET institutions is generally reliant on three main processes:

(1) the ongoing monitoring of performance and mainly outputs and outcomes;

(2) self-evaluation by VET institutions' QMSs;

(3) external quality audits.

VET institutions are responsible for the quality of their own courses. They are expected to undertake regular internal reviews and self-evaluations. Internal reviews enable VET institutions to assess their own performance against good-practice criteria and to determine their compliance with the requirements of registration and accrediting agencies.

External quality audits verify the performance of VET institutions as a whole, their management processes for achieving quality learning and their success as VET organizations. Each audit usually involves a visit to the institution by an audit panel on behalf of the external quality assurance agency.

A balance has to be found between quality assessments prior to training delivery (such as accreditation) and subsequent and ongoing quality assessments (such as quality audit). Over recent years, regulatory checks on quality have tended to emphasize accreditation prior to training delivery. This focus has been criticized as placing too much emphasis on proposals and not enough on actual performance. Quality audits that look at post-delivery performance would address this criticism.

Indeed, although audit alone could be used to validate quality, it might take several years before discoveries of poor quality delivery were corrected, since it takes time for large VET institutions to make changes. For this reason, educational quality assurance has tended to move away from an audit-only approach in preference to an upfront standard for accreditation and subsequent quality audit against this standard. This is also the preferred option of the authors of this handbook.

Using the same quality standards for audit as for accreditation enables audit findings to be fed back into VET institutions' ongoing practices for monitoring and improving the quality of their VET delivery.

For details on certification, approval, accreditation and audit processes in different countries, go to **Unit 10.1: Quality management systems** on your CD-ROM.

Unit 10.2

ASSURING
THE QUALITY OF LEARNING

10.2.1 ASSURING THE QUALITY OF COURSES

Assuring the quality of courses delivered by VET institutions is the first step that needs to be taken to assure the quality of learning. VET courses are structured learning experiences with specified outputs. A VET course involves a number of features, the major of which are the curriculum reflecting the detailed learning content of a course and the way a course is delivered and student progress assessed. Learning content may be structured into modules and research activities.

Assuring the quality of a course involves assessing the:

- course design (the quality of the way the course is structured and the way the delivery process is designed);
- course curriculum (the quality of the course's detailed content);
- course delivery.

Course design

The following major course design features need to be clearly determined:

- the name/title of the course;
- the name/title of the qualification to which the course leads;
- a summary of course objectives (the provision of knowledge and skills recognized by an award);
- anticipated outcomes (for example the relation of the course to employment opportunities);
- the course duration, for example in hours/days/weeks/years;

- the course level (such as pre-entry, entry, graduate, post-graduate, or expressed numerically according to a defined scale of levels);
- a list of course modules (if a modular course) where each module has its own credit value, and so on.

Some or all of the above features may be registered on the national qualifications framework.

For more details on course design features, refer to **Unit 8.1: Developing a course for a national VET qualification**.

Course curriculum

The degree of involvement of VET providers in curriculum development varies from country to country. Within a national qualifications framework, the curricula may be strongly determined by national VET qualifications requirements as they consist of endorsed units of competency standards and skills assessment procedures. This may leave individual providers with little freedom to develop curricula for the national qualifications that they wish to be accredited for delivering.

The curricula of provider courses are developed by a particular VET provider on its own initiative. In this case, a VET institution may establish course/curriculum development committees that cover the relevant vocational fields.

The VET institution's teaching staff are intimately involved in course and curriculum development and the institutional academic board generally exercises academic oversight. It may also be responsible for approving the proposed curricula prior to course delivery.

For details on developing and implementing a VET curriculum, refer to **Unit 8.3: Curriculum development**.

Course delivery

The quality of the course delivery can be assured through the following arrangements:

- the course is leading to a national or provider VET qualification that is quality assured;
- the provider is accredited to deliver the course;
- the skills assessment process for the awarding of the qualification is quality assured.

For more details on approval, accreditation and audit processes, refer to **Unit 10.1: Quality management systems**.

Course accreditation means that a VET institution has the necessary teachers, resources and equipment to deliver the course and assess students' achievements. These conditions and resources can be set out in a report of the accreditation panel following an inspection and/or perhaps by referring to the institution's asset register or whatever documentation the panel may request.

The curriculum should include sufficient information to enable the teaching staff to develop individual teaching plans for each session or period of training course delivery.

In addition to clearly defined objectives and the other course features listed above, course materials need to be produced. These may include anything that is required to support the teaching of a new programme – textbooks, teacher guides, online materials.

In some countries, a total learning support package is produced centrally. In some other countries, where teachers are expected to adapt their own training support materials to suit their own approaches, the development of a total support package for a complete qualification is unlikely.

For more details on developing a national vocational training course, refer to **Unit 8.1: Developing a course for a national VET qualification.**

Course review

VET courses and the curricula leading to them and the way they are delivered need to be reviewed from time to time. The curriculum is particularly sensitive to changing job requirements, while course delivery processes may need to be reviewed and updated in order to maintain the quality of the course.

The scope of a course evaluation can vary according to its purpose, but the following general issues may be explored:

- ☐ Course relevance – Is the course continuing to meet the needs of industry, enterprises and community groups? Are the course objectives appropriate and achievable? Is the content appropriate, both in subject and level? Have there been any changes in national competency standards?

- ☐ Course design – How well is the course structured? Did the content fit the time allocated to it? Do additional course modules need to be developed?

- ☐ Course delivery – Has delivery been successful? Were the delivery methods appropriate? Have students encountered any unexpected difficulties?

- ☐ Skills assessment – Was student assessment appropriate and fit for purpose? Did it deliver what was intended in terms of student success?

A VET provider might set up an internal evaluation team, consisting of teachers, managers and companies' representatives to review the course content and delivery and assess its effectiveness.

For details on course evaluation, refer to **Unit 8.4: Course evaluation**.

For details on assuring the quality of VET courses in different countries, go to **Unit 10.2: Assuring the quality of learning** on your CD-ROM.

10.2.2 ASSURING THE QUALITY OF STUDENT SELECTION, MONITORING AND GUIDANCE

The second step that needs to be taken to assure the quality of courses is to ensure that student selection processes admit suitable students, who, once admitted, receive adequate monitoring and guidance.

Enrolment practices

To ensure that enrolment decisions are based on informed choice, potential students need to be given information and support to make them aware of the requirements for attendance, assessment and participation and also of the potential progression opportunities once the course has been successfully completed.

A publicly funded VET institution is required to attract, select and enrol its trainees in accordance with an enrolment policy determined by the government. The greater the autonomy granted to the institution, the more likely it is that the VET institution will set its own enrolment conditions.

In principle, the enrolment policy is usually one of open entry, that is, any prospective student who wishes to enrol in a training course may do so without restriction. This policy is usually subject to the student meeting certain minimum entry standards, which are introduced to ensure that a prospective student has the prerequisite knowledge to cope with the requirements of the course.

The enrolment policies may operate restricted entry to publicly funded training places. Restricted access does, however, have serious consequences for equity. Competition-based enrolment systems are, at least in principle, equitable to the extent that competition is based on merit. Students of equal merit have an equal chance of participating.

Merit in this context is based on the training providers' assessments of the applicants' academic ability or recognition of their prior learning or competencies and skills achieved. Such a policy ensures that the most able prospective students are successful in gaining enrolment. However, it also assumes that the most able students will derive the greatest private benefit from further training, resulting in the greatest public benefit.

Attracting potential students

Autonomous VET institutions can attract student enrolments in a number of ways. A common approach is to use the media, by advertising in community and national newspapers, on local radio and (for particularly well-resourced institutions) through television commercials. Providers may also organize special events or attend community venues, such as shopping centres and career forums.

A more selective approach to attracting students is through careers counsellors, who are well-placed to advise students in their final year(s) of schooling on their future options for training and/or employment. In some jurisdictions, a government agency maintains a comprehensive web site that offers generic information for school leavers on their employment options and the required levels of skills and competencies.

For more details on these information services, refer to **Unit 6.4: Vocational guidance and job placement assistance**.

Applying the course requirements

The selection of students is commonly based on system-wide entrance assessment and examination requirements, particularly for young people who are leaving school. Students will express their preferences for courses and institutions, with admission based on their examination results.

The selection of students may also be linked to specific course requirements. These will be developed by the VET institution's departments with reference to individual courses or levels of study. Some courses may require the presentation of a portfolio of work to demonstrate competence and potential, others may require previous industry experience, the completion of subjects at a specified level or the demonstration of a defined level of literacy and numeracy skills.

Some training providers may elect to interview all their prospective students for particular courses, while others will only interview those students who are neither well qualified, nor unqualified for a particular course, and who may need more careful selection. Interviews may also disclose desirable personal attributes for a particular course that may not be well assessed by traditional end-of-schooling qualifications (for example the maturity required for some paramedical professions).

Other training providers may conduct entry tests in order to rank prospective students, and allow selection to be undertaken on the basis of ranking indicated by such tests. These tests at least have the benefit of consistency, that is, all students are ranked according to the same criteria.

For more details on the methods of attracting and selecting students in different countries, consult **Unit 6.1: The student enrolment process**.

Student guidance and monitoring processes

The guidance and monitoring processes may include procedures related to induction, recognition of prior learning, student progress assessment, programme evaluation, record keeping and managing students at risk of non-completion.

Once a student begins a course, a teaching team is then responsible for monitoring that student's progress against the expected course outcomes. Regular interaction with a teacher is an important element of learner success.

Student guidance generally begins with students being provided with information which helps them to choose an appropriate training course that meets their expectations and training needs and that they have the ability to complete successfully. Pre-entry information should cover the following aspects:

- □ course prerequisites (if any);

- □ course objectives and content (a syllabus outline);

- □ mode(s) of course delivery (lectures, workshops, practical instruction, field trips, self-directed study, assignments, projects, and so on);

- □ learning support options and available institutional resources (teaching and support staff, classrooms, workshops, libraries, computer networks, other resources);

- □ the cost of the course for students (tuition fees, other course-related costs including textbooks, stationery, course materials purchased by students, and so forth);

- □ course assessment requirements and industry standards;

- □ course certification (what a student will receive as evidence of course completion);

- □ personal counselling, literacy support, disability support, equal opportunity and anti-discrimination provisions, grievance and complaints procedures, appeals processes.

Students generally continue to need some guidance after enrolment has been completed. The information provided at the start of the course should cover the following aspects:

- □ timetables and training schedules;

- □ procedures used by the provider to monitor progress throughout the course (for example class tests and assignments, individual competency-based assessment, and so on);

- □ procedures used by the provider to determine course outcomes (for example examinations, projects, competency-based assessment, and so forth);

☐ the standard of behaviour expected of staff and students, and sanctions that may be applied for unacceptable behaviour;

☐ advice or counselling on effective study methods;

☐ tutorial contacts and other forms of study support to enable students to overcome any difficulties they may experience.

Measuring student performance

A VET provider will have procedures in place for monitoring the progress of its students. This will allow for the early identification of students who are not coping and who are at risk of failing or dropping out. Student performance will be measured against the course of study and the planned sequence of learning and achievement. The learning achievement should be clear to all and communicated and understood by everyone.

The criteria against which assessment tasks are measured are particularly important and will guide students to a clear understanding of what is required of them. In all cases, progress and assessment attainment should be based on objective observations against observable and measurable factors.

The processes of measuring student performance should be conducted:

☐ throughout the duration of a course to monitor students' progress, to provide students with information on how they are performing, and perhaps to enable staff to intervene if students are not coping with the demands of the course;

☐ at the conclusion of a course to determine whether students have met the course's requirements for successful graduation and, if so, are entitled to recognition of their achievement by appropriate certification.

For more details on evaluating student performance, refer to **Unit 6.2: Guiding and monitoring student progress**.

For details on assuring the quality of student selection, progress monitoring and guidance in different countries, go to **Unit 10.2: Assuring the quality of learning** on your CD-ROM.

10.2.3 ASSURING THE QUALITY OF STAFF

The third step that must be taken to assure the quality of courses delivered by VET institutions is to ensure the quality of the staff. Relevant prior workplace experience is necessary if a teacher is to have the specialist knowledge and skills required to deliver quality VET that will prepare students for the workplace.

In addition to a prerequisite level of specialist knowledge and skills, teaching staff will also need to have adequate teaching skills (a teacher certificate) if they are to be effective as teachers. These teaching skills may include the ability to:

☐ contribute to curriculum development and course design;

☐ plan for training sessions;

☐ develop knowledge, skills and work-related attitudes with their students through effective communication and the use of training aids;

☐ monitor and assess student progress.

Prior teaching and workplace experience and trade/professional and teaching qualifications may be recognized through graded teaching positions, for example associate teacher, teacher, senior teacher and principal teacher.

Assessing the quality of the staff of a VET institution can involve some quantitative data as well as professional judgements. The quantitative data may include:

☐ the overall number of staff related to the number of students and range of courses;

☐ the number of staff qualified as teachers;

☐ the number of staff with different levels of vocational qualifications in their own trade or profession;

☐ the number of staff applying for each vacant post;

☐ staff turnover (the numbers leaving and joining each year);

☐ the relative proportions of managers, full-time teachers and part-time teachers.

Professional judgements are required to assess matters such as:

☐ the impact on teaching quality of different types of staff qualifications;

☐ staff turnover – is high staff turnover necessarily a bad thing? (There may be a lot of people without recent industrial experience who need to move on.);

☐ the importance of the current industry experience of those who work as part-time teachers;

☐ the quality of leadership offered by senior managers, and how this is demonstrated.

VET institutions should have a consistent approach to attaining and monitoring the quality of their staff, which includes:

☐ a clearly stated institutional mission or purpose, values and strategic plan that are communicated to and shared by all the staff;

☐ adequate recruitment and selection policies and practices;

☐ appropriate academic and vocational qualifications according to the work position;

☐ clear and accessible job descriptions;

☐ performance monitoring and reporting;

☐ knowledge and participation in a quality management system (QMS);

☐ human resource policies that include reward and recognition;

☐ inclusion and respect for staff associations and unions;

☐ an active professional development programme;

☐ good communications throughout the organization.

Staff training systems should ensure that teaching staff have the skills and competencies necessary for them to carry out their functions. Processes are required for:

☐ the induction of new staff;

☐ training needs analyses to identify lacking skills and competencies;

☐ requisite staff training to address identified gaps in skills;

☐ the development of individual staff training plans;

☐ the certification of teaching staff through credentials and awards that attests to skills and competencies that may be taken into account in staff recruitment and remuneration;

☐ career guidance that enables individual staff members to progress within the VET institution.

For more details, refer to **Unit 7.1: Staff selection, recruitment and appointment** and **Unit 7.2: Staff training and career guidance**.

Managers in autonomous VET institutions should routinely undertake periodic staff performance appraisals to promote quality assurance. These appraisals also provide an objective basis for salary reviews and promotions as well as provide useful feedback to staff on their teaching performance.

For more details, refer to **Unit 7.3: Staff remuneration and benefits** and **Unit 7.4: Staff performance appraisal and promotion**.

Assessing the quality of staff should be part of pre-delivery accreditation and post-delivery quality audit processes as well as regular performance reviews.

For more details on accreditation and audit processes, refer to **Unit 10.1: Quality management systems**.

The selection of non-teaching specialist staff (IT, library, public relations, technical support, and so forth) and student support staff (vocational guidance, counselling, recreation and health, and so on) needs to be done carefully to ensure the best possible services for prospective, current and graduate students.

For more details on staff composition, refer to **Unit 7.1: Staff selection, recruitment and appointment**.

Where an autonomous VET institution has the authority to select its own staff, selection should be carried out through due process in accordance with an explicit selection policy that ensures transparency and facilitates the selection of the most suitable candidate. VET sector-wide agreements on the qualifications and grades of staff, pay systems and other conditions of work should be made known to the candidates.

10.2.4 ASSURING THE QUALITY OF TEACHING

The fourth step that must be taken to guarantee the quality of courses is assuring the quality of teaching delivery. This includes monitoring teaching processes and assessing the adequacy of equipment, learning technologies and teaching space.

The quality of teaching is, in the first instance, determined by the context in which teachers operate. The roles of teachers have altered greatly in recent years as the changes to curriculum structure, delivery and assessment modes, work-based training, industry liaison, the commercialization of training, the growth of a diverse student group and project-based work have taken place. At the same time, teachers may be impelled to incorporate equity principles into their approaches to ensure equal learning opportunities for all client groups. These new activities have all had an impact on the definition of quality teaching and the skills and knowledge required.

The external world of work has also given VET teachers a new range of challenges, since they now need to prepare students for a technological society, for periods of unemployment, lifelong learning and career changes rather than for one specific job. Business management practices impinge on teachers' roles as globalization, information exchange, innovation and competition need to be addressed in most work contexts.

Professional development and monitoring

Professional development is used to introduce the latest teaching techniques, preferably through practice-based research. The processes of moderating teaching and assessment tools and learning outcomes, and regular course meetings, as well as membership of professional associations all assist in teacher networking and development.

Some jurisdictions undertake the systematic monitoring of instructional performance – in essence the monitoring of inputs to student learning – within VET institutions, which includes the internal and external monitoring of teaching delivery.

An important aspect of teaching is the extent to which the teaching conforms to the course curriculum. Compliance with the curriculum may, in some cases, be an internal matter for a VET provider, and should be assessed as part of its internal QMS. Compliance is also relevant for a quality audit, which should be undertaken periodically by the VET quality assurance body.

The monitoring of teaching delivery evaluates the ability of teachers to transform curriculum into knowledge and competences acquired by their students. The benefits of such monitoring include feedback to teachers on their performance and the quality assurance of teachers' pedagogical skills. Monitoring may be internal to the VET institution (for example part of a teacher's performance review) or external (for example carried out by inspectors from an external monitoring agency).

An assessment of teaching quality can essentially only be made by those who experience it, either as learners or observers. Therefore, the views of learners can and should be taken into account.

In some country systems, it is usual for managers to evaluate lessons as part of the staff appraisal system. Teaching observation forms part of the evidence for an individual teacher's performance appraisal. The data from these observations can be accumulated into a picture of the overall quality of teaching in the institution. This assumes that a sufficient proportion of staff is observed each year, which is a time-consuming activity for managers. A clear framework is needed for such observations, so that staff can be judged fairly against an agreed standard, and those observing should be trained for the role.

Judgements about teaching quality should include:

☐ the preparation of the lesson and the materials used;

☐ the fitness/suitability of lesson objectives to the course design;

☐ the appropriateness of the delivery to the ability and level of the students;

☐ the availability of learning resources, and the skill with which they are used;

☐ the pace, timing and style of the lesson;

☐ the quality and appropriateness of the accommodation;

☐ the evidence of student learning in students' discussions and written work.

For more details on monitoring teaching delivery, refer to **Section 10.2.2: Assuring the quality of student selection, monitoring and guidance** above.

The effective delivery of education and training requires that a VET institution not only has adequate teaching spaces such as classrooms, workshops and laboratories but also adequate learning technologies and a range of equipment. Various traditional and newer teaching aids are available that enhance teacher-centred learning.

For more details on teacher-centred learning and the management of teaching spaces, equipment and learning technologies, refer to **Unit 9.3: Managing capital assets**.

Assessing the adequacy of teaching spaces, equipment and learning technologies should be part of pre-delivery accreditation and periodic post-delivery quality audit processes.

For more details on accreditation and audit processes, refer to **Unit 10.1: Quality management systems**.

For details on assuring the quality of teaching in VET institutions in different countries, go to **Unit 10.2: Assuring the quality of learning** on your CD-ROM.

10.2.5 ASSURING THE QUALITY OF KNOWLEDGE AND SKILLS ACQUIRED

The final step that needs to be taken to guarantee the quality of courses delivered by VET institutions is assuring the quality of knowledge and skills acquired. Some jurisdictions place greater reliance on assuring the quality of knowledge and skills acquired through monitoring student learning outputs and outcomes (output monitoring) than on assuring the quality of courses, student selection, staffing, teaching delivery (input monitoring). The QMS of a VET provider should include procedures to monitor outputs and outcomes so that reliable and comparable judgements can be made. Some countries conduct annual national evaluations of VET providers' outputs and, particularly, outcomes through sample surveys. These data can be used as benchmarks for individual providers and courses.

The VET course's outputs include enrolment numbers, volume of training delivery expressed as the equivalent full-time students (EFTSs) or annual hours of curriculum (AHC), and the numbers of course completers and successful graduations. All these proxy measures of VET outputs have some limitations.

The course's final outputs are the knowledge, skills and competencies acquired by its successful graduates. The quality of knowledge and skills required is outlined in the description of a qualification/curriculum and endorsed at certification. Some of these outputs, such as knowledge, skills and competencies, are, however, somewhat intangible and, therefore, difficult to measure and certify.

The learning outcomes of a VET course include the graduates' enhanced employability (or employment), their capacity for further learning and intangibles such as an enhanced ability to function in the labour market and a knowledge society.

Measures of the quality of the learning outcomes of a VET course are provided by:

☐ graduate satisfaction surveys;

☐ graduate destination surveys;

☐ surveys of employer satisfaction.

Graduate satisfaction surveys may be completed by graduates at the conclusion of their courses. However, successful graduations are not necessarily translated into successful employment or other desirable outcomes.

Graduate destination surveys or tracer studies determine the outcomes for samples of graduates from particular VET courses (or institutions). Reverse tracer studies or surveys of career paths of the current workforce help to identify the role of VET providers and their courses over a longer period of time in supplying skilled labour to the economy.

Surveys of employer satisfaction with VET graduates provide measures of the quality (relevance or fitness for purpose) of courses (or VET institutions) for their own particular skills needs.

For more details on proxy measures for outputs and on surveys of graduate satisfaction, graduate destinations and employer satisfaction, refer to **Unit 6.2: Guiding and monitoring student progress**.

For details on assuring the quality of knowledge and skills acquired in different countries, go to **Unit 10.2: Assuring the quality of learning** on your CD-ROM.

Unit 10.3

QUALITY MONITORING
AND ASSESSMENT

10.3.1 EXTERNAL QUALITY MONITORING

Quality in VET often refers to three aspects: VET qualifications, courses and providers. Furthermore, quality itself can be defined in three ways:

(1) quality as *excellence* makes comparisons between similar qualifications, courses and providers – those that score highly on a determined scale are judged as excellent and, therefore, of high quality;

(2) quality as *fitness for purpose* assesses the performance of qualifications, courses and providers against their stated outcomes or intentions;

(3) quality as *value for investment* is based on stakeholders' perceptions of whether qualifications, courses and providers meet or exceed expectations, taking into account the time and money invested in them.

On balance, quality defined as fitness for purpose is generally considered by most jurisdictions as the most workable approach, without precluding the definitions of quality as excellence and as value for investment in appropriate circumstances.

For more details on the distinctions between VET qualifications, courses and VET providers and on the concepts of quality, refer to **Unit 10.1: Quality management systems**.

Quality assurance may be either external, that is, undertaken by an external agency and external process, or internal, that is, undertaken through a VET institution's own internal QMS, involving its own staff and internal processes.

A balance has to be found between external quality assessments prior to training delivery (certification, approval and accreditation) and subsequent and ongoing external quality assessments (quality audit). Over recent years, regulatory checks on quality have tended to emphasize VET providers' accreditation prior to training delivery. However, it has been found that this focus places too much emphasis on the provider's readiness to deliver and not enough on its actual performance. External quality audits, focusing on post-delivery performance, could address this issue.

External quality assurance includes assessments of the quality of inputs to learning, such as the quality of courses, student selection/monitoring/guidance processes, and the quality of staff and teaching delivery. External quality assurance also includes assessments of the quality of outputs and outcomes from learning, such as knowledge and skills acquired, the employability of students and their capacity for further learning.

For more details on assessing the quality of inputs to learning and the quality of outputs and outcomes of learning, refer to **Unit 10.2: Assuring the quality of learning**.

Quality assurance – whether external or internal and irrespective of how quality is defined – requires the setting of benchmarks or standards against which qualifications, courses and providers can be assessed, particularly for quality defined as excellence, which introduces elements of ranking.

Benchmarks or standards may be developed:

☐ for individual VET institutions to be applied to their own internal quality assurance processes (see **Section 10.3.2: Internal quality monitoring** below);

☐ by external quality assurance agencies with responsibilities for VET systems;

☐ by international standard-setting agencies for international generic applications (for example ISO 9000 provisions).

External quality assurance agencies generally carry out quality audits of VET institutions for their compliance and effectiveness against benchmarks or standards, which are developed by the agencies themselves in consultation with stakeholders. The benchmarks or standards represent the minimum quality requirements that the agencies regard as appropriate to protect the interests of students and also the reputation of VET systems and institutions within their ambits.

The standards are generally grouped under a number of themes relating to different dimensions of the VET delivery. Each quality standard customarily includes a statement of quality practice, which is expanded into measurable terms by one or more evidential statements. The latter identify the evidence needed to demonstrate that the stated quality practice is being carried out to the satisfaction of the external quality assurance agency.

In addition to quality benchmarks and standards that are specific to VET and to a particular jurisdiction, external quality assurance agencies may also use generic quality benchmarks and standards developed by international standards organizations. The most commonly used is ISO 9000, a generic management standard developed by the ISO.

ISO 9000 contains eight quality management principles, with broad statements of the principles that underpin quality management. They can be used by the senior management of any organization – including a VET institution – as a framework to guide their organization towards improving performance.

Aligned with the ISO 9000 family are the European Standards (EN) of the European Committee for Standardization (CEN), which mainly recognize ISO standards as applicable in the EU (the ISO 9000 family is referred to as EN/ISO 9000). Individual jurisdictions may have their own standards organizations, which usually handle ISO standards on behalf of businesses in each country.

There is, therefore, a high degree of international harmonization of industry and commercial standards. They go well beyond quality management into some very specific areas of interest to those working in VET. Some standards cover the practice in individual trades and professions; others relate to educational practice, such as the teaching of IT. Each of the standards organizations can offer an assessment service for clients to judge the extent to which standards are being met. A successful assessment results in accreditation or certification for the relevant activity.

External monitoring may also be implemented by government inspectorates covering various groups of education and training organizations or areas of education and training provision. A national inspectorate may cover general education schools that deliver VET courses, while some other inspectorates may cover colleges and adult learning programmes. It is important that these bodies use a common inspection framework that takes into consideration the extent to which VET providers meet the needs of learners and produce quality outcomes.

For an outline and statements of the quality management principles underlying ISO 9000, go to "**Quality management principles underpinning ISO 9000**" on your CD-ROM (see "Resource Documents").

For details on external quality monitoring in different countries, go to **Unit 10.3: Quality monitoring and assessment** on your CD-ROM.

Implementing external quality audits

External audits for VET institutions' quality monitoring and assessment are usually a requirement of their continued registration and are the responsibility of the quality agency. Quality accreditation agencies have a range of different approaches to audits in terms of frequency and requirements. An audit may also need to be undertaken in response to a complaint.

An audit is a systematic, independent and documented process that is carried out to obtain evidence on whether the structures, processes and outcomes of a VET institution comply with the standards of the certifying agency. An audit involves a thorough review of the QMS's operations by measuring the attainment of agreed indicators. For an institutional management system, these indicators may involve leadership, strategic planning, human resources and customer satisfaction, whereas for a training process they could involve learner support, infrastructure, teacher qualifications or financial and strategic planning.

The monitoring of QMSs usually follows these phases:

☐ planning the audit;

☐ developing comprehensive checklists based on the auditee's management system documents and appropriate quality standard;

☐ complying with the audit's code of conduct;

☐ preparing comprehensive reports that detail audit findings and provide an objective assessment of the suitability of the QMS.

Those undertaking audits need to be appropriately qualified and have a thorough knowledge of the QMS requirements. They must be able to communicate well and will, in most cases, need to have undertaken training. Audit checklists are prepared prior to the audit based on the QMS indicators and the VET provider's documentation. The preparation of the checklist may also involve a desktop audit of the documentation to determine the level of compliance with the QMSs and processes.

Audits are conducted on site if there are matters that cannot be followed up through desktop documentation audits. If areas of non-compliance are identified, the training provider agrees to rectify the issues of non-compliance within a designated time frame. This agreement, termed a corrective action request (CAR), provides details of the non-conformance detected and is signed by the auditee as confirmation of the non-conformance.

The audit report should be prepared in the period immediately following the on-site audit, and the required number of copies of the report should be made available for distribution to the nominated parties.

10.3.2 INTERNAL QUALITY MONITORING

Quality monitoring in a VET institution may be entirely voluntary or subject to a range of stringent requirements, either imposed by government or adopted voluntarily by the institution itself. VET institutions' management and staff are responsible for the quality of their own courses and they are commonly expected to undertake regular internal reviews and evaluations of their organizations.

One of the duties of the governing council of an autonomous VET institution is monitoring performance against its strategic objectives, many of which will reflect the quality of training delivery. The governing council is distinct from management and should, therefore, take a dispassionate view of the organization. Its monitoring takes the form of a set of performance indicators, agreed on with management, and may involve financial, academic and business development indicators as well as institutional outputs and outcomes.

In jurisdictions that have devolved autonomy to VET institutions, most quality assurance processes – including course approval and provider accreditation – may be delegated by the external quality agencies to the institutions' own academic boards. In these autonomous institutions, the academic boards normally have overall responsibility for internal QMSs, and delegations to them are subject to periodic audits by external quality assurance agencies.

Internal reviews undertaken through internal QMSs enable institutions to determine their compliance with the requirements of external quality assurance agencies. Internal audits are also used to identify areas for improvement. Internal audits compare actual practice with what is stated in the procedure. It is conducted a as data-gathering and information sharing exercise that will add value to the area being audited, to the operations of the institution as a whole and to its QMS. It encourages an ongoing cycle of continuous improvement by measuring current performance against a documented set of standards. Consequent changes in procedures and documentation may be identified.

The internal QMSs within VET institutions should match the external quality requirements. These will include:

☐ agreement on which standards to adopt;

☐ the adoption of agreed performance indicators;

☐ the consideration of comparator data from similar institutions;

☐ decisions about management responsibilities for monitoring;

☐ communicating quality requirements and training to all members of staff;

☐ internal quality assessments and records, with reports produced to an agreed cycle that matches the planning cycle;

☐ action plans for improvement, to be built into the business cycle;

☐ recognition and rewards for good quality provision.

Where responsibility for quality assurance – including course approval and provider accreditation – is delegated to the VET institutions themselves, the role of the external quality agencies is simplified and includes only regular audits of the effectiveness of the institutions' internal QMSs and relatively infrequent external quality audits. The delegation of quality assurance processes to the academic boards reduces the compliance costs of quality assurance, encourages the development of a "quality culture" within VET institutions and also respects institutional autonomy.

For more details on course approval and accreditation processes, refer to **Unit 10.1: Quality management systems.**

Just as for external quality assurance, a balance has to be found between the internal quality assessments of the inputs to training and the outputs and outcomes of training. Irrespective of how quality is defined, internal quality assessment generally involves consideration of both inputs to learning (for example quality of courses, students, staff and teaching delivery) and of outputs from learning (for example knowledge and skills acquired, graduates' employability and capacity for further learning).

For more details on assessing the quality of inputs to learning and the quality of outputs and outcomes of learning, refer to **Unit 10.2: Assuring the quality of learning**.

The registration and certification of QMSs usually involve agreeing to an annual internal audit programme. Internal auditors will need to undertake training provided in-house or by an external expert. Irrespective of how quality is defined, internal quality assurance – like external quality assurance – also requires benchmarks or standards against which course approvals, provider accreditation and quality audits can be carried out.

These internal benchmarks or standards are normally the same as – or at least consistent with – those used by external quality assurance agencies. Consistency is necessary to ensure compliance with the requirements specified by external quality assurance agencies and used for the external quality audits that they carry out.

In addition to quality benchmarks and standards developed for VET, providers of VET may also use generic management standards developed by international standards organizations to benchmark the quality of their own management. The most commonly used is ISO 9000, outlined in **Section 10.3.1: External quality monitoring** above.

ISO 9000 may be used by the management of VET institutions as a benchmark for the quality of institutional management. This is normally in addition to the use of quality benchmarks and standards that have been developed specifically for VET.

Internal audits should be conducted in a supportive way, and should be seen as a fact-gathering rather than a fault-finding exercise. The role of the audit is to communicate clearly and to clarify the requirements to the auditees. During the process, auditors should document their observations clearly and accurately, since they will be required to prepare a report for senior management.

The audit team needs to be skilled in the necessary technical language as well as be open-minded, culturally sensitive and fair. Confidentiality is important and the auditor should reassure participants of this approach. The audit team needs to have a broad understanding of the operations of the VET provider.

Internal audits are planned by identifying the lead auditor and the audit team, deciding on the scope, reviewing previous audits and identifying relevant documents. Evidence is gathered by:

- examining documents and systems such as institutional policies and procedures;

- examining the records of actual education and training conducted;

- perusing a sample of student files;

- analysing resources for VET delivery and assessment, including assessment tools;

- questioning the auditee to gain further evidence;

- holding interviews with management, teachers, students;

- observing processes, such as skills assessment and learning activities;

- observing the facilities and equipment used during education and training.

For more details on internal VET quality monitoring in different countries, go to Unit **10.3: Quality monitoring and assessment** on your CD-ROM.

MODULE 11

Performance monitoring and reporting

Unit 11.1

ACCOUNTABILITY
OF VET INSTITUTIONS

11.1.1 THE CONCEPTS OF ACCOUNTABILITY

The greater the degree of autonomy granted to a VET institution within its national system, the more it needs to be externally accountable for activities undertaken independently. The concept of accountability involves explaining, reporting and comparison-making with others and with established standards or benchmarks, so that performance can be assessed fairly and reliably. National legislation may set out the accountability framework to which VET providers will be held at national and/or local levels.

A consideration of accountability raises three issues:

(1) To whom is a VET institution accountable?

(2) For what is a VET institution accountable?

(3) How is a VET institution held accountable?

By definition a public VET institution is accountable to the government on behalf of the public. It is also accountable to other stakeholders who are users of the services delivered by the institution. These include students, who may invest considerable time (opportunity cost) and often money (tuition fees) in following courses, and also the end-users of the knowledge and skills acquired by students, that is, industry, enterprises and the professions.

The government has three interests in public VET institutions:

(1) as funder (services purchase interest);

(2) as owner (ownership interest);

(3) as quality guarantor.

Financial accountability

Public VET institutions commonly receive a substantial proportion of their funding from the government, either directly as funding that covers the costs of training delivery or indirectly as support provided for their students through grants or loans. Funding to cover the costs of training delivery may be provided as input funding to meet salaries, materials, maintenance, and so forth, or as funding linked to training outputs. In output-funding systems, governments are purchasing services from VET institutions.

For details on funding systems, refer to **Unit 5.1: Efficient, effective and equitable funding mechanisms**.

Accountability to the government as funder includes financial accountability for public funding received, that is, expenditure should match the purpose for which funding was allocated. Financial accountability is simplified in input-funding systems, where funding is allocated to meet input costs.

For more details on financial accountability, refer to **Unit 5.5: Standard financial statements and the financial audit**.

The VET institution is accountable to the government as its owner for the:

☐ financial viability of the VET institution – the government bears the financial risk of institutional failure;

☐ stewardship of institutional assets – the VET institution is accountable for maintaining and developing institutional assets, possibly including a calculated return on (capital) investment.

In some VET systems where constituent institutions have significant financial autonomy and the government bears a corresponding ownership risk, a government agency may have the task of undertaking ownership monitoring to minimize this risk (see **Section 11.1.2: Quality and performance monitoring** below).

Accountability for performance

Accountability also depends on the clear definition of expectations, standards, responsibilities and requirements against which VET institutions' performance will be judged. The standards embodied in legislation may relate directly to VET institutions or may be those that apply to organizations and enterprises in general, such as compliance with occupational health and safety regulations, accounting and governance rules, privacy requirements, and so on.

Accountability for performance should include accountability for outputs and outcomes. This broader understanding of accountability is simplified in output-funding systems, where funding is allocated to prescribed training outputs on the basis of established funding rates, for instance, per hour of curriculum delivered. Some governments have developed national perform-ance standards and benchmarks to assess and measure the performance of VET institutions.

Accountability for quality of services

A government also has an interest in public (and sometimes private) VET institutions as a quality guarantor. In this context, quality often refers to three aspects – VET qualifications, courses and VET providers. Quality itself can mean different things: quality as excellence, quality as fitness for purpose and quality as value for investment.

For more details, refer to **Unit 10.1: Quality management systems**.

The VET provider that delivers national qualifications will require registra-tion and accreditation to conduct the training course in accordance with the quality procedures. Provider-developed courses will be subject to the internal accreditation and quality assurance mechanisms of the institution. Licensed courses will also be advertised and conducted according to defined and pub-lished quality standards.

The quality guarantor role protects the government's investment in VET by extending accountability beyond simple accounting for financial expenditure to include accountability for the quality of outputs and outcomes achieved. In particular, outcomes are dependent on the quality of VET delivery – an investment in VET is wasted if it is of poor quality.

The quality guarantor role also serves to protect the interests of other stakeholders as users of VET services, especially vulnerable students who may invest considerable time and money in VET training, but also stakeholders in industry, enterprises and the professions, who require the knowledge and skills of students.

For these reasons, one or more government agencies may be assigned the task of assuring the quality of VET delivery through the certification, approval and accreditation processes or through the audit processes.

Incentives and sanctions

Accountability systems in the VET sector may be ineffective unless there are provisions for incentives, sanctions and other government interventions.

Financial incentives and sanctions for superior or poor performance can be applied through the funding system by increasing or reducing a VET insti-tution's entitlement to the recurrent, growth and capital funding. Poor-quality VET courses may be closed down by withdrawing course approval or provider accreditation as appropriate.

A range of additional measures may be applied if VET institutions are underperforming, including:

☐ supplying additional resources to improve VET delivery, for example teaching space, equipment, instructional technologies;

☐ mandatory additional training (or dismissal) for underperforming teaching and administrative staff;

☐ the appointment of additional (external) members to governing councils to strengthen them;

☐ the replacement of a failing council with a statutory manager or equivalent.

The ultimate sanction for a poorly performing public VET institution is dis-establishment or merger. For more details on these processes, refer to **Unit 1.1: The legal environment for autonomous public VET institutions.**

For concepts of institutional accountability in different countries, go to **Unit 11.1: Accountability of VET institutions** on your CD-ROM.

Accountability and good governance

Good governance is important for demonstrating accountability. The governance system should be transparent, accountable, just, fair, democratic and responsive to stakeholder needs. The transparency expected in public-sector organizations has to be reflected in a VET provider's governance practices. Good governance supports accountability through:

☐ compliance with specific and general legislative requirements;

☐ governance arrangements through an independent VET institution's governing council;

☐ comprehensive and transparent representation of stakeholders in the governing council;

☐ following ethical principles in conduct and business;

☐ using the institution's performance data to inform decision-making and planning for continual improvement;

☐ achieving well-defined annual and/or longer term financial, management and operational objectives;

☐ compliance with annual financial and performance reporting requirements.

In order to be accountable, the VET institution's governing council must perform its functions and exercise its powers subject to:

☐ a performance and funding agreement with the government (the funder and owner of the institution);

- □ any economic and social objectives established from time to time by the government;

- □ national education and training policies;

- □ any requirements of the national legislation and regulations.

A VET institution establishes practices for accountability through a process of strategic planning that involves stating a mission (or purpose) and related objectives covering the range and scope of activities to be undertaken and reported. Performance targets and other measures by which the performance of the institution may be judged are then assessed. The principal stakeholders should be involved in this process, so that their views are incorporated into the overall strategy.

Risk management

As part of the concept of accountability, each VET institution needs to develop a risk management framework; its operational strategies should be based on elements of good practice, including:

- □ risk management policy;

- □ the allocation of risk management responsibilities;

- □ a formal process for identifying and analysing risks;

- □ the identification and assessment of the main risks relating to each objective and goal;

- □ risk management treatment plans;

- □ documented contingency plans for disaster recovery and business continuity;

- □ a formal review and evaluation procedure.

The VET institution's governing council is the main link in the accountability chain to outside bodies. The modern concept of corporate governance stresses that the council's control is best effected through agreement on principles and monitoring activity rather than interference and micromanagement.

The VET institution's managers must be prepared to explain how they have reached key management decisions and they need to provide regular routine reports on their operations. Some of these issues are dealt with in Unit 1.4: Main regulatory areas of public VET institutions and Unit 3.1: The governing council and its procedures.

For quality monitoring aspects of accountability systems, see also Module 10: Quality assurance in education and training.

11.1.2 QUALITY AND PERFORMANCE MONITORING

Systems are necessary in order to ensure that VET institutions are held account-able to their various stakeholders (governments, students, industry, enterprises and the professions) for their inputs (public funding, tuition fees, and so forth), actual performance (the way institutions conduct their business) and for their delivered outputs and outcomes (knowledge and skills of graduates, their employability, and so forth). Accountability systems generally involve quality and performance monitoring systems.

Quality monitoring

Quality monitoring focuses on the quality of courses delivered by VET institu-tions and the quality of outputs and outcomes that result from these courses. Such monitoring involves the quality assurance of VET qualifications and courses by course approval and provider accreditation processes as well as by provider quality audits.

Quality assessment generally covers both:

☐ inputs to learning (for example the quality of the curriculum, students, staff and teaching delivery); and

☐ outputs and outcomes of learning (for example the knowledge and skills acquired, enhanced employability, the capacity of graduates to engage in further learning and employer satisfaction with graduates).

For more details on the quality of learning, refer to **Unit 10.2: Assuring the quality of learning** and **Unit 10.3: Quality monitoring and assessment**.

For more details on approval, accreditation and quality audit processes, see **Unit 10.1: Quality management systems**.

In many jurisdictions, quality monitoring by course approval and provider accreditation processes is the responsibility of a dedicated external quality assurance agency.

External quality audits verify the performance of VET institutions as a whole as well as the performance of their management processes in achieving quality learning. Each audit usually involves a visit to a VET institution by a panel on behalf of the external quality assurance agency. The quality audit is necessary to safeguard the interests of stakeholders, namely current and pro-spective students and also industry, enterprises and the professions.

In jurisdictions that have devolved systems of autonomous VET institutions, most quality assurance processes – including course approval and provider accreditation – may be devolved by the external quality agencies to the institu-tions' academic boards. In these autonomous institutions, the academic boards usually have overall responsibility for internal QMSs. Delegations to them are subject to periodic quality audits by the external quality assurance agencies.

Performance monitoring

Monitoring performance involves reviewing the achievement or non-achievement of an institution's objectives, which are derived from the key focus areas of the strategic plan and the departmental action plans that emerge from these areas. Key performance indicators (KPIs) form the benchmark for institutional accountability, linking government policy objectives with institutional outputs and budget processes.

At each level in the organization, KPIs need to be identified, agreed on and refined as part of the management process. On a day-to-day basis, the VET institution's chief executive is finally accountable for the operations of the institution and the implementation of relevant policies and practices determined by the governing council. All staff are to be informed of their responsibilities within an operational framework, so that there is a whole-of-organization approach to accountability. Training programmes and a good communications strategy help staff to understand their responsibilities. In recent years, communications and policy awareness have improved thanks to the use of Intranet systems in VET institutions.

Performance monitoring systems generally focus on the major input and output streams for each VET institution, including:

☐ student enrolments, hours of curriculum delivered, drop-out rates, completions, graduations, and so on, with reference to performance measures, such as quality, timeliness and cost;

☐ finance – government funding, other revenues, expenditure, surpluses/deficits, cash flows, reserves, and so forth;

☐ capital assets – capital value, net equity, depreciation, expansion, disposal, and so forth;

☐ achievement of specifically targeted government objectives, such as, for instance, a rise in the participation of women in trade and technical training programmes.

External and internal monitoring mechanisms are commonly implemented through:

☐ a regular course review by staff and students;

☐ staff observation and appraisal;

☐ graduate and employer surveys;

☐ departmental self-assessment and action plans for improvement;

☐ external inspection and reporting.

To be effective and fair, monitoring mechanisms should encourage:

☐ opportunities for course team meetings;

☐ anonymity and ease of analysis;

☐ an agreed system and criteria for teaching observation with links to individual appraisal and staff development;

☐ the use of local and national standards and benchmarks; and

☐ staff self-assessment, with a regular cycle of reporting.

Some VET institutions use a performance management and measurement tool such as *Balanced Scorecard* or other proprietary or local strategic planning methodologies. The balanced scorecard is a management system that enables providers to clarify their vision and strategy and put them into action. It is used as a continuous improvement system that focuses everyone's attention on critical issues and provides feedback on internal and external outputs and outcomes. Involvement in such a strategic planning exercise is a powerful way of educating and involving staff in what drives current and future success.

External audits

An external audit of VET providers is commonly conducted against agreed standards underpinned by a programme of internal audit. External audits need to be carried out by a certified auditor and rely on the VET institution demonstrating that it has complied with the agreed performance standards.

VET providers may have to undergo audits in a number of areas:

☐ a financial review to ascertain compliance with regulatory framework and accounting standards;

☐ compliance with the requirements of national qualifications frameworks;

☐ the achievement of outputs and outcomes against a performance agreement contracted with the government with regard to the delivery of agreed products and services;

☐ risk management frameworks and operation.

Internal audits

The more internalized the monitoring processes are, the better. Good managers create an atmosphere in which staff are proud of good performance, and consequently assume responsibility for it themselves. Well-managed VET institutions have routine ways of monitoring themselves, because they genuinely want constant feedback on their quality and performance, and always seek to improve. It is bad practice only to monitor quality because someone outside the organization might want information, or to wait for external "threats" before taking note of quality and performance issues.

Regularly occurring internal audits are used to prepare for the external audit and, more importantly, to build and reinforce good practice and continual improvement. Institutional policies, procedures and processes should be continually reviewed and updated to reflect current practice. The outcomes of internal audits will provide the basis for the review and revision of practice.

Performance monitoring of VET providers is normally shared between government departments or agencies that have responsibilities for gathering statistical information on a VET sector to support policy development and to help operate the VET funding system. In many jurisdictions, VET institutions are required to provide statistical information to central agencies as a condition of receiving public funding.

In some VET systems where institutions have significant financial autonomy and the government bears a corresponding ownership risk, the statistical information may also be used to make assessments of institutions' financial viability. Useful financial performance indicators include projected operating surplus, returns on income and assets, operating cash flows, liquid assets, working capital and debt ratio.

Statistical data can also be used for forming judgements on the stewardship of institutional assets by their governing councils and management. The information includes data on the maintenance and development of institutional assets, often expressed as changes in net equity (net value of assets minus outstanding debts) from year to year following standard business practice in the private sector.

For more details on institutional monitoring, refer to **Unit 11.2: The monitoring of institutional performance.**

For details on accountability concepts in different countries, go to **Unit 11.1: Accountability of VET institutions** on your CD-ROM.

THE MONITORING
OF INSTITUTIONAL PERFORMANCE

11.2.1 MONITORING INPUTS, OUTPUTS AND OUTCOMES

Monitoring for accountability

Monitoring systems are necessary for ensuring that autonomous VET institutions are held accountable to their various stakeholders for both their inputs and their outputs and outcomes. Being monitored to ensure accountability is a necessary concession that autonomous VET providers must make in return for being granted autonomy.

By definition a public VET institution is accountable to the government. It is also accountable to other stakeholders who are users of the VET services delivered by the institution. These include students, who may invest considerable time (opportunity cost) and often money (tuition fees) in VET training. They also include the end-users of the knowledge and skills acquired by graduates, that is, industry, enterprises and the professions, who rely on graduates' knowledge and skills and who may also invest in VET.

Accountability through monitoring involves accounting for funding inputs but should also extend to the consideration of outputs – both quantitative (the number of graduates, and so forth) and qualitative (the quality of knowledge and skills acquired). It should also differentiate between the government's funding (the purchase of VET services from the institution) and ownership interests (since public VET providers are owned by the government).

Institutional management must allocate resources effectively by ensuring that:

☐ VET delivery targets are achieved;

☐ budgets and business plans are developed and managed to targets;

☐ institutional facilities are used to their maximum effect;

☐ the educational quality and use of resources are optimized;

☐ the accounting system can predict cash flows and end-of-year outcomes with a reasonable level of accuracy.

For more details on the concept of accountability, go to **Unit 11.1: Accountability of VET institutions**.

Accountability systems involve the quality and performance monitoring of inputs, outputs and outcomes. Monitoring involves keeping track of changes, analysing developments and evaluating progress against benchmarks. Quality monitoring generally focuses on the quality of inputs to the courses delivered by VET institutions and the quality of the resulting outputs and outcomes. Performance monitoring generally focuses on the quantitative measures of inputs, outputs and outcomes of VET institutions.

Quality monitoring

Quality monitoring is used for the quality assurance of VET courses through course approval and provider accreditation processes and through provider quality audits. Quality monitoring generally involves taking into consideration both the inputs to learning (for example the quality of courses, students, staff and teaching delivery) and the outputs of learning (for example the knowledge and skills acquired, enhanced employability and capacity for further learning).

For more details on assuring quality, go to **Unit 10.2: Assuring the quality of learning**.

In many jurisdictions, quality monitoring by course approval and provider accreditation processes is the responsibility of a dedicated external quality assurance agency.

For more details on approval, accreditation and quality audit processes, see **Unit 10.1: Quality management systems**.

External quality audits verify the performance of VET institutions as a whole, the performance of their management processes in achieving quality learning and their success as VET organizations.

In jurisdictions that have devolved systems of autonomous VET institutions, quality monitoring processes may be devolved by the external quality agencies to the institutional academic boards that are responsible for the institutions' own internal QMSs.

For more details on quality monitoring, refer to **Unit 10.3: Quality monitoring and assessment**.

Monitoring performance through inputs

It is usual in some VET systems to regard the education and training process as a production model with inputs and outputs. These are measured and quantified so as to create performance indicators in much the same way as a production plant might do. Although such measures have their uses, they need to be considered in the context of human behaviour. The controls available within an education and training process do not always lend themselves to such precise measurement.

Inputs are factors that have an impact on the VET delivery process: funding, staffing, enrolments, quality of teaching, teaching and learning equipment and materials, accommodation, support and infrastructure (catering, transport), and so on. For monitoring purposes, some of these inputs are not easily quantifiable and are usually measured as costs.

Statistical information commonly collected through input monitoring includes:

☐ the number of student enrolments (expressed as the number of equivalent full-time student (EFTS) enrolments);

☐ the number of teaching and support staff;

☐ the number of courses;

☐ revenue through public funding allocations;

☐ revenue through tuition fees;

☐ revenue from other sources;

☐ expenditure on salaries;

☐ expenditure on teaching space;

☐ expenditure on equipment and learning technologies;

☐ areas of teaching space;

☐ areas of non-teaching space, and so forth.

Quantitative performance monitoring is normally shared between government departments or agencies that have responsibilities for gathering and collating statistical information on a VET sector to support policy development and to help operate the VET funding system. In many jurisdictions, VET institutions are required to provide statistical information on inputs, outputs and outcomes to central agencies on a routine basis as a condition of receiving public funding. The information gathered – predominantly about students or finance – is used by central agencies to monitor institutional performance and to inform policy development.

Care is required when interpreting these input-based performance indicators, particularly when they are used to make comparisons between VET institutions. For example, VET institution "A", which has a higher staff/student ratio than VET institution "B", is not necessarily more efficient than "B", since the quality of teaching at "A" may be much lower than the quality of teaching at "B". A useful notion is the "system norm" or mean (or median) value for each of the performance indicators. Significant deviations from system norms may merit further investigation to determine why these deviations have occurred and whether they require any remedial intervention. System norms are also used as the basis for normative funding systems (see also Unit 5.1: Efficient, effective and equitable funding mechanisms).

Where VET institutions have significant financial autonomy and the government bears a corresponding ownership risk, the statistical information on financial inputs may also be used to assess the financial viability of VET institutions. Useful financial performance indicators include projected operating surplus, returns on income and assets, operating cash flows, liquid assets, working capital and debt ratio. More details on financial (ownership) monitoring are contained in Section 11.2.2: Financial monitoring below.

Output monitoring

A VET course's outputs are the knowledge, skills and competencies acquired by its successful graduates. These outputs are somewhat intangible, variable and, therefore, difficult to measure. For reasons of simplicity, various proxies are used as measures of these outputs.

Statistical information collected through output monitoring includes:

☐ the number of student enrolments;

☐ the number of EFTSs delivered;

☐ the number of SCHs of curriculum delivered;

☐ the number of dropouts;

☐ the number of course completers (or student retention rate);

☐ the number of successful graduations (or student graduation rate).

Some of the items used to measure inputs to the performance of VET institutions, such as the number of student enrolments (expressed as the number of EFTSs) are also used to measure their outputs. Not surprisingly, monitoring proxy measures of VET outputs has its limitations. Dropout rates provide no information on why students have not completed their courses, and so further assessment is required, particularly of course quality, to interpret them.

An EFTS is a planning measure of training volume. It is the workload undertaken by a VET provider to train a student in a full-time course for a full year. Obviously, a full-year course will require more resources than a one-week course. Accordingly, an output of 1.00 EFTS delivered for courses in particular training fields and at different qualifications levels will require different resources. Therefore, 1.00 EFTS is also a funding category on which basis the budgeting and resource allocation for institutions is arranged. The planning indicators and definitions of the full-time and full-year training are determined by the national government/funding agencies.

The calculation of SCHs for planning, funding and reporting purposes is based on the following. Each training package or curriculum nominates the number of hours that an average student under normal conditions might be expected to take to demonstrate a particular competency or set of learning outcomes in a module or course. The calculation of SCHs takes the predicted hours of training for a course within a year and multiples it by the benchmark class size.

EFTS is a better measure of student volume than course enrolments as it takes into account course length, although not the number of students who fail to complete their courses or the number of students participating in various VET courses. Course completions do not take into account those students who fail course assessments. Counting graduations as an output measure may provide a perverse incentive for institutions to pass all their students.

For more details on SCHs and EFTSs, consult **Unit 4.1 Supply and demand factors in planning for training delivery**.

Various performance indicators may be gleaned from this information. They are often expressed as ratios, so that value for money can be measured, and may include:

☐ (teaching) staff/student ratios;

☐ support staff/teaching staff ratios;

☐ teaching cost/administrative cost ratios;

☐ total cost per EFTS (or SCH of curriculum) delivered;

☐ teaching cost per hour taught;

☐ teaching cost per graduate student (qualification gained);

☐ public funding per EFTS;

☐ m^2 of teaching space per student;

☐ operational costs per m^2 of teaching space, and so on.

Areas of undue expense can be scrutinized, and their value re-assessed. For example, the full cost of the courses for particular customers should be proved. Sometimes the true cost of the course can be much higher, as the VET institution carries some infrastructure costs that are not passed on to the customer. Where there is a full measure of input costs, this can be avoided. Similarly, courses with low enrolments are often carried as an expense, and their costs balanced against more popular courses. Proper input and output monitoring allows a full examination of the costs to be recouped, and decisions to be made about the relative value of all courses offered. By linking input and output measures, other interesting monitoring possibilities emerge, such as the input costs per qualification acquired or comparisons between courses of the teaching costs per qualification gained.

The monitoring of outputs is also important in funding mechanisms. Most VET systems recognize student enrolments as at least one indicator of the funding needed for a VET institution. There are examples of funding mechanisms that are also tied to outputs.

The overall monitoring of the VET institution's staff utilization and other efficiency measures is necessary to maintain a picture of the institution's viability and efficiency. Its costs should be lower than its income, and its outputs justified against its costs. Internally, some of the same efficiency measures should be used for individual courses as for the institution as a whole. If the operational efficiency of departments/schools is kept under control, the whole VET institution will remain viable. It is for managers to decide how far inefficient units are necessary to the whole institution, and need to be supported.

For details on the efficiency of staff utilization, see **Unit 9.2: Managing staff resources**.

For details on the efficiency of institutional assets, see **Unit 9.3: Managing capital assets**.

Outcome monitoring

Outcomes are the impact that training has had on the employability of students and their capability to continue education and training; their salary levels achieved (improved); employer satisfaction with the quality and productivity of graduates, and the relevance of their training.

Outcome monitoring of a VET course is commonly implemented through:

☐ graduate satisfaction surveys;

☐ graduate destination surveys;

☐ surveys of employer satisfaction.

VET institutions have considerable (but not full) control over their outputs but much less ability to manage their outcomes, since many other factors then come into play. Nevertheless, these outputs and outcomes should be measured, where possible, to enable the impact of the VET institution to be assessed. The achievement of outcomes, however, is often measurable only in the medium to long term. Short-term outcomes may provide inadequate or skewed information.

These surveys are generally undertaken by the VET institutions themselves or by service organizations. Alternatively, they can be undertaken by government departments or agencies with monitoring and funding responsibilities in the VET sector.

For more details on outcome surveys, consult **Unit 9.4: Monitoring course progress and outputs.**

The monitoring process

If a government is to be able to measure its progress towards the achievement of outcomes over time, VET institutions must have the ability to formulate and realize targets, measure actual performance and develop measures of continuous improvement.

The monitoring process should:

☐ be planned, focused and continuous;

☐ be used to inform planning and decision-making;

☐ produce interpreted and accessible monitoring records;

☐ share its results with appropriate stakeholder groups.

Significant organizational effort should be directed at collecting monitoring information, while the use of technology in the gathering, storage and interpretation of data is essential.

More immediate feedback takes place when VET providers create an open culture, where debate and suggestions regarding ongoing performance in all aspects of the institution's operations are welcomed. VET providers also need to undertake client and employer satisfaction surveys to gain information on the services they offer. Local advisory structures may also exist, such as course monitoring committees comprising representatives of local and regional industry groups, teachers and students. This is particularly common in the piloting stages of a course or programme. Regular targeted self-evaluations and external inspections also provide valuable insights into the monitoring process.

For details on arrangements for the monitoring of VET institutions in different countries, go to **Unit 11.2: The monitoring of institutional performance** on your CD-ROM.

11.2.2 FINANCIAL MONITORING

Financial monitoring is one of the most crucial aspects of performance monitoring and reporting. A necessary condition for a public VET institution to have a level of financial autonomy is that its governance and management be accountable for the use of public and private resources allocated to the institution.

Autonomous VET institutions are increasingly being expected to be more entrepreneurial and attract non-government funds, spend government funds wisely and efficiently, deliver training efficiently and offer a selection of fee-paying courses. Strategic objectives to address these issues include:

☐ maximizing the utilization of facilities;

☐ maximizing the income from resources (assets and staff) employed;

☐ increasing fee-for-service revenue;

☐ setting priorities for public expenditure and maintaining financial viability.

These all result in the following types of financial performance indicators:

☐ the percentage of government and other funding sources;

☐ fee-for-service courses relying on government funding and commercial funds;

☐ the amount of revenue raised by student fees;

☐ revenue raised from investments.

These measures may be reviewed against benchmarks for the entire system derived from good practice and optimum performance of VET providers.

Through their agencies, governments routinely undertake the financial monitoring of autonomous VET institutions to protect their interests as funder and owner as well as the interests of other stakeholders, including students and industry.

The autonomous VET provider is commonly required to prepare a standard set of financial statements for a prescribed period, customarily a financial year. Usually, the set of standard financial statements will include corresponding sets of data for previous financial years to allow trends (over timescales longer than one financial year) to be identified.

The standard sets of financial statements are generally prepared in accordance with generally accepted accounting practices (GAAP) that pertain to each jurisdiction. Professional bodies representing accountants and auditors within each jurisdiction often have codified this practice. Accounting requirements may be made more explicit through specific (VET) legislation, generic (public finance) legislation or government regulation.

Although details of GAAP might differ between jurisdictions, a standard set of the autonomous VET institution's financial statements will usually include the following:

☐ a Statement of Financial Performance – compares the total operating income with the total cost of operations; the difference is the net operating result (surplus or deficit);

☐ a Statement of Financial Position – compares total assets with total liabilities; the difference is net assets (public equity);

☐ a Statement of Movement in Equity – compares initial net assets with final net assets after adjustments for revaluations and operating surplus or deficit have been made;

☐ a Statement of Cash Flows – provides summaries of operational cash income and expenditure, investment cash income and expenditure, and financial transactions, for example loan repayments;

☐ a Statement of Commitments and Contingent Liabilities – provides summaries of future financial commitments and liabilities;

☐ a Statement of Revenues and Expenditure – provides summaries of actual and budgeted income and expenditure by cost centre (for example faculty or service unit).

For more details on a standard set of financial statements, refer to **Unit 5.5: Standard financial statements and the financial audit.**

Autonomous VET institutions may have systems in place for the internal audit of their financial transactions. In larger institutions, a position of chief internal auditor (or equivalent) may be created to carry out this function. A necessary condition for annual financial statements to be credible, even for VET institutions with robust internal audit systems, is that they be accompanied by independent audit reports from qualified external auditors. External audit reports should certify that the statements give a fair reflection of the financial positions and operations of VET institutions.

Financial risk analysis

Financial monitoring is normally shared between government departments or agencies that are responsible for gathering statistical information on a VET sector to support policy development and to help operate the VET funding system. For VET institutions deemed to be financially sound, annual monitoring through a risk analysis of their annual financial statement may be considered all that is necessary to protect the government's interests.

Risk can be assessed through key financial indicators, which are often expressed as ratios of two types of financial information. Some examples include:

☐ the total cost per EFTS (training unit cost);

☐ public funding per EFTS;

☐ the institution's surplus (or deficit) compared with the total operating income;

☐ the change in net equity compared with net equity;

☐ the surplus compared with net equity (rate of return on equity).

Interpreting some of these financial indicators requires care, particularly if they are to be used to make comparisons between VET institutions. There is a potential trade-off between, for example, unit costs or surpluses and quality, and so increasing quality (desirable) may also have the effect of increasing unit costs and reducing surpluses (undesirable).

Performance targets (benchmarks) may be set for key financial indicators, and attention may then be given to VET institutions with financial performances that fail to meet these benchmarks. VET institutions that fail to do so only marginally (that is, they are at slight risk) may be required to report twice yearly and be monitored on the financial information, which is, under normal circumstances, collated annually into sets of financial statements. Those VET institutions that fail substantially to meet benchmarks (that is, they are at substantial financial risk) may be required to report and be monitored more frequently, for example on a quarterly or even monthly basis.

Within the regulatory framework, there should be provisions for intervening in those institutions that are regarded to be at risk. Funding bodies must keep the level of risk under review and be prepared to step in with capital injections or soft loans as bridging finance if circumstances warrant it. Other interventions may include powers for the government to remove members of the governing council, to replace removed members, or to appoint additional members; to appoint an interim chief executive; to enforce a merger with another institution or enforce closure.

To reduce financial risks, national legislation may also set constraints on the financial powers of a governing council by placing restrictions on whether it may borrow, on the amount it may borrow or on the value of institutional assets it intends to dispense with. All new ventures that are undertaken by autonomous VET institutions require a risk management assessment and a well-developed business plan to reduce the potential for financial loss.

The collecting and processing of monitoring data are costly, and care needs to be taken when developing and using a set of data that allow the performance of institutions to be monitored.

For details on financial monitoring in different countries, go to Unit 11.2: The monitoring of institutional performance on your CD-ROM.

Unit 11.3

REPORTING
ON INSTITUTIONAL PERFORMANCE

11.3.1 A FRAMEWORK FOR INSTITUTIONAL REPORTING

Reporting processes are the means by which relevant information is communicated to those that are able to use the information for making decisions and judgements about future investment and funding. Reporting is also used to inform the various stakeholders about the performance of a VET institution.

Obligatory reports on a VET institution commonly include:

☐ quarterly statistical data reports to the funding bodies;

☐ monthly reports to the funding body;

☐ monthly reports to the institutions' governing council;

☐ an annual report.

In a number of jurisdictions, the chief instrument for monitoring the autonomous VET institutions for their inputs, outputs and outcomes is the annual report. The customary content of an annual report is outlined in **Section 11.3.2: The VET institution's annual report**.

A national enabling legislation may include requirements that the governing council of each autonomous VET institution provide the responsible minister with an annual report – including financial statements – on the operation of the institution for the year that is being reported. The reporting period may be the VET institution's academic year or the government's financial year, which in some jurisdictions may not coincide.

Public finance legislation may require that each annual report contains a statement of service performance (SSP) or equivalent (see below).

Public finance legislation may also prescribe how the financial statements are to comply with GAAP in each jurisdiction and that they must include statements that represent the financial position of the VET institution and its cash flows fairly. Non-financial reporting must include the results of a VET institution's service performance in the year being reported.

The financial statements included in an annual report are normally accompanied by an auditor's opinion attesting that they give a fair representation of the financial situation of the VET institution. They also normally include a statement of responsibility, declaring that the institution's management accepts responsibility for the financial statements and for the integrity and reliability of financial and operational reporting.

An autonomous VET institution should be operating within the policy framework established by the government and other stakeholders for VET. This framework may include particular priority areas for VET. An annual report is normally expected to show how VET outputs align with and support these policy objectives.

To ensure that VET outputs align with government objectives, some jurisdictions require their VET institutions to include a SSP as part of their annual reports. The SSP discloses the outputs of a VET institution against its performance objectives and performance indicators. These outputs, performance objectives and performance indicators may be set out in an institutional performance (service) agreement, which is negotiated with the funding agency and becomes the basis of the institution's funding allocation.

Annual reports and financial statements provide useful information on the performance of VET institutions, and opportunities for the government's financial monitoring agency to assess ongoing financial risk (that is, ownership monitoring).

Ownership risk assessment provides a government with the opportunity to take pre-emptive action in the governance and management of a VET institution assessed to be at risk of financial failure.

For more details on financial risk (ownership) monitoring and the available intervention strategies, go to Unit 11.2: The monitoring of institutional performance.

In addition to regulatory requirements, there may be good-practice conventions that determine the type of reports issued to autonomous VET providers. There may be requirements for efficiency measures to be reported publicly. Countries have different public information requirements; details of input funding from public sources and costs such as the salary of the VET institution's chief executive may also be publicized. Papers from the governing council must usually be publicly available, and these will include details of regular financial and other performance monitoring.

Institutional staff may be involved in ongoing reports at departmental meetings and in a formal way at advisory structures such as the academic board, fee-for-service review meetings and regular performance monitoring reviews. These avenues cover a range of issues related to the development and delivery of VET programmes and associated activity. Reports to the governing council may be produced by its subcommittees and may include audit and risk management, resource management and strategic development issues.

For details on reporting processes in different countries, go to Unit 11.3: Reporting on institutional performance on your CD-ROM.

333

11.3.2 THE VET INSTITUTION'S ANNUAL REPORT

VET institutions are required to satisfy various statutory requirements and to produce an annual report. This document can also be used as a marketing tool by the provider when developing partnerships or strengthening links with industry. An annual report is a record of an organization's activities during the previous year. It sometimes includes predictions about the next 12 months but its main purpose is to record the past.

The format of the annual report is generally up to the VET institution to decide. An annual report will include a summary of objectives, their progress, details of staff changes, accommodation developments, details of qualifications gained and other awards to students, national awards given to the VET institution, and possibly some data which allow comparisons (usually favourable) to be made with other VET institutions. It is now much more common for such information to be posted on the VET institution's web page and be made widely available through the Internet.

The areas covered in an annual report commonly include:

☐ the vision (purpose) and strategy, with a statement from the chief executive and discussions on the organization's sustainability and future;

☐ a profile of the VET institution, including the organization, operations, stakeholders and the scope of the report;

☐ the governance structure, organization and management systems, policies, and stakeholder participation in them;

☐ performance indicators in the economic, environmental and social areas of activities;

☐ a financial report;

☐ a staffing report.

If there has been external scrutiny, such as an inspection, the outcomes of this will be summarized. It is natural for such reports to put a positive gloss on the achievements of the institution over a year. There may be other, more objective, reports on the institution's status and progress, such as those created by funding bodies for government scrutiny.

In some jurisdictions, enabling legislation may require the governing council of an autonomous VET institution to produce in their annual report the audited financial statements for the year being reported.

The legislation may also prescribe that an annual report includes an SSP that involves reporting against clearly defined and measurable outputs. These outputs are normally defined in the institution's service (performance) agreement, which is negotiated annually with the funding agency.

An annual report may also include corresponding data sets for previous reporting years to allow longer term trends to be identified. Although details of accounting practice may differ between jurisdictions, a standard set of financial statements will generally include:

☐ a Statement of Financial Performance;

☐ a Statement of Financial Position;

☐ a Statement of Movement in Equity;

☐ a Statement of Cash Flows;

☐ a Statement of Commitments and Contingent Liabilities;

☐ a Statement of Revenues and Expenditure.

For more details on financial statements, refer to **Unit 5.5: Standard financial statements and the financial audit**.

Finally, a VET institution's annual report also generally includes:

☐ a statement of responsibility in which the governing council accepts responsibility for the accuracy of the annual report;

☐ a report of an independent auditor that attests that the financial statements give a fair reflection of the financial position of the VET institution.

For more details on the annual reports of VET institutions in different countries, go to **Unit 11.3: Reporting on institutional performance** on your CD-ROM.

INDEX

Managing vocational training systems: A handbook for senior administrators,
by Vladimir Gasskov
This essential handbook addresses the multiplicity of challenges facing public
vocational education and training (VET) programmes around the world. An essential guide for VET administrators, it provides state-of-the-art materials and frameworks for coordinating important management and structural reforms. It offers
practical guidelines for managing budget and finance, evaluating performance,
and developing strategic operational plans, along with other valuable methods
and techniques for running effective VET systems.
ISBN 92-2-110867-8   2000   30 Swiss francs

**Corporate success through people: Making international labour standards work
for you,** by Nikolai Rogovsky and Emily Sims
In today's global economy, corporate managers are in the front line when it comes
to transforming management principles from an abstract vision into reality. International labour standards (ILS) can be effective and powerful tools around which
managers can build their corporate policies and practices. This volume, through
numerous case studies and examples from both large and small companies all over
the world, presents convincing evidence that implementing ILS in any company is
not only a wise code of conduct, but makes sound business sense as well.
ISBN 92-2-112718-4   2002   25 Swiss francs

Policies for small enterprises: Creating the right environment for good jobs,
by Gerhard Reinecke and Simon White
Around the world, millions of people work in micro and small enterprises (MSEs),
often in unsafe working conditions receiving low pay and little social protection.
As a result, many of these workers live in poverty. Drawing on studies carried out
in diverse countries, this comprehensive book reveals how national policies, laws
and regulations can be used to create more and better jobs in MSEs and combat
poverty as well.
ISBN 92-2-113724-4   2004   35 Swiss francs

**Implementing codes of conduct: How businesses manage social performance in
global supply chains,** by Ivanka Mamic
Based on interviews with hundreds of managers, activists, government officials,
factory workers and workers' representatives, this compendium represents the
most extensive research conducted to date into the emerging nature of corporate
social responsibility and global supply chains. Typically, codes of conduct draw on
international labour standards. The objective of this book is to provide useful
examples and lessons learned to companies, policy-makers and others interested in
implementing their own code of conduct or who are actively involved in this field.
Co-published with Greenleaf Publishing, United Kingdom.
ISBN 92-2-116270-2   2004   80 Swiss francs

Prices subject to change without notice.
Order ILO publications securely online at www.ilo.org/publns